The Internet Message

Prentice Hall Series in Innovative Technology

Dennis R. Allison, David J. Farber, and Bruce D. Shriver   *Series Advisors*

Bhasker	*A VHDL Primer*
Blachman	*Mathematica: A Practical Approach*
Johnson	*Superscalar Microprocessor Design*
Kane and Heinrich	*MIPS RISC Architecture, Second Edition*
Lawson	*Parallel Processing in Industrial Real-Time Applications*
Nelson, ed.	*Systems Programming with Modula-3*
Nutt	*Open Systems*
Rose	*The Internet Message: Closing the Book with Electronic Mail*
Rose	*The Little Black Book: Mail-Bonding with OSI Directory Services*
Rose	*The Open Book: A Practical Perspective on OSI*
Rose	*The Simple Book: An Introduction to Management of TCP/IP-Based Internets*
Shapiro	*A C++ Toolkit*
Slater	*Microprocessor-Based Design*
SPARC International Inc.	*The SPARC Architecture Manual, Version 8*
Strom, et al.	*Hermes: A Language for Distributed Computing*
Treseler	*Designing State Machine Controllers Using Programmable Logic*
Wirfs-Brock, Wilkerson, and Weiner	*Designing Object-Oriented Software*

The Internet Message
Closing the Book with Electronic Mail

Marshall T. Rose

P T R PRENTICE HALL
Englewood Cliffs, New Jersey 07632

Editorial/production supervision: *Brendan M. Stewart*
Prepress buyer: *Mary Elizabeth McCartney*
Manufacturing buyer: *Susan Brunke*
Acquisitions editor: *Mary Franz*

ISBN 0-13-092941-7

Prentice-Hall International (UK) Limited, *London*
Prentice-Hall of Australia Pty. Limited, *Sydney*
Prentice-Hall Canada Inc., *Toronto*
Prentice-Hall Hispanoamericana, S.A., *Mexico*
Prentice-Hall of India Private Limited, *New Delhi*
Prentice-Hall of Japan, Inc., *Tokyo*
Simon & Schuster Asia Pte. Ltd., *Singapore*
Editora Prentice-Hall do Brasil, Ltda., *Rio de Janeiro*

for Wrong is Right

Contents

List of Tables

List of Figures

Foreword

This last book of the Marshall Rose trilogy takes us back to his original point of entry into the Internet community. Back to his roots, so to speak. Those early days in 1981 and 1982 are deeply engraved in my memory, as I played the role of *pied piper* with ARPANET mail to lure Marshall into the technology and politics of internetworking, and then together we drew the Department of Information and Computer Science at the University of California at Irvine into the great world of academic networking. First with an early CSnet dialup "phonenet" connection for network mail, and then with a home-grown split IP gateway research project. The rest is history.

To be brief, you can only ignore Dr. Marshall T. Rose at your peril. As many of his friends (and enemies) like to say, he is very large in the industry.

Little did you all know what was being hatched for the Internet community, for the OSI movement, for internet network management, for OSI directory services, and for computer network mail. I should admit that we did not really see it all coming, but I cannot say that we were blind to the directions that were taken. All along, it was clear that "the game was afoot", and that Marshall was going to play a major role in shaping the future of global networking.

Of course, we had no detailed roadmap. We only had a few critically important strategic notions about how things should be done. Central to these themes was the notion of horizontally-oriented service-based emulation, as opposed to protocol translation. End-to-end integrity and layering became sacred. Good and simple, lean and mean engineering was something that grew out of Marshall's natural ability to see through extremely complex things to find essential simplicity.

I should say that this whole process of growing up was not one sided. Marshall also took a great deal from the Internet community. The whole idea of standardizing on only working technology was a lesson well learned. Only the Internet was teaching that lesson back then. Is anyone else teaching it now?

Other good lessons were taken from OSI, drawn from those early working papers from IFIP Working Group 6.5 that I was privileged to receive. Marshall devoured them all. Some gave him a bit of indigestion. Occasionally, he tried to explain some details to me, but my head was often too thick. I had to learn more slowly.

The decade since I introduced Marshall Rose to ARPANET mail has been an intriguing adventure. Together we have romped through the meadows and cut a few paths through the thickets of internetworking and OSI (both the technology and the politics), from top to bottom, front to back, and side to side. It has been first rate to be along for the ride. We hope you enjoyed it too.

So here we are, with Marshall telling us all about Internet mail, and between the lines educating us about networking issues in general, and explaining many general principles of how things should (and should not) be done in networks.

I am sure you will find *The Internet Message* both educational and entertaining. This whole networking business is much too deadly serious to be presented without some delicious humor. You will find it packaged as *soapboxes*, which reminds me of yet another interesting story...

Cheers!

Einar A. Stefferud
Huntington Beach, California

Preface

This is a book about the technology which provides us with the most
pervasive of all network services, electronic mail. In particular, this is a
book about the mechanisms and techniques used to provide electronic
mail in a special community called the *Internet*. The Internet community has an electronic mail infrastructure which is rich and widespread.

This infrastructure is rich because it offers a variety of services,
from personal messaging to distribution lists to exotic mail-based applications, and from simple textual memos to voice-mail to complex
multi-media objects, all across local area networks to intermittent dial-
up lines to dedicated high-speed links. The infrastructure is widespread
because it connects the commercial, government, research, and education sectors in every continent on the globe (with varying levels of
penetration). Despite the tremendous differences in end-user equipment, interconnection equipment, messaging formats, and the like, it
all (somehow) manages to work together.

Electronic mail is a unique network service in that it has seen
the most success in allowing communities, running different sets of
protocols, to communicate with each other. A *protocol* is simply a set of
rules used by computers to communicate with each other, and a *protocol
suite* is a group of these protocols all related to a common framework.
In the last decade, there has been much interest in standards-based, or
so-called "open", systems for computer-communications. There are in
fact two: the current *de facto* standard for open systems, the Internet
suite of protocols (commonly known as "TCP/IP"), and the *de jure*
standard Open Systems Interconnection (OSI) suite, which some hope
will become the open protocols of the future.

Each protocol suite has one or more protocols which provide an
electronic mail service. However, electronic mail is so valuable that

communities running different suites often put aside their differences to build mail gateways which connect their communities. That is, a user in an environment running one set of protocols is often able to exchange electronic mail with others who are not running the same set of protocols. As we shall see, electronic mail has special architectural features which make this interaction possible.

This book focuses on the protocols which provide electronic mail in the Internet. The *Internet community* is a large collection of networks under autonomous administration, but sharing a core set of protocols, the Internet suite of protocols.

In the past, the test of membership in the Internet community was whether one had a dedicated line for carrying Internet traffic. This is called being *IP-connected*. (IP, or the *Internet Protocol*, is the one protocol which ultimately carries all Internet traffic.)

Today however, the test is much broader: namely whether one's hosts are present in the Internet community's naming hierarchy. This is called being *DNS-connected*. (DNS, or the *Domain Name System*, is the Internet community's naming service for hosts and networks.) Loosely speaking, the test has changed from

> *"Can anyone in the Internet community send any kind of IP-based traffic to you?"*

to

> *"Can anyone in the Internet community send electronic mail to you?"*

The terms I use for today's taxonomy are:

small-i internet: any collection of networks which uses protocols from the Internet suite;

capital-I Internet: the subset of the Internet community which shares IP-connectivity; and,

mail-Internet: the subset of the Internet community which shares DNS-connectivity.

Of course, the mail-Internet is larger than the capital-I Internet, as the number of hosts which can exchange Internet mail is not restricted to hosts with IP-connectivity. There are two reasons for this: first, some sites administratively restrict IP-connectivity to only a small number of their hosts; second, some sites have no IP-connectivity whatsoever, and use some other means for moving Internet-mail from their private small-i internet to the capital-I Internet.

Finally, this book is intended to serve both as a graduate-level text and also as a professional reference. It is expected that the reader has a modest background in networking. And now, since the remainder of this preface is a personal note, you might wish to skip ahead to the first chapter of *The Internet Message*. (However, several readers of my previous works have indicated that the non-technical portions of my books are often the best parts. So, perhaps you might want to continue reading here.)

Last year, in the preface of *The Little Black Book*, I indicated that I would not be writing any books for a long, long while. I *lied*. I had hoped to publish a revised edition of *The Open Book* in 1992. However, that project has been postponed until early '93, when the International community publishes its 1992 series of standards and recommendations.

Originally, *The Little Black Book* was going to be on both electronic mail and directory services. Unfortunately, although I had been working in directory services for quite a while, when I sat down to write that work, I had been out of the inner loop of electronic mail for nearly five years. So, *The Little Black Book* dealt exclusively with directory services.

Fortunately, since that time, I've increased my activity in electronic mail quite a bit, in terms of helping to develop and then implement multi-media electronic mail for the Internet community. Thus, this gives me the opportunity to close the circle on my efforts in computer-communications. As an added bonus, *The Internet Message* is being published on the 10$^{\underline{th}}$ anniversary of the key standard that has made global electronic mail possible — RFC-822 was published in August of 1982! (For people new to the Internet community, RFCs are the series which document Internet technology, and RFC-822 is the one which defines the format for electronic mail messages.)

At this point, I could cut-and-paste about half of the text I've written for my previous prefaces as they also detail my struggle with electronic mail. I'll forgo that temptation and instead shamelessly plug my previous three books. If you're interested and haven't already done so, then go read the prefaces in these three works: First, there is *The Open Book*, which presents a practical perspective on Open Systems Interconnection (OSI). There are still people in the world who think that OSI is going to happen. I suppose that there are also people in the world who think that the moon is made of cheese. However, I wouldn't necessarily trust the judgement of either kind of optimist. Second, there is *The Simple Book*, which introduces internet management using the Simple Network Management Protocol (SNMP). A lot of people have commented that *The Simple Book* is easier to read and that my writing abilities are improving. Actually, my writing abilities were poor then, are poor now, and will always be poor. The difference is in the subject matter. Finally, there is *The Little Black Book*, which describes the most promising of OSI technologies, Directory Service.

Some might wonder why I haven't mentioned anything about OSI's Message Handling System (MHS), sometimes called X.400. *The Internet Message* will discuss MHS from time to time, but primarily when the text needs an example of how *not* to do something. Despite the fact that MHS is OSI's landmark application, the market is beginning to realize that it is really a non-starter. There are a lot of reasons for this, and throughout *The Internet Message* in several *soapboxes*, we'll find out why.

What's a soapbox? It's a typographical convention I use to offset personal opinion from the rest of the text. Look for text bracketed between the symbols `soap...` and `...soap`, which appear in the margin. Soapboxes appear intermittently in each book, as things like the Preface are meant to reflect a personal perspective anyway.

So, what's next? Well, next year a revised edition of *The Open Book* will be published. Enough has changed in the OSI world (sadly the changes are mostly in the form of new standards rather than production code of existing standards), to warrant a revision. Further, there might also be a revised edition of *The Simple Book* available. A lot has happened in the world of internet management since 1990.

Acknowledgements

My interest in electronic mail was fueled by working with some very forward-thinking Internet software called the Rand Message Handling System (MH). So, I gladly credit the people who designed MH at the RAND Corporation, Bruce Borden, Stockton Gaines, and Norman Shapiro, along with my University mentor and friend, Einar Stefferud, of Network Management Associates, who set me to work with MH at the University of California at Irvine (UCI). A lot of the work was done with the help of a colleague at UCI named John L. Romine, Norman Shapiro, MH advocate Phyllis Kantar, and another UCI colleague, Jerry N. Sweet. They all deserve a lot of credit for helping to make MH the useful and powerful tool it is today, over a decade after its introduction. The description of MH found in Section 3.2 is partially based on a manuscript which John and I wrote, but never finished, back in 1986. The amusing thing about this manuscript, *MH: Lessons in Message Handling*, is that it predicted the death of Internet mail and MH, at the hands of OSI's Message Handling System (X.400). Ah, how naive one is in one's youth!

The non-standard facilities for the Post Office Protocol discussed in Section 5.2.4 were developed by the author. However during the development phase, the comments of Alfred J. Grimstad and Neil Ostroff of Bellcore, and Keith McCloghrie of Hughes LAN Systems, greatly improved the final results.

There have been many reviewers who have spent considerable time pouring over countless manuscripts to help me produce the snappy prose contained herein: Nathaniel S. Borenstein of Bellcore, James M. Galvin of Trusted Information Systems, Paul V. Mockapetris who is currently assigned to the US Defense Advanced Projects Research Agency, John L. Romine of the University of California at Irvine, Einar A. Stefferud of Network Management Associates, Michael D. Zisman of Soft•Switch, and, J. Darrow Linder, Suzanne K. Schaefer, Frances J. Tong, all students at the University of California at Irvine.

Ole J. Jacobsen, Editor and Publisher of ConneXions — The Interoperability Report® was kind enough to perform the copy-editing on *The Internet Message*. His efforts brought this work to print in time for the INTEROP® 92 Fall conference and exhibition.

Paul, Ole, and Stef contributed the title and sub-title for *The Internet Message*.

Keeping with tradition, the final note is about Cheetah, my much-lionized cat. (No pun intended.) Cheetah is down to 10 kg, but continues to cause far more than his weight in trouble!

/mtr

Las Vegas, Nevada

Chapter 1

Introduction

Electronic mail provides a means for users to collaborate towards some goal. In the simplest cases, this collaboration may be solely for the dissemination of information. In other cases, two users may work on a joint research project, using electronic mail as their primary means of communication. In a public forum, electronic mail might allow hundreds or thousands of interested parties to exchange their views on topics of mutual interest. In a business setting, electronic mail might be used as a means for the automated exchange of business transactions.

The common theme running through all these examples is that electronic mail provides an automatic delivery service allowing users, separated by location and time, to exchange information objects.

So, we now begin by looking at a generic model for electronic mail. Although there are a number of systems which claim to offer "mail", in order to be an electronic mail service, a system must exhibit the architectural qualities present in this reference model.

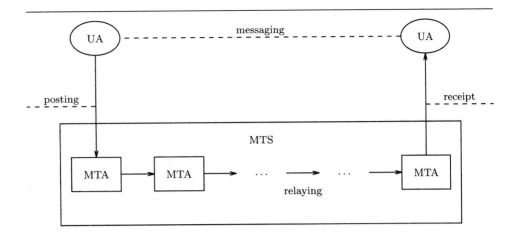

Figure 1.1: A Model for Electronic Mail

1.1   A Model for Message Handling

In 1979, IFIP, the International Federation for Information Processing, a pre-standards organization, developed a model for message handling. This model was eventually adopted and expanded by the the International Telephone and Telegraph Consultative Committee (more commonly known as the CCITT), which developed the X.400 series of recommendations, OSI's Message Handling System (MHS).

As shown in Figure 1.1, electronic mail messages are transported by a *message transfer system* (MTS), which is composed of one or more *message transfer agents* (MTAs). The message transfer system is distributed in nature, and not under a single administrative entity; in contrast, a collection of message transfer agents are usually controlled by a single administrative entity. At the edges of the system, a *user agent* (UA) acts on behalf of a user and interfaces to its local message transfer agent.

From the perspective of the message transfer system, the electronic mail message being sent is called the *content*, and all delivery information associated with the message is called the *envelope*. In theory, the message transfer system is ignorant of the structure of the content it transports; the user agents bilaterally agree as to what this structure is. Although there are no strict requirements as to the structure, there are usually two types of contents in each electronic mail message: control information (often called the *headers*), and data information (often called the *body*). A convenient way of thinking about all these terms is:

- the envelope is meaningful to the message transfer agents;

- the headers are meaningful to the user agents; and,

- the body is meaningful to the users (which may be people or programs).

When an electronic mail message is sent from one user to another, the following activities occur: The originating user indicates to the user agent the address of the recipient; the user agent places the destination address and the sender's address into the envelope and then posts the message through a *posting slot* to a message transfer agent, which involves a posting protocol in which the validity of those addresses and the syntax of the electronic mail message are considered. Upon successful completion of the submission protocol, the message transfer agent accepts responsibility either to deliver the electronic mail message, or, if so requested and if delivery fails, to inform the originating user of the failure by generating an *error report*.

After accepting responsibility to deliver the electronic mail message, a message transfer agent must decide if it can deliver the message directly to the recipient; if so, it delivers the electronic mail message through a *delivery slot* to the recipient's user agent, using a delivery protocol. If not, it contacts an adjacent message transfer agent, which is closer to the recipient, and negotiates transfer of the electronic mail message. This process repeats until some message transfer agent is able to deliver the electronic mail message, or some message transfer agent determines that the message is undeliverable.

Given this model for electronic mail, two things are clear:

- mail transfer is *third-party* in nature

  Once an electronic mail message passes through the posting slot, the user agent has no claims on the message. The message transfer system takes responsibility for the electronic mail message at posting time and retains that responsibility until delivery time.

- mail transfer is *store-and-forward* in nature

  The user agents for the originator and recipient need not be "on-line" simultaneously for mail to be submitted, transported, and delivered. In fact, only the node currently responsible for the electronic mail message, and the "next hop" taking responsibility for the message, need be connected in order for the message to be transferred.

To summarize, there are three general protocols involved in the model:

- a *messaging* protocol used between two user agents;

- a *relaying* protocol used between two message transfer agents; and,

- a *submission/delivery* protocol used between a message transfer agent and a user agent.

Of course, an electronic mail service exists in the context of a protocol suite. So, before we can study such a service in greater depth, we must now take a step back and look at a family of technologies which provide computer-communications.

1.2 The Internet Suite

The need for standardized networking technology has long been recognized. Computers must adhere to a common set of rules for defining their interactions, i.e., how they talk to one another. How computers talk to one another is termed a *protocol*. Protocols defined in terms of a common framework and administrated by a common body form a *protocol suite*.

Conventional theory holds that a single, non-proprietary suite of protocols is required to achieve information mobility. To ensure that all computers within an enterprise can communicate with each other (regardless of their manufacture), there has to be exactly *one* protocol suite. The protocol suite has to be *open* so that no one vendor can have an unfair competitive advantage in the market. Free market forces are critically important.

At present, the market has chosen the Internet suite of protocols as the *de facto* standard for open systems. Some hope that the OSI suite of protocols, as promulgated by the International Standards community, will become the *de jure* standard for open systems. Although both suites started development at roughly the same time (the late-'70s), unlike OSI, the Internet suite of protocols has seen extensive deployment — throughout the world, across the entire spectrum of user organizations. This is particularly interesting since only the OSI suite has received broad international support and governmental mandate. In contrast, the Internet suite has simply proceeded to dominate the market, based solely on its availability and the simple fact that it works!

For the purposes of *The Internet Message*, it is unnecessary to consider a full treatment of the Internet suite here. Instead, we begin with a brief synopsis of the factors which led to development of the Internet suite. Following this, we'll look at the architectural model for the Internet suite of protocols, and then examine how Internet technology is developed and standardized.

1.2.1 The Early Years

The Internet suite of protocols grew out of early research into packet-switched networking sponsored by the US Defense Advanced Research Projects Agency (DARPA). In the beginning, there was only one network, called the ARPANET, which connected a few dozen computer systems around the country. With the advent of different networking technologies, such as Ethernet, packet radio, and satellite, a method was needed for reliable transmission of information over media that do not guarantee reliable, error free delivery. (Information transmitted using these technologies can be lost or corrupted as the result, e.g., of radio propagation or packet collision.) Thus, the Internet suite of protocols was born.

Although, the Internet suite might be thought of as the property of the US military, this is an entirely pedantic view. The protocol suite is administered not by the US military, but by researchers sponsored by many areas of the US government. All computer users, regardless of nationality or profession, have benefited tremendously from the Internet suite.

The best term to use when describing the Internet suite of protocols is *focused*. There was a problem to solve, that of allowing a collection of heterogeneous computers and networks to communicate. Solving the internetworking communications gap required a good deal of cutting edge research. The Internet researchers made open systems a reality by limiting the problem, gauging the technology, and, by and large, making a set of well thought out engineering decisions.

1.2.2 Architectural Model

The architectural model for the Internet suite of protocols is defined in [1]. For our purposes, it is useful to view the Internet suite of protocols as having four layers:

- the *interface* layer, which describes physical and data-link technologies used to realize transmission at the hardware (media) level;

- the *internet* layer, which describes the internetworking technologies used to realize the internetworking abstraction;

- the *transport* layer, which describes the end-to-end technologies used to realize reliable communications between hosts; and,

- the *application* layer, which describes the technologies used to provide end-user services.

The major emphasis of the Internet suite is on the connection of diverse network technologies. As such, the current generation of protocols is *primarily* based on:

- a connection-oriented transport service, provided by the Transmission Control Protocol (TCP) [2]; and,

- a connectionless-mode network service, provided by the Internet Protocol (IP) [3].

There are several application protocols available for production use in the Internet suite. Of these, the mail-specific applications are:

- the Simple Mail Transfer Protocol (SMTP) [4, 5], which provides store-and-forward service for textual electronic mail messages, and RFC-822 [6], which defines the format of those messages;

- the Post Office Protocol (POP) [7] which provides a simple mailbox retrieval service;

- the Network News Transfer Protocol (NNTP) [8] which provides store-and-forward service for news messages (termed *articles*); and,

- the Domain Name System (DNS) [9, 10] which primarily provides mappings between host names and network addresses.

In terms of the three generic protocols introduced on page 4, RFC-822 corresponds to the *messaging* protocol, and SMTP corresponds to the *relaying* protocol. In the Internet suite, *submission* and *delivery* are local matters. However, use of SMTP and POP can provide this functionality.

Figure 1.2 on page 8 shows the relation between the core Internet electronic mail protocols. This figure also shows a protocol called

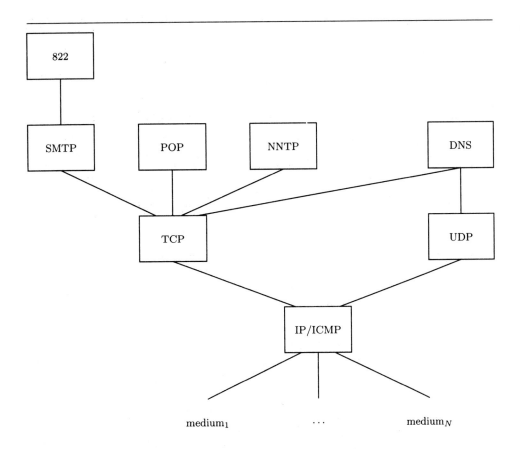

Figure 1.2: **Relationship of the core Internet Electronic Mail Protocols**

the User Datagram Protocol (UDP), which is a connectionless-mode transport protocol that is little more than a simple pass-through to IP, and a protocol called the Internet Control Message Protocol (ICMP) which is used to report on the "health" of the internet layer.

There are two key aspects of the Internet architecture which are germane to *The Internet Message*, IP-addressing and the application layer structure. Each is now discussed in turn.

IP-Addressing

An IP address is a 32–bit quantity, divided into two fields: a *network-identifier*, and a *host-identifier*. The network-identifier refers to a particular physical network in an internet, and the host-identifier refers to a particular device attached to that physical network. Because of this, an IP address precisely identifies where a network device is attached to an internet. Thus, a network device with multiple attachments will have multiple IP addresses associated with it (usually one IP address per attachment). Such a device is termed a *multi-homed* device. Finally, note that unlike media addresses, an IP address is said to be a *logical* artifact. It bears no relation to hardware, media, or any other physical conundrum.

The 32 bits of an IP address must be divided between network- and host-identifiers. This is by done by categorizing IP addresses into classes:

	bits for identifying	
class	network	host
A	7	24
B	14	16
C	21	8

Thus, there are potentially 128 class A networks, each containing up to $(2^{24} - 2)$ hosts; potentially 16384 class B networks, each containing up to 65534 hosts; and, potentially 2^{21} class C networks, each containing up to 254 hosts.[1]

---

[1]There are actually two other classes, D and E, but these are not germane to the current discussion.

As one might expect, choice of a fixed-length address field allows for an efficient encoding at the hardware level:

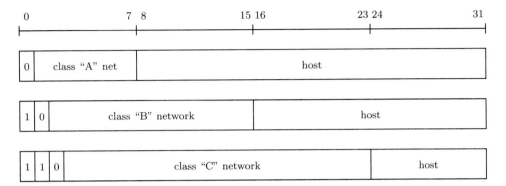

Because these 32–bit quantities appear in many packets, it is crucial that the ordering of the octets is consistent amongst implementations. In the Internet suite of protocols, the term *network byte order* is used to refer to octet ordering which is used by *all* implementations. When an IP address is transmitted, a "big endian" scheme is used. The most significant byte (the one with bit 0 in the figure above) is sent first, then the next significant byte, and so on.

Finally, when writing IP addresses in textual form, the *dotted quad* (or *dotted decimal*) notation is used: each octet is expressed as a decimal number, separated by a dot, e.g.,

```
192.103.140.1
```

At the application layer, when referring to a host whose name is unknown, a similar notation, the *domain literal* notation is used to write the IP address of that host, e.g.,

```
[192.103.140.1]
```

The Application Layer Structure

Most of the applications in the Internet suite are based on a client-server model. In brief: a server process listens on a well-known transport endpoint (termed a TCP or UDP port), and then performs actions based on the requests from a client process.

In the case of most connection-oriented applications, once a TCP connection is established, the server sends an initialization response and then awaits commands. When the service is to be released, the client sends a termination message, awaits a response, and then closes the TCP connection. Usually, both the commands and the responses are textual, terminated by a carriage-return/line-feed pair.

To describe the interaction between client and server, three conventions must be introduced: the repertoire used for the interactions (NVT ASCII), the syntax used to describe the commands and responses (BNF grammar), and the format of the commands.

NVT ASCII

NVT (Network Virtual Terminal) ASCII is the US variant of the ASCII repertoire [11]. This means that although each byte sent is 8 bits wide (an octet), the high-order (or parity bit) is zero when transmitted and ignored when received. The NVT ASCII character set (originally defined on Pages 10–11 of [12]) divides the character codes into three groups:

- control codes (values 0 through 31, decimal);

- graphic codes (values 32 through 126); and,

- uncovered codes (values 127 through 255).

From an applications perspective, the most important concern is line-termination. In the NVT ASCII repertoire, a line is terminated by a two-character sequence, carriage return (CR, value 13) followed by line-feed (LF, value 10), or CR-LF. To send a "literal" carriage-return or line-feed, the character is followed by a null (NUL, value 0).

BNF Grammar

Usually, a simple grammar is used to describe interactions, written using an augmented BNF (Backus-Naur Form) language in which *production rules* are defined that ultimately resolve into a collection of *terminal* symbols.[2] A production rule, `lhs`, is defined as

```
lhs ::= rhs
```

where `rhs` consists of one or more elements.

The possible elements are:

alternative: to indicate one of two choices, use

```
choice1 / choice2
```

grouping: to form a compound expression from two or more elements, use

```
(expression1 expression2 ...)
```

repeating: to specify an element repeating within some range, use

```
<lower>*<upper>element
```

If `<lower>` is not present, then the lower-bounds of the range is zero. Similarly, if `<upper>` is not present, then the upper-bounds of the range is infinity. As a short-hand notation,

```
<n>element
```

is equivalent to

```
<n>*<n>element
```

---

[2]This convention was formalized in RFC-822 and is used extensively throughout *The Internet Message.*

optional: to specify that an element might be present, use

```
[element]
```

which is equivalent to

```
*1element
```

list-repeating: as a short-hand notation,

```
<lower>#<upper>element
```

is equivalent to

```
element <lower-1>*<upper>("," element)
```

As a short-hand notation,

```
#<upper>element
```

is equivalent to

```
[1#<upper>element]
```

and

```
<lower>#element
```

is equivalent to

```
<lower>#<infinity>element
```

Ultimately, all production rules resolve into a collection of so-called *terminal* symbols.

Finally, any text appearing to the right of a semi-colon (";") is considered a comment.

Command Format

Commands usually consist of a keyword followed by zero or more arguments, separated by white-space. Responses consist of a success-indicator (termed a reply-code) and some textual information, usually a diagnostic meaningful to a human.

In the simplest case, consider a brief interaction between server(S) and a client(C):

```
S: <wait for connection on TCP port 109>
C: <open connection to server>
S: +OK dbc.mtview.ca.us POP server ready


...


C: QUIT
S: +OK
C: <closes connection>
S: <closes connection>
```

Actually, reply codes can be much more complicated. In the Simple Mail Transfer Protocol, for example, a reply code is a three digit number indicating not only the level of success or failure, but also operation-specific information.

If the argument to a command is multi-line (such as an electronic mail message), then a data-stuffing algorithm is used. The algorithm is simple: since the argument is expressed in NVT ASCII, it is sent line-by-line. If the beginning of a line begins with a dot-character ('.'), then the client inserts a second dot-character before sending the line. Whenever the server receives a line beginning with a dot-character, it strips it. If there are characters in addition to the CR-LF sequence, then the line is appended to the argument buffer. Otherwise, the server knows that it has received the last line of the argument.

1.2.3   Development and Standardization

The technical body that oversees the development of the Internet suite of protocols is termed the *Internet Activities Board* (IAB). There are two subsidiary bodies of the IAB: the *Internet Engineering Task Force*

(IETF), which is responsible for short-term engineering; and, the *Internet Research Task Force* (IRTF), which is responsible for longer-term research. Each task force is managed by steering groups, namely the Internet Engineering Steering Group (IESG), and the Internet Research Steering Group (IRSG), respectively. The IAB, per se, produces very few documents. Any person or group can design, document, implement, and test a protocol for use in the Internet suite. The IAB requires that protocols be documented in the *Request for Comments* (RFC) series, a convenient place for the dissemination of ideas. Protocol authors are encouraged to use the RFC mechanism regardless of whether they expect their protocol to become an Internet-standard.

Each RFC is assigned a number by the *RFC Editor* (a member of the IAB). If the text of the RFC is revised, a new number is assigned. In order to prevent confusion, if an RFC supercedes or updates any previous RFCs, this is clearly stated on the cover of the newer RFC. In addition to the RFC Editor, there is an *Internet Assigned Numbers Authority* (IANA), which is responsible for keeping the authoritative list of values used in the Internet suite of protocols (e.g., protocol numbers).

In addition to RFCs, there is a second set of documents, the *Internet Draft* series. These are produced by working groups in the IETF, and have no standardization status whatsoever, being viewed only as work in progress. At some point, if an Internet Draft matures (usually after some revision), it may be considered for standardization. In fact, Internet Drafts are not archival documents, they are available for a relatively short period of time, and are then usually removed. Finally, it should be noted that vendor product and user procurement literature should cite only RFCs and *not* Internet Drafts. In particular, note that the phrase "adherence to an Internet Draft" is oxymoronic.

It is problematic to list or even categorize all of the RFCs which have been published. However, in Appendix A starting on page 307, the RFCs relevant to the topics discussed in *The Internet Message* are listed. This appendix also discusses how RFCs and Internet Drafts may be obtained.

Internet Standards

The IAB assigns to each RFC a "standardization state". The vast majority of RFCs are termed *informational* — they enjoy no level of standardization status at all. That is, the majority of RFCs are research notes intended for discussion. In order to reduce confusion, the RFC Editor has introduced a second document series, the standard (STD) series [13]. This series is composed of RFCs which have some level of standardization associated with them.

[14] describes, in detail, the Internet standardization process. For our purposes, only the highlights are of interest: If an RFC is placed on the standards-track, it must progress through three states: from *proposed* standard, to *draft* standard, and finally to (full) *Internet-standard*. At each step, the RFC is reviewed along with implementation and deployment experience. In between each step, proponents of the document are given a six-to-nine month deadline to demonstrate implementability and usefulness. To transition from proposed to draft standard, there must be significant experience with implementation, and two independent implementations (with preferably at least one openly-available reference implementation). Similarly, to progress to full standard, there must be several independent implementations, along with extensive deployment, and considerable interoperability experience. During the course of each review, changes may be made to the documents. Depending on the severity of the changes, the document is re-issued at its current state, or is reduced back to a *proposed* standard, and the appropriate deadline is set once again.

It is critical to observe that implementation, deployment, and interoperability are all important criteria that are considered as a document progresses through the Internet standardization process. Further, note that an openly-available reference implementation is also required in order to foster understanding and availability.

In addition to assigning each RFC a standardization state, a *protocol status* is also assigned. This states the level of applicability for the technology documented in the RFC:

required: a system must implement this protocol.

recommended: a system should implement this protocol.

elective: a system may, or may not, implement this protocol. In a given technology area (e.g., routing) there are usually multiple elective protocols. A system may implement at most one of the elective protocols in the area.

limited use: a system may implement this protocol only in limited circumstances, because the protocol has a specialized nature, usually of limited functionality.

not recommended: a system should not implement this protocol.

Official Standards and Assigned Numbers

The *IAB Official Protocol Standards* document summarizes the positions of all protocols on the standards track. This RFC is issued quarterly with a strong warning to retrieve the next version when the current document reaches its expiration date. As of this writing, the latest version was [15]. As of this reading, that version is obsolete.

In addition, the *Assigned Numbers* document is a registry of assigned values used for various purposes in the Internet suite of protocols [16]. Both documents are periodically updated. As with the rest of the RFC series, the most recent document always takes precedence.

Host Requirements

There has been an on-going effort to provide technical explanation and expertise in the form of *Internet Router Requirements* and *Internet Host Requirements* documents. At present, the two documents detailing Internet Host Requirements are stable, and the document detailing Internet Router Requirements has just undergone revision with a new publication due out soon, probably by the time you are reading this book. In addition, there is increasing interest in developing requirements for specific application domains, such as electronic mail gatewaying. As of mid-1992, this work has not yet begun.

[17] provides a brief overview to the Internet Host Requirements. There are two Internet Host Requirements documents:

- one dealing with applications issues, [18]; and,

- one dealing with communications issues, [19].

Further, the original "Internet Gateway Requirements" document [20] is often referenced. Among other things, this document provides guidance on link-layer issues along with generic IP issues. (Note that the Internet community now uses the term "router" in place of "gateway".)

Although there were many motivations for writing the Internet Requirements documents, the author finds it useful to focus on one key observation:

> *during normal operations, it is difficult to distinguish between mediocre and optimal implementations — it is only when the network comes under stress that quality becomes important.*

This means that proper realization of the Internet suite of protocols requires that an implementor be familiar with the Internet Requirements documents. These documents contain much implementation and fielding experience which can be leveraged into high-quality, commercial-grade products. The goal is to maximize the robustness of the Internet in the face of stress.

1.3 Technology Perspective

When exploring a technology, it is useful to provide a view of a similar technology in order to appreciate how design decisions affect functionality, performance, and resource utilization.

For the purposes of *The Internet Message*, our contrasting technology will be OSI's *Message Handling System* (MHS). Most of the chapters which follow will conclude by comparing the OSI and Internet approaches to electronic mail. Beyond this, very little will be said about MHS.

Some readers familiar with the OSI effort in electronic mail may be wondering why *The Internet Message* spends such little time on OSI. The reason, in brief, is that the author feels that OSI is effectively dead, and is therefore unlikely to exhibit any positive influence on the market. Readers interested in pursuing this argument in great detail are encouraged to skip ahead to Appendix C starting on page 321. For now, the author merely notes that, although he has spent a lot of time working with OSI, he's come to the conclusion that OSI is now more of a problem than a solution. True, there are some good ideas there, but these are overshadowed by many more bad ideas. So, perhaps the future of OSI is that we will scavenge bits and pieces of it, but the author believes that OSI as a whole has already reached its apogee and is now approaching the "crash and burn" phase.

| soap... |

| ...soap |

1.3.1 OSI's Message Handling System

The first version of OSI's Message Handling System was released by the CCITT in 1984, some five years after IFIP developed the model for message handling introduced back on page 2. At that time, it was known as either X.400 (the series of CCITT recommendations which defined it), or MHS [21]. MHS exhibits the usual third-party transfer facility that is common to all message transfer systems.

After X.400's introduction, the CCITT began joint work with the ISO/IEC to refine and extend the standard [22, 23]. Perhaps the most important addition was the introduction of a new entity, the *Message Store* (MS). The task of the message store is to act as an intermediary between a user agent and its local message transfer agent. When performing final delivery, the message transfer agent places electronic mail in the message store. Later, the user agent can retrieve the electronic mail. For user agents which aren't constantly available (e.g., those residing on laptop computers), this allows final delivery to occur without delay. Further, the user agent might even use the message store to submit electronic mail. This would lessen the load on the computer supporting the user agent. This is termed *indirect submission*. In theory, this split of functionality allows user agents to be relatively less intelligent, by having the message store be responsible for the interactions with the MTA.

A lot of time could be spent on MHS, but let's focus the discussion back to the three generic protocols introduced earlier on page 4.

When the user agents are acting on behalf of a human user, the messaging protocol employed is called P_2 or P_{22} (depending on whether one is referring to the the 1984 or 1988 version, respectively), and the service provided is called the *interpersonal message service* (IPMS). There are other messaging protocols defined, or under development, each specifying the syntax and semantics of the content exchanged over the message transfer system. The relaying protocol is called P_1. Unlike the approach in the Internet community, the submission and delivery protocols are standardized, and are called P_3 or P_7 (again, depending on whether one is referring to the the 1984 or 1988 version).

Whenever *The Internet Message* considers MHS, discussion will focus primarily on the 1988 version.

1.4 Roadmap

The discussion in *The Internet Message* will look at several technologies for providing an electronic mail service. Further, attention will be given to a pioneering implementation of electronic mail software, MH, designed and initially implemented at the RAND Corporation, and then subsequently extensively developed and now maintained at the University of California at Irvine.

The Internet Message focuses on messaging technology, but not the ethics nor etiquette which humans should employ when using this technology. For an excellent treatise on these issues, the author highly recommends [24].

The first part of the book, Chapters 1 through 5, presents the basic technology providing electronic mail services. We began with the usual, terse discussion of a model for electronic messaging, in Chapter 1, and then go on to look at naming and addressing, the basic format for electronic mail messages, transport services for electronic mail, and finally mailbox retrieval services.

The second part of the book, Chapters 6 through 8, deals with technology which enhances the basic services: namely multi-media mail, privacy-enhanced mail, and finally mail gatewaying.

Finally, *The Internet Message* speculates about where things might be going with electronic mail.

Chapter 2

Naming and Addressing

A *naming convention* is a discipline for identifying entities within a network. In contrast, an *address* identifies where an entity resides within a network, and a *route* indicates how to traverse the network to talk to that entity. It is key to appreciate that these terms are always relative to the context of usage. For example, a telephone number can be viewed as either a route, address, or name, depending on how it is being used.

For our purposes, we focus on how users of electronic mail are named. In the Internet community, such a user is named by an electronic mail address. The textual format of an such an address is

    local@domain

where "`domain`" identifies an administrative authority responsible for naming entities, and "`local`" is a string which has meaning only within that authority.

In this chapter, we consider the semantics of the `domain` component. Following this, we look at how name-to-address mapping occurs in the Internet community. Finally, we look at how organizations and persons can be located, and then close this chapter with a technology comparison.

2.1 Domain Names

Perhaps the most important feature of a naming scheme is that of scalability. In brief,

> *always plan for your worst success*

This means that any well-used naming scheme must provide excellent support for distributed assignment, execution, and maintenance. A natural approach for realizing these characteristics is to use a hierarchical naming scheme. So, a *domain name* identifies an administrative entity using a hierarchical structure.

2.1.1 Writing Domain Names

A domain name is written as one or more ordered, textual labels. Conceptually, the domain name space is a tree. This means that all of the immediate subordinates to a node must have unique names. That is, in order to assign a label to a particular node, none of the node's siblings may use that label. As a consequence, to uniquely name any node, one simply concatenates the labels found by starting at the node and stopping at the root of the tree. By convention, the root of the tree is the empty label, and labels are separated by the dot-character ("`.`").

The BNF specification for domain names is shown in Figure 2.1. Since this is the first example of augmented BNF, let's look at it line by line. First, the production rule `domain` is defined as one or more occurrences of a `label` element, with a dot-character ("`.`") used for separation. Next, a `label` is a string starting with an alphanumeric character followed by zero or more alphabetic, numeric, hyphen, or underscore characters appear.

```
domain     ::= label *("." label)

label      ::= (ALPHA / DIGIT) *(ALPHA / DIGIT / "-" / "_")

ALPHA      ::= <any alphabetic character, "A" through "Z" and
               "a" through "z">
DIGIT      ::= <any numeric character, "0" through "9">
```

Figure 2.1: Domain Name Syntax

Note that it is permissible for labels to begin with a digit, e.g.,

```
3com.com
```

However, some software from the mid-'80s recognize a restrictive format, e.g.,

```
label      ::= ALPHA [*(ALPHA / DIGIT / "-" ) (ALPHA / DIGIT)]
```

So, some care must be taken when using older, non-conforming, software.

For example, the domain name

```
dbc.mtview.ca.us
```

refers to a node, dbc, whose parent's name is

```
mtview.ca.us
```

Continuing along, the grandparent's name is

```
ca.us
```

and the great-grandparent's name is

```
us
```

This final domain name is termed a *top-level* domain name because its parent is the root.

Each country is assigned a top-level domain name, and the two-letter ISO 3166 code is used as the label.[1] Table 2.1 on page 26 shows these codes. As of this writing, less than 60 of these domain names are in actual use.

---

[1]The only exception is that the United Kingdom uses a top-level domain name of **uk** instead of its rightful code of **gb**. This is due to historical (some say hysterical) reasons.

ad	Andorra	gn	Guinea	nt	Neutral Zone
ae	United Arab Emirates	gp	Guadeloupe	nu	Niue
af	Afghanistan	gq	Equatorial Guinea	nz	New Zealand
ag	Antigua & Barbuda	gr	Greece	om	Oman
ai	Anguilla	gt	Guatemala	pa	Panama
al	Albania	gu	Guam	pe	Peru
am	Armenia	gw	Guinea-Bissau	pf	French Polynesia
an	Netherlands Antilles	gy	Guyana	pg	Papua New Guinea
ao	Angola	hk	Hong Kong	ph	Philippines
aq	Antarctica	hm	Heard & McDonald Islands	pk	Pakistan
ar	Argentina	hn	Honduras	pl	Poland
as	American Samoa	hr	Croatia	pm	St. Pierre & Miquelon
at	Austria	ht	Haiti	pn	Pitcairn
au	Australia	hu	Hungary	pr	Puerto Rico
aw	Aruba	id	Indonesia	pt	Portugal
az	Azerbaijan	ie	Ireland	pw	Palau
bb	Barbados	il	Israel	py	Paraguay
bd	Bangladesh	in	India	qa	Qatar
be	Belgium	io	British Indian Ocean Terr.	re	Reunion
bf	Burkina Faso	iq	Iraq	ro	Romania
bg	Bulgaria	ir	Iran	ru	Russia
bh	Bahrain	is	Iceland	rw	Rwanda
bi	Burundi	it	Italy	sa	Saudi Arabia
bj	Benin	jm	Jamaica	sb	Solomon Islands
bm	Bermuda	jo	Jordan	sc	Seychelles
bn	Brunei Darussalam	jp	Japan	sd	Sudan
bo	Bolivia	ke	Kenya	se	Sweden
br	Brazil	kg	Kyrgyzstan	sg	Singapore
bs	Bahamas	kh	Cambodia	sh	St. Helena
bt	Bhutan	ki	Kiribati	si	Slovenia
bv	Bouvet Is.	kk	Kazakhstan	sj	Svalbard & Jan Mayen Islands
bw	Botswana	km	Comoros	sl	Sierra Leone
by	Byelorussian SSR	kn	St. Kitts & Nevis	sm	San Marino
bz	Belize	kp	Dem. People's Rep. of Korea	sn	Senegal
ca	Canada	kr	Rep. of Korea	so	Somalia
cc	Cocos (Keeling) Islands	kw	Kuwait	sr	Suriname
cf	Central African Rep.	ky	Cayman Islands	st	Sao Tome & Principe
cg	Congo	la	Lao People's Dem. Rep.	su	USSR
ch	Switzerland	lb	Lebanon	sv	El Salvador
ci	Cote d'Ivoire	lc	St. Lucia	sy	Syrian Arab Rep.
ck	Cook Islands	li	Liechtenstein	sz	Swaziland
cl	Chile	lk	Sri Lanka	tc	Turks & Caicos Islands
cm	Cameroon	lr	Liberia	td	Chad
cn	China	ls	Lesotho	tf	French Southern Terr.s
co	Colombia	lt	Lithuania	tg	Togo
cr	Costa Rica	lu	Luxembourg	th	Thailand
cs	Czechoslovakia	lv	Latvia	tj	Tajikistan
cu	Cuba	ly	Libyan Arab Jamahiriya	tk	Tokelau
cv	Cape Verde	ma	Morocco	tm	Turkmenistan
cx	Christmas Is.	mc	Monaco	tn	Tunisia
cy	Cyprus	md	Moldova	to	Tonga
de	Germany	mg	Madagascar	tp	East Timor
dj	Djibouti	mh	Marshall Islands	tr	Turkey
dk	Denmark	ml	Mali	tt	Trinidad & Tobago
dm	Dominica	mm	Myanmar	tv	Tuvalu
do	Dominican Rep.	mn	Mongolia	tw	Province of China Taiwan
dz	Algeria	mo	Macau	tz	United Rep. of Tanzania
ec	Ecuador	mp	Northern Mariana Islands	ua	Ukrainian SSR
ee	Estonia	mq	Martinique	ug	Uganda
eg	Egypt	mr	Mauritania	um	US Minor Outlying Islands
eh	Western Sahara	ms	Montserrat	us	United States
es	Spain	mt	Malta	uy	Uruguay
et	Ethiopia	mu	Mauritius	uz	Uzbekistan
fi	Finland	mv	Maldives	va	Vatican City State
fj	Fiji	mw	Malawi	vc	St. Vincent & The Grenadines
fk	Falkland Islands	mx	Mexico	ve	Venezuela
fm	Micronesia	my	Malaysia	vg	British Virgin Islands
fo	Faroe Islands	mz	Mozambique	vi	US Virgin Islands
fr	France	na	Namibia	vn	Viet Nam
ga	Gabon	nc	New Caledonia	vu	Vanuatu
gb	United Kingdom	ne	Niger	wf	Wallis & Futuna Islands
gd	Grenada	nf	Norfolk Is.	ws	Samoa
gf	French Guiana	ng	Nigeria	ye	Yemen
gg	Georgia	ni	Nicaragua	yu	Yugoslavia
gh	Ghana	nl	Netherlands	za	South Africa
gi	Gibraltar	no	Norway	zm	Zambia
gl	Greenland	np	Nepal	zr	Zaire
gm	Gambia	nr	Nauru	zw	Zimbabwe

Table 2.1: ISO 3166 Alphabetic Country Codes

In addition, there is a small number of other top-level domain names assigned:

Domain Name	Meaning
com	commercial
edu	educational
gov	(US) government
int	international organization
mil	(US) military
net	network provider
org	non-profit organization

Unlike the geo-political top-level domain names, these domain names identify the organizational mission of their immediate subordinates.

Historically, the majority of administrations based in the US were assigned mission-oriented domain names. However, owing to the somewhat US-centric basis of these labels and the growing international nature of the Internet community, some new sites in the US are opting to be placed under the **us** top-level domain. This accounts for the large number of hosts registered under the mission-oriented top-level domains and the rather poor showing of the **us** top-level domain.

One price of success is massive growth — the Internet community is so large that it appears to be impossible to accurately determine the number of hosts which share either IP- or DNS-connectivity. However, Table 2.2 on page 28 shows the *estimated* distribution of hosts[2] named under the existing top-level domains, as of April, 1992. This table was taken from [25]. (Interested readers should consult [26] which explains the collection methodology, as it attempts to estimate the growth of the Internet community for the last decade.)

2.1.2   Topological Independence

An important property of domains is that they are administrative, *not* topological, entities. That is, one must not infer any network connection between two sibling domains. This is true regardless of the choice of a geo-political or mission-oriented top-level domain name.

---

[2]For the purposes of this table, a host is an entity with at least one IP address.

Size	Domain Name	Size	Domain Name
284500	edu	1329	hk
217964	com	1138	pt
52900	gov	1046	be
39867	au	809	sg
39696	mil	536	gr
39356	de	533	mx
33183	ca	522	ie
28862	uk	407	pl
22410	org	285	is
18769	se	269	br
18623	nl	180	cs
16145	fr	171	us
14637	ch	88	cl
14565	fi	78	lu
12831	no	43	hu
12439	jp	36	int
4677	at	13	yu
4575	net	8	tn
2560	il	8	arpa
2524	es	6	aq
2312	dk	5	ve
1794	tw	5	in
1537	nz	2	ar
1498	za	1	it

Table 2.2: Host distribution by Top-level Domain

For example, given the two domains:

    well.sf.ca.us

and

    asylum.sf.ca.us

there is no basis for assuming any connectivity relationship between the two — the entities identified by these domains may be connected to different service providers and could be quite IP-distant. This is a very important property of domain names: because they are topology-independent, they are, by definition, independent of changes in topology.

2.1.3 Delegation of Authority

Another important property of domains is that each naming level allows for the possibility of delegation of authority.

For example, suppose an organization is assigned the domain name

    foo.sf.ca.us

Then that organization is allowed to make further assignments under this suffix, e.g.,

    bar.foo.sf.ca.us

All the organization need do is ensure the uniqueness of all labels assigned immediately subordinate to

    foo.sf.ca.us

Of course, authority can continue to be delegated downward, as long as it is convenient or necessary.

In addition to assigning names within the domain, a naming authority is responsible for defining administrative guidelines on how the information in the domain is used. Beneath each of the top-level domains, most entities impose a simple organizational structure reflecting their internal organization. This is usually adequate for applications requiring name to address translation.

However, specialized applications may require specialized domain structures. For example, one normally thinks of a name service as providing a mapping from a name into its associated attributes. However, some applications might require an inverse mapping from a particular attribute value to a name. Later on, in Section 2.2.5 on page 54, we'll see how one can map an IP address into its corresponding domain name.

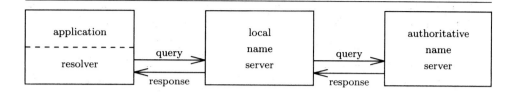

Figure 2.2: A Typical Interaction with the DNS

2.2 The Domain Name System

It is now time to consider how a domain name is mapped into its associated attributes. This is done by the *Domain Name System* (DNS). The discussion which follows tries to give the reader a good understanding of the capabilities of the DNS, whilst still avoiding a lot of the underlying complexity. The author isn't entirely sure that the presentation which follows strikes the right balance.

In order to put things in perspective, consider Figure 2.2 which shows a typical interaction with the DNS. Three application entities are involved:

- a *resolver*, which acts on behalf of an application to interrogate the DNS;

- a local *domain name server*, which knows who to ask to find out where information is kept in the DNS; and

- a remote name server, which is authoritative for the information in question.

In the interests of brevity, the term *name server* will be used when referring to a domain name server.

It must be emphasized that Figure 2.2 is highly simplified, and is presented only to give the reader a feeling of things to come.

2.2.1   Design Criteria

When designing a name service, one must usually balance functionality, performance, and consistency. In terms of functionality, the DNS:

- provides a uniform naming service for use by numerous applications;

- supports a small set of "standard" attributes which may be associated with names;

- allows for the definition of new attributes to support future applications and other protocol suites;

- provides for both interrogation and off-line modification of information;

- uses either connectionless-mode or connection-oriented transport service for communication, depending on the needs of the application; and,

- allows the application to (loosely) control which name servers are contacted for information.

In terms of performance, the DNS:

- maintains information in a distributed fashion, using replication to speed response;

- allows for replication via shadowing, so that multiple name servers may be authoritative for a collection of information; and,

- allows for replication via caching, so that an application may use information that it has learned earlier to answer later questions.

In terms of consistency, the DNS:

- allows for transient inconsistencies in the service, provided the frequency of updates is small compared to the number of queries and,

- allows the information source to define the policy for consistency.

Independent of these design goals, the DNS also strives to be simple enough to facilitate wide deployment.

2.2.2 Domain Name Space

Earlier, Section 2.1 introduced the syntax and semantics of domain names, in a fashion which was protocol-independent. From the perspective of the DNS, this presentation must be augmented with some additional discussion.

Domain Name Representation

In order to make the DNS more tractable for implementation, it explicitly limits the size of a domain name and each label. In particular, a label contains from 1 to 63 characters, with the exception of the label at the root, which is zero-length. Further, the total length of a domain name (including the dots) may not exceed 256 characters.

This allows an implementation to treat a label as a length/value pair, where the length of each label is represented in a single octet. Further, a domain name can be represented as a sequence of contiguous length/value pairs, in no more than 255 octets.

Although the protocol's length/value representation might lead one to believe that labels can be arbitrary binary information, labels currently use the US ASCII repertoire. Further, when examining two labels for equality, a case-insensitive comparison is made. Despite this, implementations should never change the capitalization of a label.

When converting the DNS representation to a string representation, because the root label is empty, the domain name ends with a dot, e.g.,

```
dbc.mtview.ca.us.
```

This form of a domain name is said to be *absolute*, and is sometimes called a *fully-qualified domain name*.

As a short-hand notation, if the trailing dot is not present, then the domain name is interpreted *relative* to the local domain, and is termed a *partially-qualified domain name*. Hence, if the local domain is

    `ca.us.`

then the partially-qualified domain name

    `dbc.mtview`

refers to

    `dbc.mtview.ca.us.`

Finally, the term *subdomain* is used to refer to a node which is the (distant) subordinate to some other node in the tree. Hence, the domain

    `dbc.mtview.ca.us.`

is a subdomain to each of these domains:

    `mtview.ca.us.`
    `ca.us.`
    `us.`
    `.`

2.2.3   Resource Records

A name service normally deals with names and their associated attributes. In the Domain Name System, these attributes are termed *resource records*. So, associated with each domain name is a set of zero or more, unordered, resource records.

A resource record contains several fields:

    class: the protocol-suite for which this record applies;

    type: the attribute type for this record;

    data: the attribute value for this record (the syntax for this field depends on both the class and type fields); and,

ttl: the number of seconds (time-to-live field) that this resource record can be cached before it should be invalidated (a value of zero indicates that resource record may be used for the current transaction, but must not be cached).

Conceptually, a resource record also has an *owner* field which identifies the domain name which contains this record.

The class and type fields are 16–bit quantities which are registered by the IANA.

There are two protocol classes which are defined, **IN** which refers to the Internet suite of protocols, and, **CH** which refers to the Chaos suite of protocols developed at MIT. Since both the class and type fields must be considered in order to make sense out of the data, we will examine them in combination. At present, there are several combinations which are in standard use. In Section 2.2.5 starting on page 45, several examples are presented to show how many of these are used. For now, each combination is now briefly introduced:

IN A: internet host addressing information

> The domain name refers to an internet host, and the value is a 32–bit IP address in network byte order.

IN CNAME: internet name aliasing information

> The domain name refers to an alias for an entity and the value is the official domain name for that entity.

IN MX: internet mail relaying information

> The domain name refers to an internet host, and the value is a preference field (interpreted as a 16–bit unsigned integer) followed by a domain name for the relay which accepts mail for the named host. The preference field indicates the relative "cost" from the mail relay to the mail service at the named host, with lower values indicating a lower cost.

IN NS: internet name server information

> The domain name refers to a subdomain, and the value is the domain name identifying a host running a name server which is authoritative for that subdomain.

IN PTR: internet name pointer information

> The domain name refers to a "back-pointer" domain, and the value is another domain name.

IN SOA: internet start-of-authority information

> The domain name refers to a subdomain, and the value defines the consistency policy for the information contained within the subdomain.

IN HINFO: internet host information

> The domain name refers to an internet host, and the value is a CPU field followed by an operating-system (OS) field. Standard values for each field are found in the Assigned Numbers RFC [16]. This information can be used by applications to tailor their behavior when communicating with the named host.

IN TXT: textual information

> The domain name refers to an arbitrary entity, and the value contains one or more arbitrary strings describing that entity.

IN WKS: internet well-known service information

> The domain name refers to an internet host, and the value is a field identifying a transport protocol (e.g., TCP or UDP), followed by a field naming the services available using that transport protocol. This latter field is a bitmap. If the bit corresponding to port number for the transport protocol is set, then that corresponding service is available on the named host.

Historically, several other DNS types have been defined. Further, new types are also defined from time to time. Interested readers might wish to consult [27, 28] for some examples.

Wildcard Resource Records

Normally, we think of a given resource record as having a single owner. However, if the owner of a resource record is a *wildcard* domain name, then the resource record is really a prototype, which may be instantiated whenever necessary.

A wildcard domain name is written as an ordinary domain name except that the first label is the wildcard-character ("*"), e.g.,

```
*.dbc.mtview.ca.us.
```

For practical purposes, this means that wildcard resource records are instantiated only when no "real" records exist at or below the wildcards. That is, a resource record with an owner subordinate to a wildcard record stops the wildcarding effect. Rather than introducing the actual semantics of a wildcard domain, later, on page 51 we'll see an example which uses wildcards. After this example, we'll spell out how wildcard resource records really work.

Writing Resource Records

The Domain Name System defines a set of textual conventions for writing resource records. The BNF specification for resource records is shown in Figure 2.3 starting on page 38.

A collection of related resource records are written by first indicating the domain name which contains them. The owner field is written at the beginning of a line. Following this are one or more resource records. After the first resource record, subsequent resource records for that owner are written, but indented from the beginning of a line.

When an individual record is written, the "ttl" and "class" fields may be omitted, in which case their values are taken from context. However, the type and value fields must be present. In the case of the **SOA** (start of authority) record, the value is written on multiple lines for clarity. (We'll find out more about these special records later on in Section 2.2.6.)

```
records   ::= owner 1*SP record CRLF *(SP record CRLF)

owner     ::= domain / wildcard

record    ::= [ttl 1*SP] [class 1*SP] type 1*SP value

ttl       ::= 1*DIGIT

class     ::= "IN" / "CH"
type      ::= "A" / "CNAME" / "MX" / "NS" / "PTR" / "SOA"
              / "HINFO" / "TXT" / "WKS"

          ; depends on class/type combination
value     ::= quad                    ; for IN A

              / domain 1*SP 1*DIGIT    ; for CH A

              / domain                 ; for IN CNAME, NS, PTR

              / cost 1*SP domain       ; for MX

                                       ; for SOA
              / master 1*SP mailbox 1*SP "(" CRLF 1*SP
                serial CRLF 1*SP
                refresh CRLF 1*SP
                retry CRLF 1*SP
                expire CRLF 1*SP
                minimum *SP ")"

              / string 1*SP string     ; for HINFO

              / string *(*SP string)   ; for TXT

                                       ; for WKS
              / transport *(*SP service)
```

Figure 2.3: Resource Record Syntax

```
quad      ::= octet 3("." octet)

octet     ::= 1*3DIGIT              ; in the range 0..255

cost      ::= 1*5DIGIT              ; in the range 0..65535

master    ::= domain
mailbox   ::= local "." domain
local     ::= label

                                   ; in the range 0..4294967295
serial    ::= 1*10DIGIT
refresh   ::= 1*10DIGIT
retry     ::= 1*10DIGIT
expire    ::= 1*10DIGIT
minimum   ::= 1*10DIGIT

string    ::= <"> <any number of characters, in which a
                   non-alphanumeric character is preceeded
                   by backslash> <">

             ; a 16-bit IP protocol number
transport ::= "tcp" / "udp" / 1*5DIGIT

             ; a 16-bit port number
service   ::= string / 1*5DIGIT

          ; trailing dot is for FQDNs
domain    ::= label *("." label) ["."]
wildcard  ::= "*"   *("." label) ["."]

label     ::= (ALPHA / DIGIT) *(ALPHA / DIGIT / "-" / "_")

ALPHA     ::= <any alphabetic character, "A" through "Z" and
                 "a" through "z">
DIGIT     ::= <any numeric character, "0" through "9">

CRLF      ::= <carriage-return followed by line-feed>
SP        ::= <a SPACE or TAB character>
```

Figure 2.3: Resource Record Syntax (cont.)

The only other interesting part of the resource record syntax is how electronic mail addresses are represented. At the very beginning of this chapter, we noted that an electronic mail address took the form

```
local@domain
```

When the DNS refers to an electronic mail address, it views it as a domain name. The `local` component is treated as a label, and the separating at-sign ("`@`") is replaced by a dot. Hence, the address

```
mrose@dbc.mtview.ca.us
```

is represented in the DNS as

```
mrose.dbc.mtview.ca.us.
```

If the `local` component contains a dot, then a backslash-character ("`\`") is used, e.g., the electronic mail address

```
internet.ietf@dbc.mtview.ca.us
```

is represented in the DNS as

```
internet\.ietf.dbc.mtview.ca.us.
```

2.2.4 DNS Interactions

The DNS uses a client-server model for providing the name service. The client portion is termed a *resolver* and issues queries on behalf of the user. The resolver is responsible for contacting the appropriate name servers in order to answer the query posed by the user. During this process, the resolver may have to deal with any number of exceptional conditions. It is beyond the scope of *The Internet Message* to detail the algorithm used by resolvers in order to provide a simple, uniform service. Suffice it to say that a resolver must be able to:

- locate which name servers are capable of answering a particular query;

- deal with situations when some name servers are unavailable; and,

- understand when it is appropriate to cache information for future use.

One topic which does merit brief discussion is whether the server or the resolver contacts a name server which has the information in question. If the resolver wants to do this itself, it issues a so-called *iterative* query to the local name server. In this case, if the local name server doesn't have the information necessary to answer the request, it responds by referring the resolver to a name server which is more knowledgeable. Otherwise, if the resolver wants the local name server to contact the more knowledgeable one, it issues a *recursive* query. It is a policy matter for the local name server as to whether it will honor such a request. If not, it returns a referral.

There are many reasons why support for recursive queries are desirable:

- a host running a name server may have better network connectivity and/or bandwidth;

- it allows the local name server to build up a cache which can be used for future queries, allowing all local resolvers to share the cached information (otherwise, the caches built would be on a per-resolver basis); and,

- since there will be wide variance in the capabilities of systems
  which implement resolvers, support for recursive queries will result in simpler resolver implementations. In theory, this will lead
  to resolvers being implemented on a large number of different
  systems.

Unlike many other Internet applications, the messages exchanged
by the DNS are not textual, but rather are represented in a concise
binary notation. Each message consists of a small, fixed-length header,
followed by four variable-length *sections*. The *header* contains these
fields:

ID: a 16–bit integer identifying a particular request/response interaction. This allows a resolver to correlate incoming responses with previous requests, and also permits a resolver
to generate multiple requests (hopefully all different) before
receiving any responses.

OPCODE: indicates the operation for this interaction.

QR: indicates whether this is a request or a response.

AA: indicates whether this response is from a name server which
is authoritative with regard to the information asked for in
the query.

TC: indicates whether this response was truncated due to size
limitations imposed by the underlying transport service. (If
UDP is used, then messages are limited to 512 octets in
length; if TCP is used, then no *a priori* length limitation
is defined.)

RD: indicates whether the resolver wants the name server to *recursively* resolve the query.

RA: indicates whether the name server is willing to recursively
resolve future queries for the resolver.

RCODE: indicates if an error occurred while processing the query.
Values include: no error, format error, server failure, name
error, operation not implemented, operation refused.

counts: four count fields, each interpreted as a 16–bit unsigned integer, indicating the number of entries in the sections which follow.

For our purposes, the *standard query* operation is the only message type of interest. For this operation, only one section is present, the *question* section, which contains one or more questions. Each question contains three fields:

QNAME: identifies the domain name to be queried.

QCLASS: identifies the class of the resource records to be retrieved. In addition to supplying a specific class, a special value may be provided to match **ANY** class. (Use of this special value is discouraged, as generally the **IN** class should be used.)

QTYPE: identifies the type of the resource records to be retrieved. In addition to supplying a specific type, a special value may be provided to match **ANY** type.

When a name server generates a response, it sets the QR bit, and, if the name server is authoritative for the information, then it sets the AA bit. If this latter bit is set, then the resolver knows that it has received complete information to the query. Otherwise, the response may be incomplete, as it comes from cached information at the name server.

The question section in the response is identical to the query, but unlike the query, one or more of the remaining sections are filled-in. The *answer* section contains resource records, if any, which matched the query. If this section is empty, but no error code is set in the header of the response, then this indicates that the domain name exists, but doesn't have any resource records which match the query.

The *authority* section contains resource records, if any, which contain information about name servers which are more knowledgeable on the query, or contains consistency policy information. For example, if a resolver asked a question about information which the name server didn't have, the answer section would be empty and the authority section would contain one or more **NS** records which identify name servers which are more knowledgeable.

A second use for the authority section is for keeping track of bad questions. For example, suppose a query is issued about a non-existent domain name. The response returned would have the "name error" code set in its header, an empty answer section, and possibly the consistency policy for the subdomain referenced in the query. By examining the consistency policy, the resolver can determine how long it should maintain a *negative* caching entry for the query. Until that cache entry expires, whenever a user asks the same question, the resolver can short-circuit the DNS interaction by simply answering "no" on behalf of the name server.

Finally, the *additional* section contains additional resource records which may be useful information. For example, if the authority section contains the name of an authoritative name server, the additional section is likely to contain the address of that name server. By having the responder anticipate how the resolver will use the information it provides, the amount of traffic generated by the resolver is greatly reduced.

2.2.5 Using the DNS

We now look at how applications can use the DNS.

Name to Address Translation

The most straight-forward activity is mapping a domain name to an IP address. The query issued indicates the desired domain name, and asks for resource records of class **IN** and type **A**. Usually one of two kinds of responses is returned:

- If the domain name exists, then zero or more resource records are present in the answer section, containing the desired information. (If zero records are returned, it means that the domain name exists, but that there aren't any resource records of the desired type.)

- If the domain name does not exist, then the reply code in the response indicates "name error", and the authority section may contain information indicating the minimum amount of time in which this condition is likely to exist. Of course, other error responses are possible as well.

For example, if the query is

```
QNAME   dbc.mtview.ca.us.
QCLASS  IN
QTYPE   A
```

then a positive response would contain an answer section that looked like this:

```
dbc.mtview.ca.us.     86400 IN A 192.103.140.1
```

Recall that the second field is the time-to-live (in seconds) that this resource record may be cached by the resolver.

If the domain doesn't exist, then the answer section would be empty and the authority section might look like this:

```
ca.us.                86400 IN SOA ca.us. us-domain.isi.edu. (
                          920406
                          43200
                          1800
                          604800
                          86400 )
```

In this case, the resolver can create a negative cache entry for the queried name, and set the time-to-live value for that entry to 86400 seconds. (Be patient! Section 2.2.6 will explain all about the **SOA** record.)

Of course, to perform general name to attribute mapping, the query could ask for some class/type combination other than **IN/A**.

Alias Handling

It is often useful to use several names when referring to the same entity. By convention, one of these names is referred to as the *canonical* name for the entity and the other names are referred to as *aliases*. To implement this, a **CNAME** resource record is used by alias names to reference the canonical name for the entity. Hence, the resource record:

```
simple-times.org.                CNAME dbc.mtview.ca.us.
```

indicates that the domain name

```
simple-times.org.
```

is really an alias for

```
dbc.mtview.ca.us.
```

When a name server answers a question about a domain name, and the name is actually an alias, the answer section always contains the **CNAME** resource record.

```
simple-times.org.      86400 IN CNAME dbc.mtview.ca.us.
```

Further, if the query's QTYPE field is neither **CNAME** nor **ANY**, and if the name server has any resource records corresponding to the canonical name, then those resource records are also returned in the answer section. So, if the query was:

```
QNAME    simple-times.org.
QCLASS   IN
QTYPE    A
```

then the answer section returned would be:

```
simple-times.org.      86400 IN CNAME dbc.mtview.ca.us.
dbc.mtview.ca.us.      86400 IN A     192.103.140.1
```

Otherwise, if the name server doesn't have any resource records corresponding to the canonical name, then the answer section would contain only the **CNAME** resource record, e.g.,

```
simple-times.org.      86400 IN CNAME dbc.mtview.ca.us.
```

The authority section would contain NS resource records for name servers which are authoritative about the canonical name, e.g.,

```
ca.us.                    172800 IN NS venera.isi.edu.
                                    NS ns.isi.edu.
                                    NS nnsc.nsf.net.
                                    NS hercules.csl.sri.com.
```

and the additional section would hopefully contain address resource records for those name servers, e.g.,

```
venera.isi.edu.       172800 IN A 128.9.0.32
nnsc.net.net.         172800 IN A 128.89.1.178
hercules.csl.sri.com. 172800 IN A 192.12.33.51
```

Two things are interesting from this response:

- first, the deepest knowledge the name server had about the query was the names of authoritative name servers for the `ca.us.` domain; and,

- second, although the name server knew the name of the name server at `ns.isi.edu.`, it didn't supply the address, perhaps because there wasn't enough space left in the response.

Because of this automatic behavior on the part of the DNS, Internet applications desiring name to address translation can usually achieve this in a single DNS transaction, by simply giving the resolver the type-in supplied by the user and asking for the usual name to address translation query.

Of course, if the query was of the form

```
QNAME    simple-times.org.
QCLASS   IN
QTYPE    CNAME
```

or of the form

```
QNAME    simple-times.org.
QCLASS   IN
QTYPE    ANY
```

then only the **CNAME** resource record would be returned.

Mail Routing

Because electronic mail is inherently a store-and-forward service, it should not be surprising that application-level routing is often necessary when relaying electronic mail messages. To implement this, an **MX** resource record is used to indicate a list of hosts which relay mail for a destination domain name. This allows mail to be automatically routed through the Internet community.

Each time a mail transfer agent attempts to relay an electronic mail message, it issues a query, indicating the target domain name, and asking for resource records of class **IN** and type **MX**.[3]

The message transfer agent must carefully scrutinize the response, both to ensure proper relaying and to avoid routing loops:

- If the DNS indicates a transient error (e.g., a response is received with error code "server failure"), then this is treated as a transient error and the message transfer agent schedules the electronic mail message for later processing.

- If a response is received, but contains an error code other than "no error" or "server failure", then this is treated as a permanent error and the message transfer agent generates an error report. (These are described much later in Section 4.1.1 starting on page 127.)

- If a response is received, but is truncated, and the message transfer agent cannot re-issue the query using a connection-oriented transport service, then this too is treated as a permanent error.

Otherwise, the answer section, which contains zero or more **MX** resource records is examined.

If no **MX** resource records are present, then the message transfer agent will try and use the target domain name directly and open an SMTP connection. (Usually this will involve issuing another query asking for a class/type combination of **IN/A**.) This is done for backwards compatibility.

---

[3]Note that the original specification of this algorithm [5] has been modified by the Internet Host Requirements document. In particular, the algorithm previously looked for **WKS** resource records to see if the SMTP service was supported by a host which an MX resource record listed as a mail relay. This step has been removed.

Otherwise, recall that each **MX** resource record contains two fields, a preference (which is a 16–bit unsigned integer) and a domain name (which should be a canonical name). So, the message transfer agent sorts the set of **MX** resource records in ascending order of preference fields. It then examines each record looking for one which contains a domain name that identifies the local domain for the message transfer agent. If one is found, then the message transfer agent discards any record containing a preference field equal to or greater than the preference field in the record naming the local domain. This helps to avoid routing loops.

Next, the message transfer agent loops through the list of remaining **MX** resource records, going in ascending order of preference field. For each, the message transfer agent will attempt direct communication with the named host. If the electronic mail message cannot be delivered, the next resource record is consulted. This continues until either the message is delivered, or the message generates an error report, or the list of resource records is exhausted. In the final case, the message transfer agent treats it as a transient error and schedules the electronic mail message for later processing, when another query asking for a class/type combination of **IN/MX** will be issued.

Let's now look at an example to put this into perspective. Suppose the resolver for a message transfer agent at

    spyder.ssw.com

was talking to a name server containing these resource records:

```
dbc.mtview.ca.us.            IN A   192.103.140.1
                                MX  0 dbc.mtview.ca.us.
                                MX 10 fernwood.mpk.ca.us.
*.dbc.mtview.ca.us.          IN MX  0 dbc.mtview.ca.us.
fernwood.mpk.ca.us.          IN A   130.93.1.2
```

If the message transfer agent wanted to deliver an electronic mail message for an address containing a domain name of

    dbc.mtview.ca.us

then its resolver would issue this query:

```
QNAME    dbc.mtview.ca.us.
QCLASS   IN
QTYPE    MX
```

The answer section returned would be:

```
dbc.mtview.ca.us.            IN MX   0 dbc.mtview.ca.us.
                                MX 10 fernwood.mpk.ca.us.
```

and the additional section would contain

```
dbc.mtview.ca.us.            IN A   192.103.140.1
fernwood.mpk.ca.us.          IN A   130.93.1.2
```

The message transfer agent would first attempt relaying using the IP address

    192.103.140.1

If no SMTP transaction could be achieved, then it would try the IP address

    130.93.1.2

If a message transfer agent at

```
fernwood.mpk.ca.us
```

was also talking to the same name server and wanted to deliver mail to

```
dbc.mtview.ca.us
```

it would get back the same response:

```
dbc.mtview.ca.us.              IN MX  0 dbc.mtview.ca.us.
                                  MX 10 fernwood.mpk.ca.us.
```

However, when examining the list of **MX** records returned in the answer section, it would remove

```
dbc.mtview.ca.us.              IN MX 10 fernwood.mpk.ca.us.
```

as this record names a message transfer agent (itself) which isn't closer than the message transfer agent doing the lookup. So, the message transfer agent would attempt relaying using a single **MX** record to guide it.

Now suppose that the message transfer agent wanted to deliver an electronic mail message for some recipient at

```
baiji.dbc.mtview.ca.us
```

then its resolver would issue this query:

```
QNAME    baiji.dbc.mtview.ca.us.
QCLASS   IN
QTYPE    MX
```

The answer section returned would be:

```
baiji.dbc.mtview.ca.us.        IN MX  0 dbc.mtview.ca.us.
```

and the additional section would contain

```
dbc.mtview.ca.us.              IN A  192.103.140.1
```

The message transfer agent would first attempt relaying using that one IP address. This illustrates two important points:

- first, when a name server uses a wildcard resource record to satisfy a query, the owner of the returned record identifies the domain named targeted by the query; and,

- second, **MX** resource records are not used recursively. For example, even though mail destined for

  ```
  dbc.mtview.ca.us
  ```

  is handled by two different hosts, both of these hosts do not necessarily relay for the destinations serviced by

  ```
  dbc.mtview.ca.us
  ```

So, based on this example, we can intuit the semantics of a wildcard domain:

- when a name server which is authoritative about a subdomain is asked a question about a domain name, and

- there aren't any resource records which are owned by that domain name, and

- there are wildcard resource records which, ignoring the wildcard label, are superior to the domain name in question, and,

- there are no resource records superior to the domain name in question, but subordinate to the wildcard resource records,

- then the wildcard resource records are used to answer the question.

Address to Name Translation

Finally, it is often useful to be able to map an IP address back into a domain name. A special portion of the domain name space,

    in-addr.arpa.

is used for this purpose. In this subdomain, entities with IP addresses are named by "reversing the quad". Hence, an entity with an IP address of

    a.b.c.d

would have a domain name of

    d.c.b.a.in-addr.arpa.

For example, the entity having IP address

    192.103.140.1

would have an entry in the DNS of

    1.140.103.192.in-addr.arpa.

The reason for this reversal is to allow ease of delegation: when written in dotted-quad format, the network portion of an IP address occurs on the left; in contrast, the most-significant labels in a domain name occur on the right. "Reversing the quad", makes it easier for the top-level naming authority for

    in-addr.arpa.

to delegate authority to individual networking administrations.

For example, the administration responsible for the class C IP network

    192.103.140

could be delegated responsibility for the subdomain

    140.103.192.in-addr.arpa.

meaning that it would be responsible for populating the subdomain with resource records corresponding to the hosts using that particular IP network.

The leaf-entities named in this subdomain typically have a single resource record, with a class/type combination of **IN/PTR**. This resource record identifies the domain name (which should be a canonical name) that has a corresponding IP address. For example, suppose an application wanted to find out the domain name of its peer that was communicating from IP address:

```
192.103.140.1
```

The application's resolver would issue the query

```
QNAME    1.140.103.192.in-addr.arpa.
QCLASS   IN
QTYPE    PTR
```

and the answer returned would be:

```
1.140.103.192.in-addr.arpa.  IN PTR dbc.mtview.ca.us.
```

2.2.6 Zones of Authority

Our discussion of the DNS closes by examining how delegation of authority is represented. This is achieved by introducing a new concept, a *zone* of authority.

In order to distribute information, the entire domain name space is divided into several, non-overlapping zones. For each zone, a single name server, the *primary*, masters the information in that zone. In addition, at least one other name server must also be configured to be authoritative about the zone. These are termed *secondary* name servers for the zone, and are used to increase availability of the DNS service.

When a delegation of authority occurs within a zone, a new zone is created, and, in order to keep the two zones disjoint, authority for information contained in the subtree rooted at the delegated domain name is removed from the parent zone. Thus, a zone is always a connected, albeit possibly irregular, portion of the naming tree, and each zone always contains at least one domain name. The technical term for the point where a zone is created is a *cut*.

The DNS uses resource records in order to describe a zone. The top of a zone is described by a single **SOA** resource record which defines the consistency policy for the zone, along with **NS** resource records naming the authoritative name servers for the zone. This resource record contains these fields:

master: the domain name of the name server that masters the information in the zone;

mailbox: a domain name identifying the electronic mail address of a person responsible for the zone;

serial: a version number (expressed as an unsigned 32–bit integer) which identifies the serial number of the master information (this value is changed each time the zone is cut or whenever information within the zone is changed);

refresh: the number of seconds (expressed as an unsigned 32–bit integer) indicating how often secondary name servers should check to see if the primary name server has changed the serial number for this zone, (and if so, the secondary will then shadow (copy) the entire zone from the primary name server);

retry: the number of seconds (expressed as an unsigned 32–bit integer) indicating how often secondary name servers should retry a failed refresh;

expire: the number of seconds (expressed as an unsigned 32–bit integer) indicating the maximum amount of time that can elapse before this zone is no longer authoritative; and,

minimum: the number of seconds (expressed as an unsigned 32–bit integer) indicating the minimum time-to-live field associated with resource records in this zone. (Among other things, this field is used by resolvers when they create negative caching entries.)

The shadowing process is termed a *zone transfer*, in which every resource record — including any wildcard resource records — associated with the zone is copied verbatim from the primary name server by each secondary name server.

Each time a cut is made in a zone, two or more **NS** resource records are added to the zone. These identify the primary name server and one or more secondary name servers for the subzone.

Using the examples we've already seen, suppose that a naming authority for the State of California is created. The authority contacts the naming authority for the US, and asks that the following cuts be added to the **us.** zone:

```
ca.us.                          IN NS venera.isi.edu.
                                   NS ns.isi.edu.
                                   NS nnsc.nsf.net.
                                   NS hercules.csl.sri.com.
```

In addition, if any of the name servers identified by the cuts are not (or are no longer) contained within the parent zone, then "glue" must be added to the parent zone. This glue takes the form of **A** resource records for those name servers.

Glue allows servers knowledgeable about the parent zone to contact the name servers directly (for recursive queries), or to hand back the appropriate addressing information (for iterative queries). (Note that this means that a zone can contain two kinds of resource records for domain names which are outside the zone, **NS** records which identify the cut, and **A** records which provide the IP addresses of the name servers.)

In this example, since none of the name servers are subordinate to `ca.us.`, no glue is needed. Further, because glue represents information available elsewhere in the DNS, it should never be used gratuitously, as this may cause anomalous behavior.

Continuing with our example, the naming authority for `ca.us.` creates the `ca.us.` zone by adding this resource record to the information kept in those name servers:

```
ca.us.                      IN SOA ca.us. us-domain.isi.edu. (
                            920406
                            43200
                            1800
                            604800
                            86400 )
```

One of the name servers is then configured as the primary for the `ca.us.` zone, whilst the others are configured as secondaries. Once the `us.` naming authority is satisfied that the `ca.us.` zone is properly configured, the cuts described above are put in the `us.` zone and the serial number field of the **SOA** resource record for the `us.` zone is updated.

There are actually many more details involved when setting up a zone. [29] presents an overview of the administrative procedures, whilst [30] outlines the operational procedures.

2.3   Finding Information

The style of name service provided by the DNS is sometimes called a
"bullet" service: you issue a query with the domain name that you're
interested in, and the DNS quickly returns an answer to your query.
However, a key problem is determining which domain name to query.
At present, there is no widely-accepted, automatic facility for achieving
this in the Internet community. However, work continues along several
avenues, including:

- since mid-1989, work has been underway to develop an OSI Directory Infrastructure for the Internet community (See Section 5.1
  of [31]);

- since the same time, work has been going on to synthesize existing
  electronic *white pages* services in order to build a meta-service,
  termed the Knowledge Information Service (KIS) [32], which has
  wide coverage, and,

- research is underway in the area of resource discovery and related
  technologies [33, 34].

In the remainder of this chapter, we'll look at three Internet services
which can be used to find sites and persons. (Before continuing, the
reader may find it useful to refer back to page 1.2.2 which describes the
structure of Internet application layer protocols.)

2.3.1   Finding a Particular Site

The *whois* protocol [35] is used to find information about a particular
resource registered with the DDN Network Information Center (NIC).
Although this NIC is supposed to provide service to just one of the networks in the Internet community, the MILNET, due to historical events,
it also maintains information about several Internet-wide resources.
The NIC maintains a centralized database, the WHOIS database, which
keeps track of these resources. Resources include such entities as:

persons
domain names

mailing lists
network numbers
organizations

and so on. Each entry is assigned a brief, alphanumeric handle which is used as a unique key into the WHOIS database. In addition, each entry is tagged as containing a certain kind of record (e.g., an organizational record).

Because the whois service is based on a a centralized database, there are the usual problems encountered when dealing with a centralized service, e.g., availability problems, performance bottlenecks, timeliness of update, and so on.

Generally, the whois service is available on the host `nic.ddn.mil`. However, several sites run their own private version of the whois service. A server process listens on TCP port 43. A client establishes a connection to the whois server and issues a single query. The whois server evaluates the query, returns whatever information is available, and closes the TCP connection. The client receives the information, displays it to the user, and then closes the TCP connection. Figure 2.4 shows the syntax of the query and response, both of which are in NVT ASCII.[4]

Evaluation of a query consists of three phases: filter construction, database search, and, output generation.

A query often begins with a keyword or special symbol that indicates the type of record to search for. The whois server can then construct a filter specialized for that kind of search, using the query's token as a parameter. In the easiest case, the keyword `handle` or bang-character ("!") is given which indicates that the token which follows is a "handle" from the WHOIS database. In this case, only a simple retrieval is necessary. Otherwise, a more complicated filter is used. If a trailing dot follows the token, then this indicates that the filter should allow for initial-substrings matching; otherwise, the filter uses case-insensitive string-equality.

---

[4]Actually, the syntax is somewhat richer than this figure indicates. However, Figure 2.4 conveys the wide range of querying options available.

```
query      ::= [kword 1*SP / ksym] [qword 1*SP / qsym]
                 *SP token [partial] CRLF

response   ::= *(*text CRLF)

kword      ::= "handle" / "name" / "mailbox" / record
                 / "partial"
record     ::= <any unique abbreviation of a record type
                 defined in the WHOIS database>

ksym       ::= "!"                    ; handle
                 / "."                  ; name

token      ::= 1*<any character except CRLF or ".">

qword      ::= "expand" / "full" / "subdisplay" / "summary"
qsym       ::= "*"                    ; expand
                 / "="                  ; full
                 / "%"                  ; subdisplay
                 / "$"                  ; summary

partial    ::= "."                    ; partial matches

text       ::= <any character, including bare CR and bare LF,
                 but not including CRLF>

CRLF       ::= <carriage-return followed by line-feed>
SP         ::= <a SPACE or TAB character>
```

Figure 2.4: Whois Query Syntax

Output generation varies, depending on whether one or more than one match was found. Here again, a keyword or special character will control the output:

expand: display complete information on each match, followed by information on any subordinate entries (i.e., if an organization is matched, after displaying information on the organization, list any of the organization's users who are in the database);

subdisplay: display one-line of information on each match, followed by information on any subordinate entries;

full: display complete information on each match; or,

summary: display one-line of information on each match.

If no directives are present, then output generation depends on the number of matches. If exactly one match is found during the search, complete information is displayed, otherwise only one-line of information is displayed for each match.

Two examples should help clarify things. Suppose we want to find out about the organization

```
Dover Beach Consulting, Inc.
```

Figure 2.5 shows a result when the query is simply

```
Dover Beach Consulting
```

The name in parenthesis,

```
NET-DOVER-BEACH
```

is the WHOIS handle for the entry being displayed. Among the more interesting bits of information is the class C IP network number assigned, along with the domain names and IP addresses of the name servers for hosts on that network.

```
Dover Beach Consulting (NET-DOVER-BEACH)
   420 Whisman Court
   Mountain View, CA 94043-2112

   Netname: DOVER-BEACH
   Netnumber: 192.103.140.0

   Coordinator:
      Rose, Marshall T.   (MTR)   mrose@DBC.MTVIEW.CA.US
      (415) 968-1052

   Domain System inverse mapping provided by:

   DBC.MTVIEW.CA.US            192.103.140.1
   FERNWOOD.MPK.CA.US          130.93.1.2
   NS.PSI.NET                  192.33.4.10
   NS2.PSI.NET                 192.35.82.2

   Record last updated on 29-Nov-91.
```

Figure 2.5: Finding an Organization

Dover Beach Consulting (NET-DOVER-BEACH)   192.103.140.0

There is one known host:

DBC.MTVIEW.CA.US   192.103.140.1

Figure 2.6: Finding Hosts in an Organization

Now suppose we wanted to find out what hosts were registered for
that network. As shown in Figure 2.6, a query of

> %!NET-DOVER-BEACH

would do the trick!

Actually, the WHOIS database is used primarily by users to find
other people, not organizations or networks. However, a lot of times,
the WHOIS database will have information on only a few persons at an
organization. Even so, being able to find out about domain names,
networks, and hosts associated with an organization is very useful.
Why? Because then you might be able to ask one of those hosts about
the person you're looking for.

2.3.2 Finding a Particular Person

The *finger* protocol [36] is used to find information about a particular
user. A server process listens on TCP port 79. A client establishes a
connection to the finger server and issues a single query. The finger
server evaluates the query, returns whatever available information is
permitted, and closes the TCP connection. The client receives the information, displays it to the user, and then closes the TCP connection.
Figure 2.7 shows the syntax of the query and response, both of which
are in NVT ASCII.

Before continuing, it is worthwhile musing on the network security
impacts of the finger service. Finger returns information about users.
Users may not want information about them to be disclosed.   For
entirely different reasons, system administrators may also not want
information about users to be disclosed. Consequently, many sites

```
query      ::= [verbose [1*SP username]] [path] CRLF

response   ::= *(*text CRLF)

verbose    ::= "/W"

username   ::= 1*<any character except SP or CRLF>

path       ::= 1*("@" domain)

domain     ::= label *("." label) ["."]
label      ::= ALPHA [*(ALPHA / DIGIT / "-" ) (ALPHA / DIGIT)]

text       ::= <any character, including bare CR and bare LF,
                   but not including CRLF>

ALPHA      ::= <any alphabetic character, "A" through "Z" and
                   "a" through "z">
DIGIT      ::= <any numeric character, "0" through "9">

CRLF       ::= <carriage-return followed by line-feed>
SP         ::= <any SPACE or TAB character>
```

Figure 2.7: Finger Query Syntax

in the Internet community no longer run a finger service. For those sites which do run a finger service, [36] outlines configuration options which should be available to the system administrator. As such, the discussion below outlines the maximum behavior of a finger server. A system administrator may selectively disable one or more of the features described. If enough features are disabled, then the finger service is effectively useless and there is little point in running it. Naturally, this leads to a soapbox!

soap... To be sure, users have a legitimate concern for privacy and system administrators have a legitimate concern for security. However, the author still fondly remembers the old days of the Internet community. If you needed to contact someone, you could finger them and find out useful things like:

- if they were currently logged in;

- if so, how long ago they had used their terminal;

- how long ago they had read their mail;

- where they were forwarding their mail to; and so on.

This turned out to be very useful when you needed to communicate with a colleague, because:

- if they were logged in, you could ask finger for their office number and call them;

- if they were forwarding mail, you could finger them on the destination to see if perhaps they were logged in there; or, at the very least,

- you could send them mail, and later see if they read it.

Today, finger is unfairly viewed as one of the culprits in the infamous Internet worm incident, and as such a dastardly threat to world peace and the ozone layer.[5] Let's take a step back: networks are supposed to

---

[5] All because a programmer at a university didn't code a finger server well, and then dozens of commercial vendors shipped product containing the server without ever giving it a second thought. Who's to blame, the protocol or the vendors? The reader can guess my answer.

help people communicate, to collaborate, to get things done together. Finger provides a valuable infrastructural service in this cause. So, here's my advice to users: get your system administrator to consult Section 3 of [36], have them check out the available finger implementations, and then *demand* that your system run a secured finger service. Remember, "we're all in this together!"

`...soap`

Finger Server Behavior

The finger server first sees if the query contains a `path` specification. If so, this indicates that the client wishes the query to be evaluated at some other host. The finger server strips off the rightmost domain in the `path` and enters the role of a client: it establishes a TCP connection to the finger server residing at the host named by that domain, and sends the initial portion of the query followed by a CR-LF sequence. Then, the now intermediate finger server simply passes back to the original client any information which is provided by the new finger server.

Of course, there may be more than one domain name contained within the original `path` specification, but eventually a finger server will receive a query which is to be evaluated locally.

At this point, the server checks to see if the query contains a `verbose` flag. If so, this is remembered when output is to be generated.

Now, the query either contains a `username` or is empty. If a `username` is specified, the finger server treats this as a specification for a local user and returns whatever publicly-available information is allowed. It is possible that the `username` specified is not a complete specification of a local user. In this case, the finger server returns a brief summary of each possible local user. The rationale for this is that the client can peruse the output and then issue a more refined finger query.

Instead, if no `username` is specified, the finger server returns a brief summary of all the local users currently logged onto the system.

```
Login        Name              TTY Idle    When    Where
mrose        Marshall T. Rose  p2   23 Thu 22:26  baiji:0.0
```

Figure 2.8: Fingering Users on a Host

```
[dbc.mtview.ca.us]
Login name: mrose              In real life: Marshall T. Rose
Directory: /home/mrose         Shell: /bin/csh
On since Apr  9 22:26:36 on ttyp2 from baiji:0.0
22 minutes Idle Time
No unread mail
Project: Computer-communications Consultancy
Plan:
Postal:  Dover Beach Consulting, Inc.
         420 Whisman Court
         Mountain View, CA   94043-2112
         US

Tel:  +1 415 968 1052
Fax:  +1 415 968 2510
```

Figure 2.9: Fingering a User

Let's look at two examples: Figure 2.8 shows a result when an empty query (one containing only a CR-LF sequence) is received by a finger server. In contrast, Figure 2.9 shows a result when a query for a particular user is issued and **path** is specified, e.g.,

mrose@dbc.mtview.ca.us CR-LF

The first line of the result is generated by the intermediate finger server, to indicate that it is contacting the next finger server in the path.

So to put things back in perspective, suppose if we were trying to find someone named "Marshall Rose" who was working somewhere called "Dover Beach Consulting, Inc." The first step would be to use the whois service to find out something about the organization. This was shown in Figure 2.5 on page 63. The next step would be to find a host, operated by that organization, which might know about the person in question. This was shown in Figure 2.6 on page 64. The final step is to try to finger the user at that host. Usually starting with the surname is best, so a finger query of

```
rose
```

directed at the server residing on

```
dbc.mtview.ca.us
```

would be the starting point. This yields the results shown in Figure 2.9 on page 68. Of course, if "**rose**" wasn't a complete specification, the server might reply instead with a list of possibilities. We could then re-issue the request using one of these.

2.3.3   An Automated Approach

Actually, there is a better way to find a particular person. As a part of his research into resource discovery, Professor Michael F. Schwartz at the University of Colorado at Boulder, has developed the *netfind* program [37].

Figure 2.10 on page 70 shows the syntax of the query and response for netfind. Typically **user** is the person's last name, and **where** identifies the institution where the person works, by name and/or geographic location.

Netfind first consults a "seed database" which relates organization names to domain names. The database is built, and continually refined, by a process which monitors several sources: public electronic mail messages, the domain name system, and so on. The database is then pruned by hand to remove irrelevant entries.

Netfind looks in the database and selects those domain names which match the locational information provided by the user (the **where** components). If more than three are found, the user is asked to select at most three for further examination.

Then, netfind asks the DNS to provide the addresses of authoritative name servers for each of those domains (i.e., it issues a query for NS resource records for the zones containing those domains). The reason is that these name servers often reside on hosts which are used for network administration purposes.

```
query      ::= user 1*(1*SP where) CRLF

response   ::= *(*text CRLF)

user       ::= 1*<any character except SP or CRLF>
where      ::= 1*<any character except SP or CRLF>

text       ::= <any character, including bare CR and bare LF,
                   but not including CRLF>

CRLF       ::= <carriage-return followed by line-feed>
SP         ::= <any SPACE or TAB character>
```

Figure 2.10: Netfind Query Syntax

Next, netfind connects to the SMTP server on each of these administrative hosts, and uses SMTP's **VRFY** command to see if the user is known, and if so, to determine which host the user receives mail on. (This command is discussed much later on in Section 4.1.2 starting on page 139.)

Finally, netfind connects to the finger server on the host where the user receives mail. If the finger service provides information about the user and other hosts, then netfind connects to those finger servers as well.

Because some sites allow finger traffic from remote hosts only to their administrative hosts, when a finger connection can't be established to the host where the user receives mail, netfind establishes a finger connection to the administrative host, and uses a finger query containing a path specification.

Finally, netfind is fairly clever about parallelizing its use of network resources — a single netfind process contains ten lightweight threads allowing it to pursue several different avenues of search concurrently. In fact, netfind is resilient in the case of unavailable services. For example, it uses a different strategy if SMTP service is not available on an administrative host.

2.4 Technology Comparison

In MHS, a user is named by an originator/recipient name (*O/R-name*). This contains either a *distinguished name* from the OSI Directory, an MHS address (termed an *O/R-address*), or both. Like the DNS, the OSI Directory provides a name service. Unlike the DNS however, the Directory offers a rich information service. Discussion of the Directory is clearly beyond the scope of *The Internet Message*. Interested readers should consult *The Little Black Book* [31] instead.

During message submission, if the O/R-name contains only a Directory name, the Directory is consulted to determine the corresponding O/R-address. Once an O/R-address is present (either supplied during submission or found later in the Directory), the O/R-address will be used as the basis for relaying. If, for some reason, a message transfer agent determines the O/R-address to be in error, and a Directory name is present in the O/R-name, then the directory is once again consulted to see if there is a new O/R address. So, for the remainder of this discussion, we'll focus on O/R-addresses. To understand them, we need to understand that MHS views the message transfer system as containing *administrative management domains* (ADMDs) and *private management domains* (PRMDs). Management domains provide a means for dividing up the message transfer system under different authorities. An administrative management domain is run by a public telecommunications authority (PTT), whilst private management domains are run by non-PTTs. ADMDs are required to have a routing capability to all other ADMDs. Outside of this characteristic, the divisions between ADMDs and PRMDs are largely artificial.

An O/R-address is a combination of several attribute/value pairs, taken from an ordered, fixed list. In the 1984 recommendations on Message Handling Systems, the components available are:

Country (C): identifies the country associated with the electronic mail address.

Administrative Management Domain (ADMD):
identifies the public-carrier associated with the electronic mail address.

Private Management Domain (PRMD): identifies
the private-carrier associated with the electronic mail
address.

X.121 Address: identifies the X.121 address of the electronic
mail address.

Terminal Identifier: identifies the terminal address of the
electronic mail address.

Organization (O): identifies the organization associated with
the electronic mail address.

Organizational Unit (OU): identifies the organizational unit
associated with the electronic mail address.

Unique User-Agent Identifier: identifies the user-process associated with the electronic mail address.

Personal Name (PN): identifies the personal name associated
with the electronic mail address, a combination of first initial,
given name, surname, and generational-qualifier.

Domain-Defined Attribute (DDA): provides an "escape
mechanism" by allowing arbitrary key/value strings to be
associated with the electronic mail address. These pairings
are meaningful in some identified context.

Only four combinations of these are allowed:

- C, ADMD, and any of: PRMD, O, OU, PN, and DDA

- C, ADMD, X.121 address, and optionally DDA

- C, ADMD, Unique User-Agent Identifier, and optionally DDA

- X.121 address, and optionally Terminal Identifier

The 1988 standard on MHS added more components, to support addressing of processes (which have a common, rather than a personal,
name) and physical-delivery addresses.

Unfortunately, there are number of inadequacies to electronic mail addressing in MHS.

First, there is no support for automatic routing. Unlike the mail system in the Internet community which uses MX resource records from the DNS, there is no standardized means for conveying mail routing information. This means that message transfer agent administrators must manually develop, maintain, and exchange routing tables among themselves.

Second, although O/R-addresses appear hierarchical, they do not provide sufficient structure to provide for hierarchical routing. Consider: MHS theory states that a given PRMD is subordinate to a particular ADMD. In practice, this works only when there is a single ADMD within a country. In countries with multiple PTTs, there are multiple ADMDs, and larger organizations with their own PRMDs often find it attractive to subscribe to several ADMDs. As such, there is no hierarchical relationship between ADMDs and PRMDs. (Of course, in countries with a single ADMD, having this component in an O/R-address is entirely superfluous, as knowledge of the country yields knowledge of the ADMD).

Third, O/R-addresses are composed from a dozen different attributes combined in four different ways. This is entirely too complex and leads to a number of problems:

- the OSI Directory is not widespread, so human users have to determine a correspondent's address manually, and type it in manually (at least the first time).

- because there is no official textual syntax for an address, formats vary between implementations, and it is difficult to enter the information from business cards or personal communication.

- implementations are unlikely to support routing algorithms for all four configurations, leading to interesting interoperability problems.

Further, it's not really clear what benefits are accrued by allowing such flexibility. For example, the most successful telecommunications number scheme in history is the one used by the international telephone system. Since international telephone numbers are actually hierarchical, they exhibit excellent qualities for hierarchical routing. Further, since most people, not just computer people, know how to write and remember phone numbers, one can even argue that phone numbers are the ideal unit of commerce for addressing users of a message transfer system.

Finally, there are few authorities in place to register ADMD and PRMD names, even though the original MHS specification was standardized back in 1984. Hence, within many countries, there is no guarantee that PRMD names will be unique. This makes it even more difficult to coordinate routing, change service providers, or (in extreme cases) even assign electronic mail addresses.

soap...   So, electronic mail addresses for OSI can't be assigned, read, written, or routed. Other than that, they're perfect. Perhaps the reader might think this is polemic. On the other hand, it is interesting to note that there are still quite a few MHS "experts" who don't seem to use electronic mail. For these people, MHS addresses really are perfect! Oh, and lest the reader be misled by those who claim that the OSI Directory will just "solve" this problem, the author makes the gentle reminder that it's now four years since the Directory was standardized and market adoption is quite low. There are many reasons for this, which are outside the scope of *The Internet Message* (Section 6.5.3 of *The Little Black Book* explains why). Just keep in mind that it's going to be a long, long time, before the OSI Directory is solving anyone's

...soap   problems in a large community.

Chapter 3

Message Formats

Now that we have explored naming in the Internet community, let's return to the model for message handling introduced back on page 2. It's now time to consider the messaging "protocol" spoken between user agents. However, this protocol is really nothing more than a common format for conveying information.

Rather than present a strict bottom-up discussion on this common format, we'll begin by discussing basic structuring rules, and then introduce capabilities which are used to support user agent functions. Of course, before looking at these capabilities, we'll have to set the context by introducing a real user agent. Finally, the chapter concludes by examining a few miscellaneous topics.

Some readers might find the style of describing headers in terms of user agent functionality to be controversial. Indeed, one of the reviewers of *The Internet Message* did not like this style of presentation at all. However, the author believes it to be the best way to convey the concepts and minimize the tedium.

3.1   A Memo-Based Format

The unit of commerce in electronic mail is a message. In general, an electronic mail message is an information object. That is, it contains an arbitrarily structured body which conveys some meaning between the originator and a recipient.

In more concrete terms, in the Internet community, an electronic mail message contains information of two types: *headers*, which are used to convey control information; and, a *body*, which is used to convey the actual data. For our purposes, the syntax of an electronic mail message is defined in a document called RFC-822 [6].[1]

As with many other Internet application protocols, an electronic mail message contains characters from the NVT ASCII repertoire. Of course, it is a local matter as to how electronic mail messages are stored at a particular site. All that does matter is that when electronic mail is exchanged, the NVT ASCII repertoire is used during the exchange. That is, as with all Internet protocols, the format of electronic mail messages places requirements on the *interchange* of information, not a requirement as to how information is locally represented or stored.

The headers of an electronic mail message are each identified by a keyword and a structured value. In contrast, the body is viewed as unstructured text.

On the surface, these choices might seem rather limiting as to the variety of electronic mail messages which can be represented. However, the use of a 7–bit, US ASCII scheme for transmission, coupled with a memo-based textual format, is surprisingly flexible. Further, as we shall see later in Chapter 6, these choices do not prevent the interoperable exchange of electronic mail messages containing arbitrarily structured binary objects.

3.1.1   Writing Electronic Mail Messages

The top-level BNF specification for electronic mail messages is shown in Figure 3.1. This specification is high-level in that the actual syntax for

---

[1]Although RFC-822 uses the term "header field", in the interest of brevity *The Internet Message* will use the term "headers" instead.

```
message    ::= 1*field *(CRLF *text)

field      ::= name ":" [value] CRLF

name       ::= 1*<any character except SP or ":">

           ; actual syntax varies depending on header
value      ::= text *(LWSP text)

text       ::= <any character, including bare CR and bare LF,
                  but not including CRLF>

LWSP       ::= CRLF 1*SP
CRLF       ::= <carriage-return followed by line-feed>
SP         ::= <any SPACE or TAB character>
```

Figure 3.1: Electronic Mail Message Top-level Syntax

a header's value depends on the keyword used to identify the header. However, the figure should illustrate these points:

- an electronic mail message starts with one or more headers;

- each header is named by a keyword and followed by a value;

- the value can span multiple-lines, but never starts at the beginning of a line; and,

- the body starts after the first blank line.

So, to separate the headers from the body, look for the first occurrence of the four characters, CR, LF, CR, LF, and the dividing line occurs right after the second LF.

The most interesting feature of these rules is the provision for multi-line values for headers. Basically, whenever a header value contains one or more adjacent occurrences of the LWSP sequence, this is treated as a single space-character (" "). This allows user agents to "fold" headers to make them more readable.

Most of the headers have a keyword-dependent syntax associated with them. However, a few do not. These are termed *unstructured*

header values, and are simply text. The only caveat associated when
dealing with unstructured headers is that white-space is significant.
Hence, although multiple adjacent occurrences of the LWSP sequence
are considered as a single space-character, this one space-character
forms a part of the header value.

One thing which Figure 3.1 on page 77 does not convey is case-
independent handling of headers. In general, the keywords which identify a header are handled in a case-insensitive fashion. That is, the
following keywords all identify the same header:

```
TO
To
tO
to
```

However, the value of a header may, or may not, require case-insensitive
handling, depending on the semantics of the header. Regardless, user
agents should always preserve the case of a header value.

3.1.2   Structured Header Values

In order to allow for automated processing by user agents, it is necessary
to define structured values for many kinds of headers. For now, we need
only consider the building blocks which go into making that structure.
Figure 3.2 on page 80 defines the syntax of these building blocks. Their
meanings are:

comment: Informational text, meaningful only to humans, delimited within matching parenthesis-characters ("(" and ")").
Comments actually nest (which is probably a worthy topic
for a soapbox), and may be multi-line values. Comments can
occur just about anywhere. When processing an electronic
mail message, the placement and content of comments should
be preserved to the largest extent possible.

domain-literal: Native addressing information, used when
"address to name" translation information is not available
from the network (e.g., a transient DNS failure), delimited
within matching bracket-characters ("[" and "]"), e.g.,

"`mrose@[192.103.140.1]`". Domain literals may be multi-line values.

quoted-string: An arbitrary collection of characters treated as a single unit, used when a single lexeme would contain white-space or one or more separator characters. Quoted strings may be multi-line values.

atom: A single lexeme used when its components contain only alphanumeric or non-separator characters. Atoms may not be multi-lined values.

word: Either an atom or a quoted-string.

specials: Separator characters.

It should be noted that within a structured header value, comments can occur between any two lexemes. Similarly, white-space can also separate any two lexemes. In the remaining BNF descriptions in this chapter, these conventions won't be explicitly brought out. So, just keep them in mind.

So, with these building blocks out of the way, let's take a step back and look at an implementation of a user agent. This will aid future discussion as to how the format of electronic mail messages supports user agent functions.

```
comment    ::= "(" *(ctext / quoted-pair / comment) ")"

ctext      ::= <any character except "(", ")", "\", CR,
                   but including LWSP>

domain-literal
           ::= "[" *(dtext / quoted-pair) "]"

dtext      ::= <any character except "[", "]", "\", CR,
                   but including LWSP>

quoted-string
           ::= <"> *(qtext / quoted-pair) <">

qtext      ::= <any character except <">, "\", CR,
                   but including LWSP>

word       ::= atom / quoted-string

           ; any characters except specials and SP
atom       ::= 1*atomic
atomic     ::= ALPHA / DIGIT
               / "!" / "#" / "$" / "%" / "&" / "'" / "*"
               / "+" / "-" / "/" / "=" / "?" / "^" / "_"
               / "'" / "{" / "}" / "~"

specials   ::= "(" / ")" / "[" / "]" / <"> / "\"
               / "," / "." / ":" / ";" / "@" / "<" / ">"

quoted-pair
           ::= "\" <any character>

LWSP       ::= CRLF 1*SP
CRLF       ::= <carriage-return followed by line-feed>
SP         ::= <any SPACE or TAB character>
ALPHA      ::= <any alphabetic character, "A" through "Z" and
                   "a" through "z">
DIGIT      ::= <any numeric character, "0" through "9">
CTL        ::= <any character with value 0(NUL) through 31(US)
                   or having value 177(DEL)>
```

Figure 3.2: Electronic Mail Message Syntactic-Sugar

3.2 MH: A "Multifarious" User Agent

The UCI version of the Rand Message Handling System, MH, is a mail user agent for the UNIX operating-system [38, 39, 40, 41, 42]. It is composed of a set of programs, each of which performs a different message handling task.

MH was originally developed by Bruce Borden, Stockton Gaines and Norman Shapiro at the Rand Corporation in 1979. The Information and Computer Science Department of the University of California at Irvine acquired a copy of MH in 1981, and began extensive development of the software.

3.2.1 The MH Philosophy

Although MH has many traits that tend to distinguish it from other systems which handle mail, there is a single fundamental design decision which influences the interface between MH and the user: MH differs from most other systems in that it is composed of many small programs instead of one very large one. This architecture gives MH much of its strength, since intermediate and advanced users are able to take advantage of this flexibility.

The key to this flexibility is that the UNIX command interpreter, called a *shell*, is the user's interface to MH. This means that when handling mail, the entire power of the shell is at the user's disposal, in addition to the facilities which MH provides. Hence, the user may intersperse mail handling commands with other commands in an arbitrary fashion, making use of command handling capabilities which the user's shell provides.

Furthermore, rather than storing electronic mail messages in a complicated data structure within a monolithic file, each message in MH is a UNIX file, and each folder (an object which holds groups of electronic mail messages) in MH is a UNIX directory. That is, the directory- and file-structure of UNIX is used directly. As a result, any UNIX file-handling command can be applied to any electronic mail message.

In addition, MH is highly customizable. Each user maintains a profile which contains default values for MH in general and also for each MH command. This allows each user to simply tailor MH for

their desired behavior. Further, these defaults are evaluated before any
command-line arguments, so a user can easily override their behavior.
To simplify matters further, a user may give a single MH command
different names, and assign different defaults to the command, based
on the name.

Finally, because the user's shell provides the interface to the UA,
MH is also extensible. A user can combine MH commands by writing
shell scripts (command files) which invoke the appropriate MH programs.

3.2.2   MH Command Handling

The syntax of each MH command is fairly regular:

```
name ["+" folder] *msg *("-" switch [argument])
```

where `name` identifies the command and `+folder` and `msg` identify the
electronic mail messages to be processed.

The default folder is called `inbox`, which is where electronic mail
messages are delivered. The `msg` identifies either a message number
or a message sequence. MH will number electronic mail messages
automatically when they are placed into a folder. In contrast, the
user may direct MH to recognize well-known or user-defined sequences.
For example, keywords such as `first`, `last`, and `cur` all have well-
understood meanings. A user might also identify several electronic mail
messages by their contents, (e.g., by identifying all the messages in a
folder from a particular recipient), assigning them a sequence name,
(e.g., by naming that collection "`select`"), and then using that name
later on with other MH commands.

Finally, MH commands recognize several options, termed *switches*,
each starting with a hyphen-character ("-"). Options are words which
may be uniquely abbreviated as desired. All commands recognize the
`-help` switch which reports the syntax of the command along with local
configuration information. Because MH runs on such a wide-range of
platforms, and because this necessitates many configuration options,
this information is invaluable when resolving problems. Figure 3.3
shows what the command

```
% scan -help
```

yields on the author's desktop.

```
% scan -help
syntax: scan [+folder] [msgs] [switches]
  switches are:
  -[no]clear
  -form formatfile
  -(forma)t string
  -[no]header
  -width columns
  -[no]reverse
  -(file) file
  -(help)

version: MH 6.7.4a #7[UCI] (dbc) of Fri Mar 27 07:57:55 PST 1992
options: [APOP='"/etc/pop.auth"'] [BIND] [BPOP] [BSD42] [BSD43]
         [MHE] [POP] [POPSERVICE='"pop3"'] [RPATHS] [SENDMTS]
         [SMTP] [SUN40] [TYPESIG=void] [UCI] [WHATNOW] [ZMAILER]
```

Figure 3.3: Getting Help from an MH command

MH provides several message handling facilities to aid the user.
MH provides commands to manipulate folders (e.g., creating folders,
examining folders, moving electronic mail messages from one folder to
another, and deleting folders and messages). MH also provides commands to manipulate sequences (e.g., creating sequences, examining
sequences, and deleting sequences). There is one other facility which
deserves special attention, the MH formatting facility.

3.2.3 MH Format Handling

Several MH commands utilize either a format string or a format file
during their execution. For example, when a reply is generated, the
MH command responsible for this examines a format file which specifies
how the headers in the reply should be constructed.

The MH formatting facility is extremely powerful, however, format
files are designed to be efficiently parsed by MH commands.[2] As a

---

[2]Van Jacobson of Lawrence Berkeley Laboratories implemented the facility which
led to the one described here. Van was responsible for many significant performance
improvements in MH, albeit at the expense of introducing the odd bug or two.

consequence, the syntax of these files can be difficult to understand and write. Fortunately, there are several "canned" format files already written, which allow for a wide range of uses. Figure 3.4 presents the grisly details.

So, let's try and explain this. A format file contains zero or more logical lines. A logical line contains zero or more directives and is terminated by a LF. In order to improve readability, any occurrence of a sequence consisting of a backslash-character ("\") followed by a LF is ignored.

A directive is either text or a %-escape. When a format file is evaluated, text is simply copied to the desired output. In contrast, when an escape is encountered, it is evaluated.

There are three kinds of escapes:

component: The input message is examined to see if it contains the named header. If so, the value of that header is copied to the output. If the value is multi-line, then multiple adjacent occurrences of the LWSP sequence are considered as a single space-character. If the component is preceded by a number, then this numeric quantity is the exact number of output positions which will be used. (A negative numeric quantity indicates right-justification instead of left-justification.)

function: The function is evaluated and its value, either a string or an numeric quantity, is copied to the output. If the function is preceded by a number, then this is the exact number of output positions which will be used. A function may take an argument, either a literal number or string, a header value, or some expression (which requires further evaluation before being supplied to the called function).

The functions provided make it possible to examine structured header values and extract individual components. For example, when looking at an electronic mail address or a date-time specification, it is possible to examine their structured components, such as the local or domain part.

```
file      ::= *lines

          ; any occurrences ("\" LF) are ignored
line      ::= *directive LF
directive ::= text / "%" escape

escape    ::= component / function / flow

          ; identifies the value of the named header
component ::= ["-" 1*DIGIT] "{" name "}"

          ; a built-in function
function  ::= ["-" 1*DIGIT] "(" name [1*SP argument] ")"
argument  ::= literal / component / escape
literal   ::= 1*DIGIT / *<any chararacter excluding "{", "(", "%">

          ; alters format execution
flow      ::= "<" condition directive *("%?" condition directive)
              ["%|" directive] "%>"
condition ::= component / function

name      ::= 1*<any character except SP or ":">

text      ::= <any character excluding LF, "%",
              and including special>
special   ::= "\b"                    ; BS
            / "\f"                    ; FF
            / "\n"                    ; LF
            / "\r"                    ; CR
            / "\t"                    ; TAB

DIGIT     ::= <any numeric character, "0" through "9">
```

Figure 3.4: MH Format File Syntax

flow: The condition associated with the flow directive is evaluated. If non-zero, the directive which follows is executed.
Otherwise, an alternative condition, if any is evaluated.

As user agent functionalities are explored in Section 3.3 starting on
page 89, we'll see several examples of MH's format handling capabilities.

3.2.4   Relationship of MH to the Model

Having reviewed the structure and facilities of MH, let's consider how
it relates to the model for message handling introduced back on page 2.
Clearly, MH is more than a user agent. As shown in Figure 3.5, MH
is really an electronic mail message handler interacting with a user
interface that defines the way the user and the message handler communicate. In fact, there are a large number of interfaces to MH; text-based,
window-based, network-based, editor-based, etc. Each serves a different
kind of user community.

The electronic mail message handler itself is divided into four components, each of which may be thought of as a client to some service:

database agent: The *database agent* manages electronic mail
messages in the user's possession (received messages,
messages being composed, and so on). This includes all
the usual database functions: retrieval, selection, etc.

The database services used by MH are provided solely by the
UNIX filesystem. This allows all of the extensive, existing
UNIX file-handling tools to be used for message handling as
the need arises.

user agent: The *user agent* provides the classical submission and
delivery services, along with the basic user agent functionality, including draft composition.

MH supports several options when interfacing to a message
transfer agent, as there is a large number of differing local
configurations. However, the preferred approach is to use
SMTP and POP for submission and delivery. This policy
tends to factor out many system-specific details and gives
MH a consistent set of message transfer primitives on which

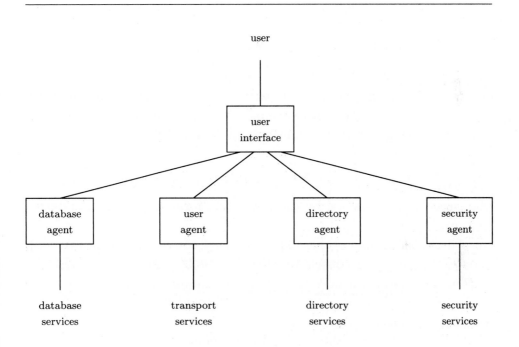

Figure 3.5: **The MH Model for Electronic Mail**

to build better services (e.g., encapsulation of failure notices, encryption, and so on).

directory agent: The *directory service agent* provides for name to address mapping.

MH provides an aliasing facility to allow a user to maintain the names and addresses of frequent correspondents, and also uses the DNS to resolve host names into canonical domain names.

security agent: The *security agent* implements special procedures for those electronic mail messages which require authentication and perhaps privacy.

There has been some early work using MH in this area [43, 44], but much more promising work is currently underway using the privacy-enhanced mail technology described in Chapter 7.

So, with our cursory discussion of MH out of the way, let's look at the capabilities provided by the messaging format used in the Internet community.

Although all user agents in the Internet community must exchange messages which are consistent with RFC-822, the Internet Host Requirements document does not define the minimal level of functionality which a user agent must exhibit. As such, readers should keep in mind that the discussion which follows describes a wide range of capabilities that may not be available with all user agents.

3.3   User Agent Functionality

The functionality provided by a user agent can be broadly divided into three categories:

- *generation*, in which electronic mail messages are created and submitted to the local message transfer agent;

- *examination*, in which electronic mail messages, after being delivered to the user agent, are examined by a user; and,

- *processing*, in which received electronic mail messages are manipulated.

(One could argue that examination is one possible processing activity, but, for the purpose of discussion in *The Internet Message*, we'll consider them separately.)

3.3.1   Message Generation

There are four basic generation activities:

- *composing*, in which a new electronic mail message is composed and sent;

- *distributing*, in which a previously received electronic mail message is sent, verbatim, to additional recipients;

- *forwarding*, in which one or more previously received electronic mail messages are combined into a single new message (perhaps with additional comments) and sent to new recipients; and,

- *replying*, in which a response to a previously received electronic mail message is generated and sent back to the originator (and perhaps any other original recipients).

```
mailbox    ::= addr-spec / [phrase] route-addr

addr-spec ::= local "@" domain

local      ::= word *("." word)
domain     ::= subdomain *("." subdomain)
subdomain ::= atom / domain-literal

phrase     ::= 1*word
route-addr::= "<" [route] addr-spec ">"
route      ::= 1#("@" domain) ":"
```

Figure 3.6: Mailbox Address Syntax

Mail Addresses

All of these activities involve electronic mail addresses. At the very beginning of our discussion on naming, we had identified an electronic mail address as being of the form

> `local@domain`

where "`domain`" identifies an administrative authority responsible for naming entities, and "`local`" is a string which has meaning only within that authority. It turns out that an electronic mail address is somewhat more complicated.

Figure 3.6 shows the syntax of an electronic mail address.[3] (This figure uses the BNF defined in Figure 3.2 on page 80.)

An electronic mail address takes one of two forms, either the simple form we've been using thus far; or, one containing the name associated with the address, an optional route to the electronic mail address, and then the familiar `local` and `domain` components. The Internet Host Requirements document has declared the `route` component in a `route-addr` to be obsolete, since the DNS is used for mail relaying. Hence, user agents must be able to recognize the `route` syntax, but must never generate it.

---

[3]This syntax differs slightly from the one given in RFC-822. The reason is that the Internet Host Requirements document modified the syntax to make the `phrase` component in a `mailbox` optional.

In the author's experience, the most commonly used syntax is:

```
phrase (comment) <local@domain>
```

where the `phrase` names the user corresponding to the electronic mail address, and the `comment` is usually absent. Hence,

```
"Marshall T. Rose" <mrose@dbc.mtview.ca.us>
Marshall Rose <mrose@dbc.mtview.ca.us>
```

are identical electronic mail addresses though they may displayed differently to the user. Of course, there are some interesting uses for the `phrase` component, e.g.,

```
the wireless terminal of Geoff Goodfellow <geoff@fernwood.mpk.ca.us>
```

Two other common formats are:

```
local@domain (comment)
local@domain
```

where the `comment` component names the user associated with the electronic mail address.

It must be emphasized that the meaning of the `local` component is strictly an issue for the domain named in the electronic mail address. It also names the user associated with the electronic mail address, e.g.,

```
Steve.Kille@cs.ucl.ac.uk
```

In addition, addresses may be collected together in a *group*:

```
group    ::= phrase ":" [#mailbox] ";"
```

which is a named collection of zero or more electronic mail addresses.

```
date-time ::= [day ","] date time

day        ::= "Sun" / "Mon" / "Tue" / "Wed"
               / "Thu" / "Fri" / "Sat"

date       ::= 1*2DIGIT month (2DIGIT / 4DIGIT)
month      ::= "Jan" / "Feb" / "Mar" / "Apr"
               / "May" / "Jun" / "Jul" / "Aug"
               / "Sep" / "Oct" / "Nov" / "Dec"

time       ::= hour zone
hour       ::= 2DIGIT ":" 2DIGIT [":" 2DIGIT]
zone       ::= "UT" / "GMT"            ; Universal time
               / "EST" / "EDT"         ; some US timezones
               / "CST" / "CDT"
               / "MST" / "MDT"
               / "PST" / "PDT"
               / 1ALPHA                ; military zone
               / (("+" / "-") 4DIGIT)  ; offset from UT
```

Figure 3.7: Date-Time Syntax

For example,

```
Reviewers:
      Nathaniel Borenstein  <nsb@thumper.bellcore.com>,
      "James M. Galvin"     <galvin@tis.com>,
      Paul Mockapetris      <pvm@darpa.mil>,
      John Romine           <jromine@ics.uci.edu>,
      Einar Stefferud       <Stef@nma.com>,
      Mike Zisman           <mdz@ssw.com>;
```

indicates a group of six electronic mail addresses, whilst

```
Reviewers: ;
```

indicates a collection of unspecified electronic mail addresses, known as a *blind list*.

Dates and Times

In addition, electronic mail message generation activities often involve dates and times. Figure 3.7 shows the syntax of a date-time specification.[4] (This figure uses the BNF defined in Figure 3.2 on page 80.)

A date-time specification consists of three parts: first, an optional indication as to the day of the week; second, a date consisting of the day of the month, the month, and the year; and, third, a time consisting of the hour and minutes, optionally the seconds, and a time zone. The time zone is either a specification of universal time, a symbolic time zone for North America, a military time zone, or a specification of the number hours and minutes relative to universal time. This latter specification is termed a numeric form.

The Internet Host Requirements document states that the year component should always be generated using 4–digit years, although 2–digit year components should continue to be recognized. Further, the Internet Host Requirements document has declared all non-numeric forms of the zone component to be obsolete, since experience has shown these forms to be highly error-prone. Hence, user agents must be able to recognize the full zone syntax, but should generate only numeric time zones. An example date-time specification might be:

```
Sun, 12 Apr 1992 11:50:40 -0700
```

---

[4]This syntax differs slightly from the one given in RFC-822. The reason is that the Internet Host Requirements document modified the syntax to allow for four-digit years in a date component.

```
To:
cc:
Subject:
--------
```

Figure 3.8: MH Composition Template

Composing

Composition is the simplest of the electronic mail message generation activities. The user agent constructs a template, which the user fills in. Immediately prior to submission, the user agent then adds a few special headers. Figure 3.8 shows the default composition template used by MH. A convention used by MH is that the headers and body are separated either by a blank line or a line consisting entirely of hyphen-characters.

In fact, there are several other headers which may be supplied during composition:

```
Bcc:
From:
Reply-To:
Message-ID:
References:
Keywords:
Comments:
```

Figure 3.9 shows the syntax of the composition headers. (This figure uses the BNF defined in Figures 3.2 and 3.6 on pages 80 and 90, respectively.) Let's consider each of these headers in turn.

To: This identifies one or more "primary" recipients of the electronic mail message. The semantics of being a primary recipient is an application-specific matter. For example, addressees listed in a **To:** field are normally expected to take some action based on the message. In such cases, these addressees would be expected to reply to the message.

```
composition
          ::= recipient / originator / others

recipient ::= "To"          ":"  1#address
          / "cc"            ":"  1#address
          / "Bcc"           ":"  0#address

originator
          ::= from [CRLF reply-to]
from      ::= "From"        ":"  1#address
reply-to  ::= "Reply-To"    ":"  1#address

others    ::= "Message-ID" ":"  msg-id
          / "References" ":"  *(phrase / msg-id)
          / "Keywords"   ":"  #phrase
          / "Subject"    ":"  *text
          / "Comments"   ":"  *text

address   ::= mailbox / group
msg-id    ::= "<" addr-spec ">"
```

Figure 3.9: Composition Headers Syntax

cc: This identifies one or more "secondary" recipients of the electronic mail message. The semantics of being a secondary recipient is an application-specific matter. For example, addressees listed in a `cc:` field are usually listed for informational purposes only (so-called FYI correspondence). In such cases, these addressees would not be expected to reply to the message.

Bcc: This identifies any number of "blind" recipients of the electronic mail message. When present, it indicates that two messages should be submitted to the local message transfer agent. The first electronic mail message is sent to the primary and any secondary recipients and does not contain the `Bcc:` header. The second message is sent to the blind recipients, and, at the option of the user agent, may contain the `Bcc:` header. This allows a user to automatically inform third-parties about electronic mail messages being sent to the primary and secondary recipients. (We'll see an example of how MH handles blind-carbon-copies later, starting on page 98. But, don't skip ahead now, the example builds on some concepts which haven't been introduced yet!)

From: This identifies the electronic mail address(es) on whose behalf this message was composed.

Reply-To: When a reply is generated, this identifies one or more electronic mail addresses to whom the reply should be sent.

Message-ID: This contains a unique identifier for this electronic mail message. This is constructed by using the originator's domain name for the **domain** component along with a locally generated string.

References: This identifies any correspondence related to this electronic mail message. If this message is related to other electronic mail messages, then the `msg-id` alternative is used. This correlates to the value of the **Message-ID:** header in those messages.

Subject: This identifies the subject of the information contained in the electronic mail message.[5]

Keywords: This contains any number of phrases which describe the topics discussed in this electronic mail message.

Comments: This allows an arbitrary textual comment to be attached to the electronic mail message.

Not all of these headers need be present. In particular, the only one from this group which is required is either a `To:` header containing at least one address, or a `Bcc:` header containing no addresses.

Figure 3.10 on page 98 shows the MH composition template for an electronic mail message filled-in recently by the author. MH will automatically supply `From:` and `Message-ID:` headers if they are not supplied. In addition, there is one other header, `Fcc:`, which is a local convention used by MH to indicate a file-carbon-copy. After MH submits the electronic mail message to the local message transfer agent, it will file copies of the message to the named folders. (The `Fcc:` will not be present in the submitted message.)

Finally, immediately prior to the submission process, two headers may be added by MH:

```
Date:
Sender:
```

Figure 3.11 on page 99 shows the syntax of the submission headers. (This figure uses the BNF defined in Figures 3.2, 3.6, and 3.7 on pages 80, 90, and 92, respectively.) Let's consider each of these headers in turn.

Date: This identifies the date and time that the electronic mail message was created. This header must always be present.

Sender: This specifies the identity of electronic mail address which submitted this message for delivery. If the `From:` header contains more than one electronic mail address, or if the electronic mail address it contains is different than

---

[5]Rather redundant, eh?

```
To: Reviewers:
     Nathaniel Borenstein <nsb@thumper.bellcore.com>,
     "James M. Galvin"    <galvin@tis.com>,
     Paul Mockapetris     <pvm@darpa.mil>,
     John Romine          <jromine@ics.uci.edu>,
     Einar Stefferud      <Stef@nma.com>,
     Mike Zisman          <mdz@ssw.com>;
Subject: Want to review a book?
Fcc: +outbox, +books/letter-book
--------
As you may have heard, I am undertaking the writing of my
fourth and final book.  The working title is

                 The Internet Letter:
          Closing the Book on Electronic Mail

(The main title being suggested by Paul Mockapetris, the
subtitle being derived from a suggestion by Ole Jacobsen.)

My goal would be to provide you with a hardcopy on May 1st.
I would need comments back by June 1st.  If you are involved
with INTEROP or IFIP this may be tight, but based on publication
schedules, this is the best I can do.

As always, reviewers get a credit in the Acknowledgements
section plus two gratis copies of the book when published.

Oops, forgot to tell you what the book is about!

It's about Internet electronic mail, something like this:

        DNS, 822/usenet, SMTP/UUCP, POP/PCMAIL/IMAP3

        MIME, PEM, bboards/lists/NNTP, gateways

Very little on X.400, except when I need to illustrate how
not to do something. (-:

/mtr
```

Figure 3.10: Completed Composition Template

```
submission
          ::= orig-date / sender

orig-date ::= "Date"       ":" date-time

sender    ::= "Sender"     ":" mailbox
```

Figure 3.11: Submission Headers Syntax

the submitting user agent (either in the **phrase** component or in the **addr-spec** component), then this header must be present.

Figure 3.12 on page 100 shows the electronic mail message which MH submits to the local message transfer agent. Because a **From:** header was not present, MH added one. Further, MH added **Date:** and **Message-ID:** headers.

```
To: Reviewers: ;
Subject: Want to review a book?
Date: Sun, 12 Apr 1992 11:50:40 -0700
Message-ID: <18597.703104640@dbc.mtview.ca.us>
From: Marshall Rose <mrose@dbc.mtview.ca.us>

As you may have heard, I am undertaking the writing of my
fourth and final book.  The working title is

                   The Internet Letter:
           Closing the Book on Electronic Mail

(The main title being suggested by Paul Mockapetris, the
subtitle being derived from a suggestion by Ole Jacobsen.)

My goal would be to provide you with a hardcopy on May 1st.
I would need comments back by June 1st.  If you are involved
with INTEROP or IFIP this may be tight, but based on publication
schedules, this is the best I can do.

As always, reviewers get a credit in the Acknowledgements
section plus two gratis copies of the book when published.

Oops, forgot to tell you what the book is about!

It's about Internet electronic mail, something like this:

        DNS, 822/usenet, SMTP/UUCP, POP/PCMAIL/IMAP3

        MIME, PEM, bboards/lists/NNTP, gateways

Very little on X.400, except when I need to illustrate how
not to do something. (-:

/mtr
```

Figure 3.12: Example Submission Draft

Distributing

Distribution occurs when a user agent re-submits an electronic mail message into the message transfer system with a new set of recipients. In order to distinguish the newly submitted message from the original message, a new set of originator, recipient, and date headers are added:

```
Resent-To:
Resent-cc:
Resent-Bcc:
Resent-From:
Resent-Reply-To:
Resent-Message-ID:
Resent-Date:
Resent-Sender:
```

The syntax of these headers is identical to the syntax of the corresponding original headers. (So take a look at Figures 3.9 and 3.11 on pages 95 and 99 to get a handle on the BNF.)

When using MH, the user fills in a template for the distribution headers which contains no body. (The default template is similar to the one shown in Figure 3.8 on page 94.) As might be expected, MH recognizes a `Resent-Fcc:` header with the obvious semantics.

Forwarding

Forwarding occurs when the user agent collects a number of electronic mail messages together and sends them in one new message. The headers of the new electronic mail message may be any which are allowed for composition.

With MH, the user fills in a template for the headers of the new electronic mail message along with the initial portion of the message body. (The default template is similar to the one shown in Figure 3.8 on page 94.) MH then appends the forwarded electronic mail messages at the end of the body, using an encapsulation scheme. MH supports two such schemes, the one specified in [45], and the one specified in [46]. Since the latter scheme is discussed later on in Section 6.1.1 on page 215, the current discussion focuses on the former approach, which is a popular convention, but not an Internet-standard, for encapsulation.[6]

Figure 3.13 shows the syntax of the encapsulation algorithm. Basically, each electronic mail message is separated by a three line sequence consisting of: a blank line, a line starting with at least two hyphen-characters ("--"), and another blank line. If a line in the body of an encapsulated message starts with a hyphen-character, then the two-character sequence "- " is prepended to the line. This technique is called a *data-stuffing* algorithm, similar to the one we encountered way back on page 14.

In addition to supplying a command to forward electronic mail messages, MH also contains a command to *burst* a message, which extracts the forwarded messages contained therein. The algorithm used by a receiving user agent is straight-forward as it can unambiguously extract the forwarded messages by looking for lines in the body starting with at least two hyphen-characters. When it copies the body of each of the forwarded messages, if a line starts with a hyphen, it ignores the first two characters of that line.

Figure 3.14 on page 105 shows how MH might construct an electronic mail message which forwards the one shown in Figure 3.12 back on page 100. Actually, forwarding with MH can be somewhat more

---

[6][45] is a formal definition of an algorithm which had been in use since the late-'70s. Readers should consult [47] for an informal description of the convention. It's anyone's guess as to why [45] was published nearly five years earlier than [47].

```
body      ::= *(CRLF line *text) *(boundary message) boundary
              *(CRLF line *text)

line      ::= <any character, including bare CR and bare LF,
                  but not including CRLF, nor including "-">

boundary  ::= CRLF 2*"-" CRLF

message   ::= 1*field *(CRLF ["- -"] *text)

field     ::= name ":" [value] CRLF

name      ::= 1*<any character except SP or ":">

              ; actual syntax varies depending on header
value     ::= text *(LWSP text)

text      ::= <any character, including bare CR and bare LF,
                  but not including CRLF>

LWSP      ::= CRLF 1*SP
CRLF      ::= <carriage-return followed by line-feed>
SP        ::= <any SPACE or TAB character>
```

Figure 3.13: Encapsulation Syntax

complicated as MH allows the user to specify which headers from the forwarded messages should be included in the body. (This isn't strictly legal, but it has proved to be a useful feature.)

MH also uses forwarding to implement the blind-carbon-copy facility described earlier on page 96. Suppose that the completed composition template in Figure 3.10 back on page 98 had an additional header line, e.g.,

```
Bcc: Mary Franz <franz@prenhall.com>
```

Then MH would submit two electronic mail messages for delivery. The first would look exactly like the one shown in Figure 3.12 back on page 100. The second would look something like the one shown in Figure 3.14, except that the `To:` header would be replaced by:

```
BCC:
```

and the encapsulation markers would be

```
------- Blind-Carbon-Copy
```

and

```
------- End of Blind-Carbon-Copy
```

respectively.

Finally, readers of RFC-822 should note that it mistakenly terms "distribution" as "forwarding". These are two entirely different concepts as illustrated by the discussion above.

```
To: Ole Jacobsen <ole@csli.stanford.edu>
Subject: As per your request...
Date: Sun, 12 Apr 1992 23:21:25 -0700
Message-Id: <20585.703146085@dbc.mtview.ca.us>
From: Marshall Rose <mrose@dbc.mtview.ca.us>

...here is the message I was referring to.

/mtr

------- Forwarded Message

To: Reviewers: ;
Subject: Want to review a book?
Date: Sun, 12 Apr 1992 11:50:40 -0700
Message-ID: <18597.703104640@dbc.mtview.ca.us>
From: Marshall Rose <mrose@dbc.mtview.ca.us>

As you may have heard, I am undertaking the writing of my
fourth and final book.  The working title is

<<in the interests of brevity, the majority of the body of
   the original message has been removed in this figure...>>

Very little on X.400, except when I need to illustrate how
not to do something. (-:

/mtr

------- End of Forwarded Message
```

Figure 3.14: **Example Forwarded Draft**

```
in-reply-to
        ::= "In-Reply-To" ":" *(phrase / msg-id)

msg-id    ::= "<" addr-spec ">"
```

Figure 3.15: In-Reply-To Header Syntax

```
%(lit)%(formataddr %<{reply-to}%?{from}%?{sender}%?{return-path}%>)\
%<(nonnull)%(void(width))%(putaddr To: )\n%>\
%(lit)%(formataddr{to})%(formataddr{cc})%(formataddr(me))\
%<(nonnull)%(void(width))%(putaddr cc: )\n%>\
%<{fcc}Fcc: %{fcc}\n%>\
%<{subject}Subject: Re: %{subject}\n%>\
%<{date}In-reply-to: Your message of "\
%<(nodate{date})%{date}%|%(pretty{date})%>."%<{message-id}
          %{message-id}%>\n%>\
--------
```

Figure 3.16: MH Reply Format File

Replying

Replying occurs when a user agent generates a reply to an electronic mail message. The headers of the new message may be any which are allowed for composition, with one additional one as shown in Figure 3.15. (This figure uses the BNF defined in Figures 3.2 and 3.6 on pages 80 and 90, respectively.) The semantics of the In-Reply-To: header is simple: it identifies the electronic mail message(s) to which this reply is being made.

With MH, a format file is used to construct the headers and initial portion of the message body. Figure 3.16 shows the default format file used.

As noted earlier, the format is amazingly cryptic. So, here is the layman's explanation:

- MH looks for the

      Reply-To:
      From:
      Sender:
      Return-Path:

  headers, in this order, until it finds one of these in the electronic mail message being replied to. If one is found, then a `To:` header is output along with any electronic mail addresses found in that header. The electronic mail addresses are output in a nicely formatted fashion, with folding, as appropriate.

- MH combines the contents of the `To:` and `cc:` headers, if any, from the electronic mail message being replied to. If the user wanted to receive a copy of the reply, then the user's electronic mail address is added to this list. If at least one electronic mail address is present, then a `cc:` header is output along with all of those electronic mail addresses. The electronic mail addresses are output in a nicely formatted fashion, with folding, as appropriate.

  In the case of the electronic mail message shown in Figure 3.12 back on page 100, note that although a group is present in the `To:` header, no electronic mail addresses are present.

- If the user specified any file-carbon-copies (on the command line or in the user's profile), then an `Fcc:` header is output along with the names of the folders.

- If a `Subject:` header is present in the electronic mail message being replied to, then a `Subject:` header is output, followed by the string "`Re: `", followed by the original subject. (MH will strip off any occurrences of "`Re: `" from the original subject.)

- If a `Date:` header is present in the electronic mail message being replied to, then an `In-Reply-To:` header is output which begins

      In-reply-to: Your message of "

If the value of the `Date:` header is valid, it is re-formatted according to the style MH prefers. Regardless, it is then output followed by the two-character sequence ""`.`".

Further, if a `Message-ID:` header is present in the electronic mail message being replied to, then a CR-LF sequence followed by some white-space is output, followed by the value of the `Message-ID:` header.

Interested readers should compare this description of MH's behavior to the definition of a reply in RFC-822. The author suspects that they will find it amazingly similar!

3.3.2 Message Examination

There are two examination facilities:

- *listing*, in which a one-line summary of an electronic mail message is displayed; and,

- *displaying*, in which the entire electronic mail message is shown to the user.

Each is now examined in turn.

Listing

Listing, often called "scanning", is a quick way for a user to summarize the contents of an electronic mail message.

MH provides a command to scan a message, based on the format file facility described earlier. After the lengthy example given in Section 3.3.1 just moments ago on page 106, the reader shouldn't be surprised at the flexibility MH provides. MH provides several canned formats, which can be selected automatically by the user. Let's consider two.

Figure 3.17 on page 110 shows the default format file used by MH. Once again, the reader's senses are assaulted by this cryptic notation. So, here's the interpretation:

- MH first prints the message number in four positions.

- Either the plus-character ("+") or a space is output, depending on whether the electronic mail message being scanned is the current message.

- If a `Replied:` header is present in the message being scanned, then the minus-character ("-") is output.

  Otherwise, if an `Encrypted:` header is present, then an "E") is output;

  Otherwise, if a `Content-Type:` header is present, then an "M") is output; otherwise, a space is output. (Don't worry! We haven't discussed these two headers yet.)

```
%4(msg)%<(cur)+%| %>
%<{replied}-%?{encrypted}E%?{content-type}M%| %>\
%02(mon{date})/%02(mday{date})%<{date} %|*%>\
%<(mymbox{from})%<{to}To:%14(friendly{to})%>%>\
%<(zero)%17(friendly{from})%> \
%{subject}%<{body}<<%{body}>>%>
```

Figure 3.17: MH Scan Format File

- The Date: header is then examined. If one is not present, the creation date of the UNIX file containing the electronic mail message is used. The month and day of the month are output. Then, either a space or a wildcard-character ("*") is output, depending on whether a Date: header is present in the message being scanned.

- Next, if the first electronic mail address in the From: header is the user's address, then the string To: is output followed by one or more of the electronic mail addresses in the To: header from the message being scanned. Otherwise, the address in the From: header is output.

  These electronic mail addresses are output into a fixed number of positions, and in a "friendly" format. This means that MH will output only the names of each address (the phrase component), if present. Otherwise, the local and domain components are output. Of course, given the small number of output positions, it is likely that only one electronic mail address will be output.

- If the electronic mail message being scanned contains a Subject: header, then it is output.

- Finally, if a non-null body is present, the beginning of the body is displayed, bracketed by "<<" and ">>".

```
%4(msg)%<(cur)+%| %>
%<{replied}-%?{encrypted}E%?{content-type}M%| %>\
%(void(rclock{date}))\
%<(gt 15768000)%03(month{date})%(void(year{date}))%02(modulo 100)\
%?(gt 604800)%02(mday{date})%03(month{date})\
%?(gt 86400) %(day{date}) %|\
%02(hour{date}):%02(min{date})%>\
%<{date} %|*%>\
%<(mymbox{from})%<{to}To:%14(friendly{to})%>%>\
%<(zero)%17(friendly{from})%> \
%{subject}%<{body}<<%{body}%>
```

Figure 3.18: Another MH Scan Format File

When MH generates a scan listing, it knows the length of the output device being used for display. Thus, it truncates the listing as appropriate. So, if we ask MH to generate a scan listing for the electronic mail message shown in Figure 3.12 on page 100, the output will be:

```
1+ 04/12 To:Reviewers:     Want to review a book?<<As you may have heard
```

Figure 3.18 shows a different format file. The difference lies in how the Date: header is output. MH calculates the difference between the current time and the date of the electronic mail message being scanned:

- If it is larger than 15768000 seconds (half a year), the month and last two digits of the year from the electronic mail message's date are output;

- otherwise, if it is larger than 604800 seconds (1 week), the day of the month and the month from the message's date are output;

- otherwise, if it is larger than 86400 seconds (24 hours), the day of the week from the message's date is output.

- otherwise, the hour and minutes from the message's date is output.

Again, referring back to Figure 3.12 on page 100, if asked to scan that electronic mail message a few hours later, MH would produce this output:

```
1+ 11:50 To:Reviewers:      Want to review a book?<<As you may have heard
```

In contrast, scanning the message during the afternoon of the next day would produce:

```
1+  Sun  To:Reviewers:      Want to review a book?<<As you may have heard
```

Displaying

Displaying, sometimes called "showing", is how a user can examine an entire electronic mail message.

MH provides a command to show an electronic mail message, using a facility similar to the format file mechanism. In addition to specifying which headers should be displayed, the user can also specify which headers should be hidden. (This facility, termed `mhl`, provided the motivation for developing the MH formatting facility described earlier.) By providing a common display mechanism, the user is presented with electronic mail messages in a consistent format. For example, the user's eye knows to look at certain parts of the screen for different kinds of information — and it is the user who may define this layout. In fact, this is a critical distinction: messages should be rendered according to the user's display preferences, but a user agent should never directly reformat a message.

Unfortunately, not all user agents are as capable as MH. Early on, this led to a plethora of complaints about RFC-822. `soap...`

For example, the reason the Internet Host Requirements document did away with non-numeric time zones is that they were terribly misused. For example, one site, in clear violation of the standard, would generate electronic mail messages with a time zone of `EVT` (Eastern Virtual Time), because system manager at that site didn't want to change the time zone string for his host since it would require re-configuring the operating-system! But, when user agents started generating time zones in numeric form, lots of people started complaining that they didn't like them. The reason: the user agent used by these people would display the `Date:` header verbatim, rather than trying to convert the information contained therein to a locally useful form.

Similarly, from a person's point of view, the amount of interesting information in the headers can be quite small. Therefore, having the ability to display only a subset of the headers present in an electronic mail message can be quite pleasing to the user.

So, it is very important that a user agent contain the ability to select which headers are of interest, and also to display structured header values in a locally meaningful form. `...soap`

3.3.3   Message Processing

Finally, we'll consider two processing facilities:

- *searching*, in which a collection of electronic mail messages satisfying some criteria are identified; and,

- *sorting*, in which a collection of electronic mail messages are ordered according to some criteria.

Each is now examined in turn.

Searching

MH provides a command to search electronic mail messages which satisfy a query criteria. Figure 3.19 shows the syntax for this command. (This figure uses the BNF defined in Figures 3.1, 3.2, and 3.7 on pages 77, 80, and 92, respectively.) In brief, MH allows the user to search electronic mail messages as if they were entries in a database, where the headers and the body are record fields.

Further, because MH uses the shell as its interface, this command can be used in interesting ways, e.g.,

```
% scan 'pick -from farber -and -before monday'
```

will produce a scan listing of all the electronic mail messages in the current folder which are from `farber` and are dated before the previous monday.

In order to facilitate this process, whenever MH distributes, forwards, or replies to an electronic mail message, it *annotates* that message by adding an appropriate header, one of:

Resent:
Forwarded:
Replied:

which contains the date of the annotation and the new recipient addresses. In addition, MH provides a command which allows a user to add an arbitrary annotation to an electronic mail message. This allows a user to add "hints" which aid searching.

```
query      ::= exp1 *(1*SP "-or" 1*SP query)

exp1       ::= exp2 *(1*SP "-and" 1*SP exp1)
exp2       ::= ["-not" 1*SP] exp3
exp3       ::= "-lbrace" 1*SP query 1*SP "-rbrace" / exp4
exp4       ::= "-" component pattern
             / "--" name pattern        ; arbitrary header
             / "-search" pattern         ; body
             / "-after" date-spec
             / "-before" date-spec
             / "-datefield" name         ; names field for
                                         ; -after/-before

component ::= "to" / "cc" / "from" / "date" / "subject"

          ; case-insensitive matching, and
          ; unix regular expressions are allowed
pattern   ::= word

date-spec ::= date-time
            / "today" / "yesterday" / "tomorrow"
            / "Sun" ["day"]  / "Mon" ["day"]
            / "Tue" ["sday"] / "Wed" ["nesday"]
            / "Thu" ["rsday"] / "Fri" ["day"]
            / "Sat" ["urday"]
            / "-" 1*digit              ; #-days ago
```

Figure 3.19: MH's Pick Syntax

Sorting

Normally electronic mail messages are numbered in the order they are filed into a folder. However, MH provides a command which re-orders the messages in a folder according to some collating sequence. The user supplies the name of one or two headers, the first being used for the major sort key, and the second, if present, as the minor sort key. Then, the values of those headers in each electronic mail message are compared and the messages are ordered accordingly.

One common usage is:

```
% sortm -limit 0 -textfield subject -datefield date
```

which indicates that the electronic mail messages in the current folder should be sorted on the basis of the values in the `Subject:` header, and that a temporal comparison of the `Date:` header should be used as the secondary key. (The `-limit` switch is used to indicate that the `Date:` header should be the secondary, rather than primary, key.)

```
trace     ::= return / received

return    ::= "Return-Path" ":" "<" addr-spec ">"
            / "Return-Path" ":" "<" ">"

received ::= "Received"      ":"
                "from"    domain
              [ "by"      domain]
              [ "via"     atom]
             *("with"     atom)
              [ "id" "<" addr-spec ">"]
              [ "for"     addr-spec]
                ";" date-time
```

Figure 3.20: Trace Header Syntax

3.4 Other Headers

Although the discussion on user agent functionality covered most of the headers used in electronic mail messages. There are a few more that require discussion.

3.4.1 Trace Headers

There are two headers which are added by message transfer agents. Figure 3.20 shows the syntax of these headers.[7] (This figure uses the BNF defined in Figures 3.1, 3.2, 3.6, and 3.7 on pages 77, 80, 90, and 92, respectively.) Let's consider each of these headers in turn.

Return-Path: This is added by the message transfer agent which performs final delivery. It contains the electronic mail address of the entity which submitted this electronic mail message into the message transfer system, which is incrementally

---

[7]This syntax differs slightly from the one given in RFC-822. First, the Internet Host Requirements document modified the syntax to allow for an empty address in a `Return-Path:` header. This indicates that the electronic mail message is an error report. (Error reports are discussed later on in Section 4.1.1.) Second, the Internet Host Requirements document mandates that a message transfer agent provide the `from` component in a `Received:` header.

built-up in the SMTP envelope as the message passes through each transfer agent. (Note that a fair number of message transfer agent implementations incorrectly add this header without the angle brackets.)

Received: This is added by each message transfer agent when it accepts responsibility for the electronic mail message. The only mandatory component is the date and time when the MTA accepted the message. With the exception of the `from` component, all of the other components are all optional:

from This identifies the message transfer agent which relayed the electronic mail message.

by This identifies the message transfer agent which received the electronic mail message.

via This identifies the physical path between the two message transfer agents.

with This identifies relaying protocol used between the two message transfer agents. (More than one of these components may be present to indicate the complete combination of protocols used for relaying, if need be.)

id If the receiving message transfer agent queued the electronic mail message prior to relaying it, this lists the queue identifier used by the receiving message transfer agent.

for If the recipient address is re-evaluated by the receiving message transfer agent, then this identifies the original recipient of the electronic mail message. (Usually this happens if the message passes through an alias expansion or a mailing list explosion — terms we will discuss later on in Section 4.1.1.)

As can be seen from the description, the information contained in these headers can be used for tracing the path of an electronic mail message through the message transfer system. Hence the term *trace* headers.

Let's look at a brief example to wrap things up.

```
Received: from andrew.cmu.edu by dbc.mtview.ca.us
          (4.1/3.1.090690)
          id AA22260; Mon, 13 Apr 92 09:25:09 PDT
```

This identifies the relaying and receiving message transfer agents (`andrew.cmu.edu` and `dbc.mtview.ca.us`, respectively), a commentary string (`4.1/3.1.090690`) which identifies the version of the receiving software, the internal queue-identitifer used by the receiving message transfer agent (`AA22260`), and the date that the electronic mail message was accepted.

3.4.2 Miscellaneous Headers

RFC-822 defines an `Encrypted:` header, which is obsoleted by new work on Privacy-Enhanced Mail which is discussed in Chapter 7.

Finally, there are two extensibility mechanisms defined for headers. If a local environment wishes to define their own headers, they can do so, simply by starting the keyword with the string "`X-`". Presumably, any header starting with this sequence has a bilaterally agreed-upon meaning.

Second, Internet-standards are allowed to define new headers as long as they do not conflict with any other standard headers (and do not start with "`X-`", of course). For example, the new standards-track document described in Chapter 6 will introduce four new headers dealing with multi-media mail!

3.5   USENET Messages

The text-oriented, memo-based format used in the Internet community has proven surprisingly tractable. As such, other communities have adopted this format for their use. Perhaps the largest of these is the *USENET* community (described in some detail on pages 235–250 of [48]). USENET can perhaps best be summarized as a large community which interworks with a single service, *news.* News is similar to electronic mail in that both employ a store-and-forward transport service. However, whilst electronic mail messages are addressed to a fixed number of recipients, a news message, termed an *article,* reaches all interested parties in the community, termed a *newsgroup.* As might be expected, there is a wide range of topics discussed in the USENET, each having its own (potentially global) distribution.

A newsgroup is identified by a hierarchical name, having a similar syntax to a domain name, e.g.,

```
rec.arts.movies
```

However, the most-significant labels in a newsgroup occur on the left. Further, there are two different kinds of hierarchies: topic-based, which relate to a particular area of discussion; and, geography-based, which relate to topics of interest to those in a particular locale.

A news-capable user agent supports three kinds of generation activities:

- *posting,* in which a new article is submitted to one or more newsgroups;

- *followup,* in which a response to a previously received article is generated and sent, as an article, to the recipient newsgroups; and,

- *replying,* in which a response to a previously received article is generated and sent, as an electronic mail message, to the originator.

So, let's see how the format of news article aids a user agent in these tasks.

```
news       ::= "Newsgroups" ":" groups
           / "Path"         ":" 1#(["@"] word *("." word))

groups     ::= 1#(word *("." word))
```

Figure 3.21: Article Header Syntax

3.5.1   USENET Headers

For the format of news articles, the USENET community uses the Internet community's format for electronic mail messages [49]. Although very few headers need be present in an electronic mail message in the Internet community, the requirements on a news article are somewhat more stringent. The mandatory headers are:

> From:
> Date:
> Subject:
> Message-ID:
> Newsgroups:
> Path:

The first four, we're already familiar with. The syntax of the other two is shown in Figure 3.21. (This figure uses the BNF defined in Figures 3.1, 3.2, 3.6, and 3.7 on pages 77, 80, 90, and 92, respectively.)

Let's consider each of these headers in turn.

Newsgroups: This identifies one or more newsgroups for which this article is intended. (Note that no headers containing recipient addresses, i.e., To:, cc:, Bcc:, are present in an article.)

Path: This identifies the path of USENET nodes which the article has traversed to reach the current node. As each node processes the article, it prepends its own identity to the beginning of the header value. This header is used for minimizing the amount of news traffic between adjacent nodes.

(Section 4.3 on page 150 explains how.) Except in older versions of USENET software, this header is not used for generating replies.

An example of a `Path:` header might be:

```
Path: fernwood.mpk.ca.us!dbc.mtview.ca.us!mrose
```

which indicates that this copy of the news article originated with

```
mrose@dbc.mtview.ca.us
```

and was then sent to the host

```
fernwood.mpk.ca.us
```

In addition, several optional headers may appear in an article. They are:

```
Reply-To:
Sender:
References:
Keywords:
Followup-To:
Expires:
Control:
Distribution:
Organization:
Summary:
Approved:
Lines:
Xref:
```

Again, the first four we're already familiar with. The syntax of the others is shown in Figure 3.22. (This figure uses the BNF defined in Figures 3.1, 3.2, 3.6, and 3.7 on pages 77, 80, 90, and 92, respectively.)

```
more        ::= "Followup-To"  ":" ("poster" / groups)
            / "Expires"        ":" date-time
            / "Control"        ":" *text
            / "Distribution"   ":" groups
            / "Organization"   ":" *text
            / "Summary"        ":" *text
            / "Approved"       ":" addr-spec
            / "Lines"          ":" 1*DIGIT
            / "Xref"           ":" word *(1*SP group ":" 1*DIGIT)

groups      ::= 1#group
group       ::= word *("." word)
```

Figure 3.22: More Article Header Syntax

Let's consider each of these headers in turn.

Followup-To: If present, this indicates the newsgroup(s) where followup articles are to be sent. Otherwise, the newsgroup(s) identified in the `Newsgroup:` header are used. If the value of this header is

> `poster`

then followups are not allowed for this article. Only replying is allowed.

Expires: This indicates when the information contained in the article is no longer useful. The articles stored at each node are removed automatically, depending on local policy. This header, if present, indicates a different lifetime for the article.

Control: This indicates that the article is actually a *control* message, used for automated newsgroup maintenance, and that the article is not meant for user consumption. (Consult Section 3 of [49] for further details.)

Distribution: This reduces the propagation of the article by restricting distribution to nodes which have agreed to transfer the named distribution. In brief, the article will be transferred only to those nodes which subscribe both to the newsgroups in the `Newsgroups` header, and the given distribution. This is used, for example, to limit articles to a specific locale by specifying a geography-based name in this header.

Organization: This indicates the textual identity of the originator's organization.

Summary: This contains a brief summary of the article.

Approved: This indicates the mailbox of the entity which approved this article for distribution.

Lines: The number of lines in the body of the article. (To allow for more efficient listing of articles by news-capable user agents.)

Xref: This contains local equivalence information when an article is stored on a USENET node. If an article is posted to more than one newsgroup, a node may keep track of where each copy of the article is stored. A news-capable user agent can then use this information to know that when the user has read the article in one newsgroup, then it is unnecessary to inform the user about the article in the other newsgroups.

And that concludes our (lengthy) discussion on the format of electronic mail messages in the Internet community.

Chapter 4

Mail Transports

Once again, let's return to the model for message handling introduced on page 2. It's now time to consider the relaying protocol used between message transfer agents.

In the Internet community, the Simple Mail Transfer Protocol (SMTP) provides this service. So, most of this chapter focuses on the store-and-forward service provided by SMTP. Following this, we'll look at another message transfer protocol, one that is based on a remote command execution paradigm. Next we'll briefly examine how news articles can be transferred in the Internet community. Finally, we'll conclude with a discussion on implementation issues for message transfer agents and then close this chapter with a technology comparison.

4.1   Simple Mail Transfer Protocol

In our discussion of SMTP, we'll look at three things:

- the SMTP envelope;

- protocol interactions; and,

- implementation issues.

However, we first need to examine an important requirement on all message transfer agents in the Internet community.[1] It is important that there be a well-known address which is valid at each site. As such, every message transfer agent must recognize and accept messages addressed to its local user `PostMaster`, regardless of the capitalization used. Electronic mail messages sent to this address are delivered to the entity responsible for the local message transfer agent. This facility has proven to be invaluable when the message transfer system is encountering difficulties.

4.1.1   SMTP Envelope

Because SMTP is a relaying protocol, it carries both the envelope and content of the electronic mail message. The SMTP envelope is very simple. It contains:

- the electronic mail address of the user which caused creation of this envelope, termed the *originator* address. This corresponds to the `Sender:` field in the headers, if present.

- one or more *recipient* electronic mail addresses, along with an indication as to mode of delivery.

In the envelope, all electronic mail addresses have domain names which are in canonical form.

It must be **strongly** emphasized that there need be no relationship between the addresses in the SMTP envelope and any recipient addresses present in the headers of the electronic mail message. In fact,

---

[1]This requirement is actually stated in RFC-822, but the author feels it is more appropriately discussed here.

it is entirely possible for the headers to contain no recipient addresses. For example, the message might have a `To:` header containing an empty group, or an empty `Bcc:` header.

SMTP offers four different modes of delivery:

- delivering the electronic mail message to the recipient's mailbox;

- displaying the electronic mail message on any terminal on which the recipient is currently logged in;

- if the recipient is currently logged in, then displaying the electronic mail message to that user's terminal, otherwise, delivering the electronic mail message to the recipient's mailbox.

- delivering the electronic mail message to the recipient's mailbox, and, if the recipient is currently logged in, then optionally displaying the electronic mail message to that user's terminal.

These last three modes are largely of historical interest: virtually all SMTP traffic carries electronic mail messages for recipient mailboxes, not terminals.

Error Reports

When the envelope's originator is the empty string, then the associated content is termed an *error report*. An error report is generated whenever a message transfer agent determines that it cannot relay or deliver the message to one or more of the recipients in the envelope. A new envelope and content are created. The new envelope's originator is the empty string, and a single recipient address is present: the originator address from the old envelope, after any path information has been removed. The delivery mode indicates recipient mailbox delivery.

The content of an error report is an electronic mail message. The `From:` header contains the address of the message transfer agent which generated the error report, and the `To:` header contains the originator's address from the old envelope (again, after any path information has been removed). There is also a `Date:` header. Beyond this, no other headers are required. The body of the error report is whatever diagnostic text the message transfer agent feels might be useful. Following this, the original content might be included. This lack of a formal structure for the content of an error report often requires a human (user or administrator) to examine the error report when it is delivered. There are situations in which this is problematic, e.g., see the discussion on interpreting error reports on page 163.

Note that an error report **must never** result in the generation of another error report. Hence, whenever a message transfer agent decides to generate an error report, it examines the envelope associated with the electronic mail message in question. If the envelope's originator is the empty string, then no error report is generated, and the message in question is discarded. (A wise implementation of a message transfer agent would log these actions.)

Observant readers will note that if an envelope contains an empty originator, then it needn't really be an error report. However, the key thing to note is that such an envelope will never result in an error report being returned.

Address Expansion and Explosion

Thus far, we've been operating under the implicit assumption that there is a one-to-one relationship between an address in an electronic mail message and a mailbox (or terminal) which receives the message. In the general case, this is perhaps true. However, when a message transfer agent accepts responsibility for a local address, that address might actually be an *alias* which resolves to one or more other electronic mail addresses, termed the alias value. Any number of these electronic mail addresses might be a local recipient, or could be reachable through a remote message transfer agent.

It is a local matter as to how a message transfer agent is configured to have aliases. However, when a message transfer agent encounters a local alias as a recipient address in an envelope, it replaces the alias address in the envelope with the electronic mail addresses given by the alias value. Note that the message transfer agent must not modify the content during this process. This is termed *alias expansion*.

Mailing Lists

Some aliases are special in that they are actually *mailing lists*. A mailing list is a collection of one or more electronic mail addresses with an administrator. When an alias corresponding to a mailing list is encountered as a recipient address in the envelope, then *list explosion* occurs. A new envelope is created with an identical content. The new envelope's originator is set to the address of the mailing list's administrator. (This redirects any subsequent error reports to the entity responsible for the mailing list rather than the originator of the electronic mail message.) The recipient addresses in the envelope are set to the addresses given by the alias value (these are termed the mailing list's *subscribers*). The original envelope is discarded and the new envelope is substituted in its place. The message is then re-examined by the MTA, as if it had just been submitted through the posting slot. Again, note that the message transfer agent must not modify the content during this process.

By convention, if an Internet mailing list is named

```
foo
```

then its administrator is named

```
foo-request
```

That is, to contact the administrator of the mailing list

```
mh-users@ics.uci.edu
```

one uses the address

```
mh-users-request@ics.uci.edu
```

As might be guessed from this example, the administrator, or so-called *request address*, for a mailing list, might actually be an alias.

Personal Aliases

User agents may also provide an aliasing facility. However, these aliases must be expanded prior to message submission. Because this is a user agent function, such aliases are removed from the relevant headers and replaced with their values. Once again, note that with the exception of trace headers, message transfer agents are not allowed to manipulate any part of the content, including the headers.

Comparison of Aliasing Methods

To summarize, the following different kinds of aliasing may occur:

What	Who	How
system alias	MTA	replace recipient addresses in envelope
mailing list	MTA	new envelope originator is administrator recipients are subscribers
personal alias	UA	expand headers prior to submission

4.1.2   Protocol Interactions

An SMTP interaction is straight-forward: An SMTP server listens on TCP port 25. A client establishes a TCP connection to the SMTP server and awaits a greeting. The server's greeting indicates the status of its local message transfer agent. If the status is acceptable to both parties, the client identifies itself and then initiates one or more SMTP transactions. When the client is finished, it issues a command to release the service, and waits for the SMTP server to return a response and close the TCP connection. The client then closes the TCP connection.

Figure 4.1 shows the syntax of SMTP interactions, which is in NVT ASCII.[2] (This figure uses the BNF defined in Figures 3.2 and 3.6 on pages 80 and 90, respectively.)

---

[2]The BNF shown is slightly different from the one in the SMTP specification. The author has taken the liberty of "regularizing" the syntax with respect to the constructs used in RFC-822.

```
          ; case-insensitive matching of string-literals
commands  ::= "HELO "        domain      CRLF
          / "MAIL FROM: " route-addr CRLF
          / "MAIL FROM: " "<>"        CRLF
          / "RCPT TO: "   route-addr CRLF
          / "DATA"                    CRLF
          / "NOOP"                    CRLF
          / "RSET"                    CRLF
          / "QUIT"                    CRLF
          / optional
optional  ::= "SEND FROM: " route-addr CRLF
          / "SOML FROM: " route-addr CRLF
          / "SAML FROM: " route-addr CRLF
          / "VRFY "        string      CRLF
          / "EXPN "        string      CRLF
          / "TURN"                     CRLF
          / "HELP"    [" " string]    CRLF

response  ::= *(code ["-"][" " *text] CRLF)
              code        [" " *text] CRLF
code      ::= ("1" / "2" / "3" / "4" / "5")
              ("0" / "1" / "2" /      / "5")
              1DIGIT

string    ::= 1*(stext / quoted-pair)
stext     ::= <any character, not including space or specials>

text      ::= <any character, including bare CR and bare LF,
              but not including CRLF>
```

Figure 4.1: SMTP Interaction Syntax

As can be seen, each command consists of a verb, possibly followed by an argument. Note that although the SMTP specification allows the full `route-addr` syntax to be used for an electronic mail address, the Internet Host Requirements document has declared the `route` component in such addresses to be obsolete. This means that the electronic mail addresses given in SMTP commands use the familiar

```
addr-spec ::= local "@" domain
```

syntax. The reason, of course, is that the DNS is used for mail relaying. Whilst SMTP servers must be able to recognize the `route` syntax, a client must never generate it. If an SMTP server encounters an address containing the `route` syntax, the Internet Host Requirements document suggests that the path contained therein be ignored.

Responses are much more interesting; they consist of one or more lines, each starting with a three-digit reply code and possibly followed by a textual explanation.

Before we can look at the individual commands, we need to better understand SMTP reply codes.

Reply Codes

A reply code is a string containing three digits, which the author terms completion, category, and instance:

completion (first digit): an indication as to whether the command completed, and if so whether it succeeded or failed. The permitted values are:

positive preliminary (1): The server is ready to perform the command, but is waiting for confirmation (or rejection) from the client. (No command in SMTP returns this code, so the description here is only for completeness.)

positive completion (2): The server has successfully performed the command.

positive intermediate (3): The server is ready to perform the command, but requires additional information from the client before proceeding.

transient negative (4): The server did not perform the command due to a transient problem. The client may re-issue the command, in identical form, at a later time.

permanent negative (5): The server did not perform the command due to a permanent problem. The client may re-issue the command but with different arguments, at a later time.

category (second digit): an indication as to why the command succeeded, failed, or didn't complete. The permitted values are:

syntax (0): The reply deals with syntax-related issues, such as unimplemented commands or syntax errors.

informational (1): The reply contains information requested by the client.

connections (2): The reply deals with the underlying transport service.

application-specific (5): The reply deals with an application-specific issue. (In the case of SMTP, the reply deals with the message transfer agent.)

instance (third digit): a value used to distinguish between reply codes having the same completion/category values.

Following the reply code is an optional, implementation-specific, textual explanation, which varies in response to each particular command and its argument. If the explanation is multi-line, then each line of the response starts with the same reply code, and all but the last line have a hyphen-character ("-") immediately following the reply code.

Commands

We now consider the various commands available in SMTP. For each command, we'll list the possible responses in a concise tabular format. In addition to listing a reply code and a meaning for each, we'll also indicate the possible actions that a client might take. Note that the algorithm described for the client is purposefully complex, to demonstrate the wide range of capabilities available in the SMTP service.

Server Identification

When a client opens a TCP connection to an SMTP server, the SMTP server returns a greeting indicating the status of its local message transfer agent. This greeting is a response, just as if the client had issued a command. However, unlike other responses, the informational text is mandated to begin with the domain name of the host associated with the SMTP server's local MTA, e.g.,

```
220 dbc.mtview.ca.us SMTP service ready
```

The possible outcomes are:

Code	Meaning	Next Action
220	MTA available	client identification
421	MTA unavailable	retry later
		close connection

Client Identification

The client identifies itself using the HELO command. The argument contains the domain name of the host associated with the client's local MTA.

Code	Meaning	Next Action
250	identity accepted	originator identification
500	command syntax error	service release;
501	parameter syntax error	try next server,
504	parameter not implemented	or generate error report
421	MTA unavailable	retry later
		service release

Originator Identification

After identifying itself, the client can initiate one or more relaying transactions.

Each transaction starts when the client identifies the originator of the next message to be transferred, along with the mode of the delivery. The client uses one of four different commands to achieve this, each corresponding to one of the delivery modes described earlier on page 127:

```
MAIL FROM:
SEND FROM:
SOML FROM:
SAML FROM:
```

[handwritten annotations: "maint" / "invokes Terminal interaction"]

The argument associated with the command identifies the originator.

Code	Meaning	Next Action
250	originator accepted	recipient identification
552	exceeded storage limits	service release;
451	local error	try next server,
452	out of local storage	or generate error report
500	command syntax error	
501	parameter syntax error	
421	MTA unavailable	retry later
		service release

In addition, if a command other than `MAIL` was given, then one other reply is possible:

Code	Meaning	Next Action
502	command not implemented	generate error report;
		next transaction,
		or release service

Recipient Identification

After identifying the originator of the next message to be transferred, the client can specify one or more recipients for the message. The client uses the RCPT TO command, and the associated argument identifies each recipient.

Code	Meaning	Next Action
250	recipient accepted	recipient identification
251	relaying to recipient	or content transmission
550	no such recipient	generate error report
553	recipient unavailable	continue
551	recipient not local	try next server
		continue
450	mailbox busy	retry later
451	local error	continue
452	out of local storage	
552	exceeded storage limit	
500	command syntax error	service release;
501	parameter syntax error	try next server,
503	command out of sequence	or generate error report
421	MTA unavailable	retry later
		service release

The action taken by the client varies depending on whether the message is being sent to more than one recipient:

- On success (code 250 or 251), the client sees if any other recipients for this electronic mail message are serviced by this SMTP server. If so, the next recipient is identified; otherwise, the client proceeds to transferring the content.

  However, if the client doesn't want the SMTP server to relay the message (code 251), the client may void the entire transaction with a RSET command, and then either begin a relaying transaction or release the service.

- On a permanent failure (code 550 or 553), the client generates an error report.

- In the case where a recipient is not local and the SMTP server refuses to relay the message (code 551), the client sees if another

SMTP server can be used for relaying (by consulting the MX resource records for the recipient's domain). If so, this response is treated as a transient error and an alternate SMTP server is tried; otherwise, this response is treated as a permanent error and an error report is generated.

- In the case of transient errors (code 450, 451 or 452), and some permanent errors (code 552), the client marks the recipient for retry during a later SMTP session.

- In the case of totally unexpected responses (code 500, 501, or 503), the client sees if there is another SMTP server that can be used for relaying (by consulting the MX resource records for the recipient's domain). If so, this response is treated as a transient error and an alternate SMTP server is tried; otherwise, this response is treated as a permanent error and an error report is generated.

- Finally, if the SMTP server's local message transfer agent has become unavailable, the client voids the entire transaction with a RSET command, marks the recipient for retry during a later SMTP session, and releases the service.

On any kind of failure, the client sees if any other recipients for this electronic mail message are serviced by this SMTP server. If so, the next recipient is identified. Otherwise, the client sees if at least one other recipient has already been accepted for this message. If so, the client proceeds to transferring the content; otherwise, the client issues the RSET command and either begins another relaying transaction or releases the service.

Content Transmission

After the SMTP server agrees to accept responsibility for relaying a message to one or more recipients, the client now uses the DATA command to initiate transfer of the content.

Code	Meaning	Next Action
354	ready for content	send content
451	local error	retry later; next transaction, or release service
554	transaction failed	generate error report; next transaction, or release service
500	command syntax error	service release;
501	parameter syntax error	try next server,
503	command out of sequence	or generate error report
421	MTA unavailable	retry later service release

If the reply code isn't 354, the client voids the entire transaction with the RSET command and either starts a new transaction or releases the service. Otherwise, if the reply code is 354, the SMTP client sends the electronic mail message (headers and body) over the TCP connection, line-by-line, and terminating each line with a CR-LF sequence. If a line from the message begins with a dot-character ("."), the client inserts a dot before sending the line. When the entire message has been sent, the client sends a three-character sequence consisting of a dot-character and CR-LF. (Observant readers will have noted that this mechanism inspired the example of the data-stuffing algorithm introduced back on page 14.)

The SMTP server creates a storage buffer (usually a disk file) for the new message, and then reads the electronic mail message from the TCP connection into the buffer. Whenever the SMTP server receives a line beginning with a dot-character, it strips that character. If any other characters remain besides the CR-LF pair, then the rest of the line is appended to the buffer. Otherwise, the SMTP server knows that it has received the last line of the message, and it issues another response:

Code	Meaning	Next Action
250	message accepted	next transaction or service release
552 554	exceeded storage limit transaction failed	generate error report continue
451 452	local error out of local storage	service release; retry later

If the reply code is 250, the SMTP server has secured the message and accepted responsibility for relaying it. The SMTP client removes those recipients from the envelope which the server SMTP accepted. If no recipient addresses remain, the envelope and content are discarded, as they have been completely processed.

On a permanent error (code 552 or 554), the client generates an error report; otherwise, on a transient failure (code 451 or 452), the client marks the accepted recipients for retry during a later SMTP session. Regardless of the outcome, the client either starts another transaction with this SMTP server, or releases the service.

Probe Commands

Any time after a client has identified itself, it may ask the SMTP server to verify that a mailbox is available for a local "user". For example, if the client issues the command:

    VRFY mrose

it is asking:

"If I asked you to deliver a message to:

    <mrose@your-domain>

. . . would you deliver it?"

In response, the SMTP server replies with one of:

Code	Meaning
250	user is local
251	user is non-local
252	willing to relay: user is non-local
550	no such user
551	won't relay: user is non-local
553	user's mailbox unavailable
500	command syntax error
501	parameter syntax error
502	command not implemented
504	parameter not implemented
421	MTA unavailable

Instead, if a client wishes to find out what recipients will receive a message addressed to a local "user", it issues the EXPN command. For example, if the client issues the command:

```
EXPN st-columnists
```

it is asking:

"If I asked you to deliver a message to

```
<st-columnists@your-domain>
```

... who would you deliver it to?"

In response, the SMTP server replies with one of:

Code	Meaning
250	user is local
550	no such user
500	command syntax error
501	parameter syntax error
502	command not implemented
504	parameter not implemented
421	MTA unavailable

In the case of a reply code of 250, the server issues a reply indicating which electronic mail addresses would receive the message, e.g.,

```
EXPN st-columnists
250-<case@utkvx.utk.edu>
250-<kzm@hls.com>
250-<waldbusser@andrew.cmu.edu>
250-<dperkins@synoptics.com>
250 <rlstewart@eng.xyplex.com>
```

This can be used to manually expand a mailing list.

Although both of these commands are optional in the SMTP specification, the Internet Host Requirements document specifies that the VRFY command must be implemented. Many implementations support these commands, but most site administrators disable them. Naturally, this leads to a soapbox!

Finger is not the only service to succumb to paranoia in the Internet community. SMTP's EXPN command, and sometimes even VRFY command, have also fallen victim. The rationale, of course, is either privacy- or security-related. However, experience has shown that use of the EXPN command provides important diagnostic help when debugging mail routing loops. Further, programs such as netfind discussed earlier in Section 2.3.3 make use of the EXPN command as a part of their algorithm for locating users. Once again, the author must appeal to the reader's community spirit: let's cooperate and try to make the network a place where we can work together, instead of spending our time erecting barriers to communication.

> soap...

> ...soap

Service Reset and Release

As already noted earlier, the RSET command can be used to void a transaction in process. If the SMTP server responds with code 250, the transaction in progress, if any, is aborted. Otherwise, if this request fails, the client should probably simply release the service.

To release the service, the client issues the QUIT command. If the SMTP server responds with code 250, the client will close the TCP connection, and then the SMTP server does likewise. Otherwise, if the QUIT command (somehow) fails, the client should simply reset the TCP connection.

Miscellaneous Commands

There are three miscellaneous commands.

The HELP command takes an optional argument, and asks the SMTP server to provide explanatory text. If the SMTP server responds with code 211 or 214, then the reply contains informative text (for a human user). Otherwise, the SMTP server might complain about the usual syntax errors, parameter errors, and the like.

The NOOP command is simply an application-layer "ping" to see if the SMTP server is still functioning. The SMTP server replies with code 250 if all is well.

Finally, the TURN command is used to request that the SMTP server deliver any mail it might have queued for the client's local MTA. The SMTP server replies with code 250 and then an SMTP command if it is willing to do so. Otherwise, the SMTP server replies with code 502. Because a host with IP-connectivity (which is necessary to run SMTP) can usually support multiple TCP connections, the TURN command is unnecessary. Further, because of the security implications, this command is usually not available. However, on sophisticated implementations, when an SMTP server receives a TURN command, it informs its local message transfer agent that the host named when the client identified itself is now accepting mail. The SMTP server's local MTA can then examine its queues and instantiate a new SMTP client if necessary.

An Example Interaction

Let's consider a straight-forward example to get the feel for the protocol. In the discussion below, (S) refers to an SMTP server, and (C) refers to the client.

Recall earlier the composition template shown in Figure 3.10 on page 98. When MH (on the author's desktop) submits this message for delivery, it establishes an SMTP session to the local server, and the SMTP session looks something like that shown in Figure 4.2. (Recall that the actual message submitted is shown in Figure 3.12 page 100.)

```
S: <wait for connection on TCP port 25>
C: <open connection to server>
S: 220 dbc.mtview.ca.us SMTP service ready
C: HELO baiji.dbc.mtview.ca.us
S: 250 dbc.mtview.ca.us says hello to baiji.dbc.mtview.ca.us
C: MAIL FROM: <mrose@dbc.mtview.ca.us>
S: 250 sender ok
C: RCPT TO: <nsb@thumper.bellcore.com>
S: 250 recipient ok
C: RCPT TO: <galvin@tis.com>
S: 250 recipient ok
C: RCPT TO: <pvm@darpa.mil>
S: 250 recipient ok
C: RCPT TO: <jromine@ics.uci.edu>
S: 250 recipient ok
C: RCPT TO: <Stef@nma.com>
S: 250 recipient ok
C: RCPT TO: <mdz@ssw.com>
S: 250 recipient ok
C: DATA
S: 354 Enter mail, end with "." on a line by itself
C: To: Reviewers: ;
C: Subject: Want to review a book?
C: Date: Sun, 12 Apr 1992 11:50:40 -0700
C: Message-ID: <18597.703104640@dbc.mtview.ca.us>
C: From: Marshall Rose <mrose@dbc.mtview.ca.us>
C:
C: As you may have heard, I am undertaking the writing of my
C: fourth and final book.  The working title is
C:
   <<in the interests of brevity, the majority of the body of
     the original message has been removed in this figure...>>
C:
C: Very little on X.400, except when I need to illustrate how
C: not to do something. (-:
C:
C: /mtr
C: .
S: 250 message sent
C: QUIT
S: 221 dbc.mtview.ca.us closing connection
C: <closes connection>
S: <closes connection>
```

Figure 4.2: Example SMTP Interaction

Now, suppose that the server SMTP had rejected one of the recipient addresses, e.g.,

```
C: RCPT TO: <Stef@nma.com>
S: 550 mail to nma.com not allowed
```

The client SMTP process has a choice. It can either try the next recipient address, or it can void the entire transaction. MH, which is using SMTP as a submission protocol, takes the latter choice:

```
C: RSET
S: 250 ok
C: QUIT
S: 221 dbc.mtview.ca.us closing connection
```

and then reports the failure to the user. In contrast, a message transfer agent would likely have chosen the first alternative, removing all but the rejected address from its envelope. Then, depending on whether there appeared to be another SMTP server providing relaying for that recipient, the message transfer agent would either try the alternate servers, or generate an error report.

Whilst SMTP provides adequate functionality when a user agent wishes to submit a message, an experimental protocol has been defined which is an SMTP subset. This is called the *Message Posting Protocol* (MPP) [50]. The MPP command syntax is shown in Figure 4.3. (This figure uses the BNF defined in Figure 3.2 on page 80.)

The **USER** and **PASS** commands are used to "authenticate" user submitting mail using a locally-significant user-identity and a plaintext password. The **DATA** command is identical to the one used in SMTP for content transmission (refer back to page 138 for the details). Similarly, the **NOOP** and **QUIT** commands also have identical semantics.

Responses in MPP have the same syntax as those in SMTP, although only a subset of the reply codes are used, with one exception: if the password supplied is invalid, a new reply code is used to signal this.

soap...   MPP is just plain silly. First, there is no concept of a user-identity within the message transfer system. So, requiring authentication for submission is completely ineffective as neither authentication syntax nor semantics are transferred with the message. Second, because there

```
                 ; case-insensitive matching of string-literals
commands  ::= "USER " string CRLF
              / "PASS " string CRLF
              / "DATA"        CRLF
              / "NOOP"        CRLF
              / "QUIT"        CRLF

response  ::= *(code ["-"][" " *text] CRLF)
                   code      [" " *text] CRLF
code      ::= ("1" / "2" / "3" / "4" / "5")
              ("0" / "1" / "2" /     / "5")
              1DIGIT

string    ::= 1*(stext / quoted-pair)
stext     ::= <any character, not including space or specials>

text      ::= <any character, including bare CR and bare LF,
              but not including CRLF>
```

Figure 4.3: MPP Command Syntax

is no envelope negotiation, the MPP server must read the headers of
the content in order to deduce the recipients to associate with the
envelope. This prevents use of the blind-carbon-copy facility discussed
earlier on page 96. Finally, a minimal client SMTP implementation is
very straight-forward to implement. It is arguable that implementing
an MPP client in a constrained environment is going to be any easier. According to an unconfirmed source, the only reason MPP was
submitted for publication was because the company that developed
MPP wanted to make the claim in their marketing literature that their
products conformed to an RFC! Of course, MPP is officially designated
as a limited-use, experimental protocol for the Internet community.
Somehow the author doubts that the product literature mentions that
factoid.

...soap

4.2   UUCP

The UUCP community is a large set of hosts (described in some detail
on pages 251–254 of [48]), which interworks using a remote execution protocol called UNIX-to-UNIX copy (UUCP) primarily over asynchronous dial-up lines.[3]   Although a generalized file transfer can be
provided with such a facility, by far the best-used service in the UUCP
community is electronic mail. The idea is straight-forward: an envelope and content are transferred as the input to a command which
executes on an adjacent node. The command examines the envelope
and determines whether final delivery or further relaying is necessary.

A UUCP node name is identified by an alphanumeric string of one
to eight characters in length, which is intended to be globally unique.[4]
In order to calculate the topology of the UUCP network, the UUCP
community has a project which runs a mapping algorithm. Thus, when
one UUCP node wishes to execute a command on another, the map
can be consulted to determine which adjacent node(s) are closest to a
destination. Note that depending on the connectivity of a node, use of
the UUCP map is not always necessary. For example, if a node has but
a single connection, topology information is largely irrelevant.

4.2.1   Transporting Mail

As described in [51], the UUCP community today largely uses domain
naming to identify electronic mail recipients. So, when a message
transfer agent on a UUCP node wishes to relay an electronic mail
message, it must derive two kinds of related information:

- which adjacent nodes are closest, and,

- what command to execute on one of those nodes.

To determine the potential next-hop message transfer agents, the node
needs a method for mapping a domain name into the UUCP node

---

[3]UUCP also runs over TCP, though discussion of this usage is far beyond the
scope of *The Internet Message*.

[4]Due to a proliferation of defective implementations, names must usually be
unique in the first six characters.

```
envelope   ::= line *(">" line)

line       ::= "From" sender uucpdate "remote from" system
               *("!" system) LF

sender     ::= domain "!" local

system     ::= ALPHA *5(ALPHA / DIGIT)

uucpdate   ::= day "," SPACE month SPACE dotm SPACE hours
               SPACE 4DIGIT
dotm       ::= (SPACE / 1DIGIT) 1DIGIT
hours      ::= 2DIGIT ":" 2DIGIT ":" 2DIGIT
```

Figure 4.4: UUCP Envelope Syntax

name for the next-hop. The UUCP map can often be used to calculate this. Otherwise, most UUCP nodes are configured to know about a "default" node. Regardless of the choice, the message transfer agent, then executes the uux program identifying the command to execute and the name of the UUCP node which should perform the execution. The input to the command is the envelope information, specified on one or more lines, followed immediately by the content, which is an RFC-822 message (headers and body).

The Envelope

The syntax of a UUCP envelope is shown in Figure 4.4. (This figure uses the BNF defined in Figures 3.2, 3.6, and 3.7 on pages 80, 90, and 92, respectively.)

The first line of the envelope identifies the originator of the electronic mail message, any remaining lines are trace information. On some UUCP nodes, the trace information is coalesced onto the end of the first line of the envelope. For example, the envelope

```
From uucp Wed Apr 15 16:21:52 1992 remote from fernwood
>From mrose Wed Apr 15 16:21:52 1992 remote from dbc
```

is equivalent to

```
From uucp Wed Apr 15 16:21:52 1992 remote from fernwood!dbc
```

Command Specification

In nearly all cases, the command executed on the adjacent UUCP node is `rmail`, which uses the envelope information to submit the message to the local message transfer agent. However, the arguments to the `rmail` command may vary considerably, depending on the version of UUCP software being run on the next-hop. Interested readers should consult Section 2.5 of [51] for the details.

A common consideration however is that the recipient identified in the arguments to `rmail` be properly interpreted. Most UUCP nodes run the UNIX operating-system, and hence UUCP invokes a UNIX shell to parse the command and arguments to be executed.

The arguments to `rmail` contain a recipient address of the form

```
local@domain
```

or more properly an `addr-spec` using the syntax in Figures 3.6 and 3.2 on pages 90 and 80, respectively. Therefore, the `local` component may contain one or more characters which the UNIX shell terms a *meta-character* — one which the shell, and not the command being run, will interpret. The solution to this problem is defined in [52]. When constructing the command line for remote execution, the message transfer agent examines the recipient address. If a `quoted-string` is present, the initial and final quotation-marks (") are removed. Regardless, each character is examined. If it appears in the left-hand column of Table 4.1 then the corresponding substitution is made. In addition, an ASCII control character (see page 80 for a definition) is output as a five-character sequence:

```
any        ::= "#" 3DIGIT "#"
```

where the number indicated is the ASCII value of the character in question. Further, if the message transfer agent knows that a particular character might cause problems on the adjacent UUCP node, it can transform that character as a five-character sequence as well. Otherwise, all other characters in the recipient address are copied verbatim.

As might be expected, reversing the mapping is straight-forward, with the exception that once a new string is generated, if the result

Character	Replacement
(	#1#
)	#r#
[	#091#
]	#093#
"	#034#
\	#b#
,	#m#
:	#c#
;	#059#
<	#060#
>	#061#
#	#h#
/	#s#
=	#e#
_	#u#
␣	_

Table 4.1: Translating NVT ASCII to Printable String

sequence of characters is not an **atom**, then quotation-marks (") are added at the beginning and end of the string.

This particular mapping was not developed specifically for the UUCP community. Rather, it defines a mapping between NVT ASCII and the *printable string* repertoire used by OSI's Message Handling System. The fact that this mapping isn't specifically tailored to the UUCP community will come as no surprise to anyone familiar with the UNIX shell — very few meta-characters actually appear in the table! Usually, these characters are also quoted as a five-character sequence:

```
meta      ::= "!" / "$" / "&" / "'" / "*" / "?" / "^"
          / "`" / "{" / "}" / "~"
```

Finally, depending on the version of UUCP software being run on the next-hop, it is possible that if a line of the input contains only a single dot-character ("."), then **rmail** might terminate its input prematurely. Unfortunately, there is no transparent way to fix this problem. If the next-hop is known to have this problem, the message transfer agent adds a character in front of the dot-character, which will ultimately be seen by the recipient.

4.3   Transporting News Articles

Recall from the earlier discussion in Section 3.5 starting on page 120 that unlike an electronic mail message, which is addressed to a fixed number of recipients, a news article reaches all parties in a community of interest (i.e., newsgroup).

The key notion of USENET is that news articles are broadcast through a flooding algorithm. The flow of news articles from one node to another is termed a *feed*. Each USENET node is configured with a list of other nodes with which it exchanges news articles, along with the newsgroups and distributions that are permitted to be exchanged with each node. This is normally, but not necessarily a symmetric relationship. That is, the newsgroups permitted to flow in the feed from one USENET node to another, are usually the same newsgroups permitted to flow in the reverse feed.

To avoid loops, two tests are used when a USENET node receives a news article. First, the node checks to see if its node name is in the `Path:` header. If so, the article has already passed through this node, and it can immediately be discarded. Second, the node checks a database of `Message-ID:` values which it has already encountered for the news group. If the `Message-ID:` value for the news article matches something in the database, the article can be discarded.

The advantage of this technique is that the USENET node providing the feed doesn't have to know which articles the downstream node has encountered. (This would be a daunting task considering that the downstream node may receive feeds from other USENET sites.)

4.3.1   Using Remote Execution or Mail

There are several ways in which news articles are transferred in the USENET community. One way, which has been in use for the longest time, is to transfer news using the remote execution facility of UUCP. By convention, the `rnews` command is used for this purpose. The input to a command is a news article.

Another way is to encapsulate a news article in an electronic mail message and send it to special electronic mail address on an adjacent node. By convention, the "rnews" recipient is used for this purpose — it bursts the news articles from the message body and posts them accordingly. The encapsulation scheme used is quite simple: a capital-N ("N") is placed at the beginning of each line in the news article prior to transmission, and the character is removed by the `rnews` recipient (thus avoiding UUCP's single dot-character problem noted earlier.)

Both of these are transaction-based approaches to transferring news. We now turn to an interactive approach.

4.3.2 Using the Network News Transfer Protocol

The Network News Transfer Protocol (NNTP) provides three services:

- identifies newly created newsgroups on the NNTP server;

- identifies, and optionally transfers, newly arrived news articles on the NNTP server; and,

- identifies, and optionally transfers, newly arrived news articles on the NNTP client.

Readers should note that as of April, 1992, the IETF is working on refining and extending NNTP. Therefore, some of the details in this section may be overtaken by events. However, the basic concepts should all remain unchanged.

Protocol Interactions

An NNTP interaction is straight-forward: An NNTP server listens on TCP port 119. A client establishes a TCP connection to the NNTP server and awaits a greeting. The greeting indicates whether the NNTP server will allow the client to post news articles. If the status is acceptable to both parties, the client initiates one or more NNTP transactions. When the client is finished, it issues a command to release the service, and waits for the NNTP server to return a response and close the TCP connection. The client then closes the TCP connection.

Figure 4.5 on page 153 shows the syntax of NNTP interactions, which is in NVT ASCII. (This figure uses the BNF defined in Figures 3.2 and 3.6 on pages 80 and 90, respectively.)

The command syntax is significantly more complex than the syntax used by SMTP. For example, some reply codes indicate that a multi-line parameter follows, using the usual data-stuffing algorithm employed by SMTP and friends. Although not shown in Figure 4.5, the responses are also more complex: many responses return one or more parameters.

Each time a news article is placed in a newsgroup, the NNTP server increments a counter and assigns the value as the local article number for that news article in that group. In addition, the NNTP server keeps track of the lowest and highest local article numbers for each newsgroup: as news articles expire, the lower-bound increases; and, as news articles arrive, the upper-bound increases.

Rather than give an exhaustive explanation for each command (interested readers should consult [8] for that treatment), let's consider them briefly:

list: Returns a multi-line parameter indicating, for each newsgroup known to the NNTP server's node, the numeric range of news articles present, and whether posting is allowed.

newgroup: Returns a multi-line parameter indicating all the newsgroups which have been created on the NNTP server's node since the indicated date and time. Each group is identified by its name, numeric range, and posting-permission.

The `distribution` parameter identifies one or more newsgroups. If present, it is used to filter the results to those newsgroups which are subordinate to those identified in the distribution.

newnews: Returns a multi-line parameter indicating all the news articles which have been received by the NNTP server's node since the indicated date and time. Each news article is identified by its `Message-ID:` header. The `distribution` parameter is used to limit the results returned.

group: Changes the "current group" used for subsequent interactions to the one indicated by the parameter to this command, and returns the number of news articles present.

```
              ; case-insensitive matching of string-literals
commands  ::= "LIST"                              CRLF
            / "NEWGROUP" 1*SP when
              [1*SP distributions]                CRLF
            / "NEWNEWS"  1*SP 1#group when
              [1*SP distributions]                CRLF
            / "GROUP"     1*SP group              CRLF
            / "NEXT"                               CRLF
            / "LAST"                               CRLF
            / "ARTICLE"  1*SP [msgid / 1*DIGIT] CRLF
            / "HEAD"     1*SP [msgid / 1*DIGIT] CRLF
            / "BODY"     1*SP [msgid / 1*DIGIT] CRLF
            / "STAT"     1*SP [msgid / 1*DIGIT] CRLF
            / "IHAVE"    1*SP  msgid              CRLF
            / "POST"                               CRLF
            / "SLAVE"                              CRLF
            / "HELP"                               CRLF
            / "QUIT"                               CRLF

              ;   YYMMDD      HHMMSS  server's zone or UT
when      ::= 6DIGIT 1*SP 6DIGIT [1*SP "GMT"]
distributions
          ::= "<" 1#group ">"
group     ::= word *("." word)
msg-id    ::= "<" addr-spec ">"

response  ::= *(code ["-"][" " *text] CRLF)
              code       [" " *text] CRLF
              [multiline CRLF "." CRLF]
code      ::= ("1" / "2" / "3" / "4" / "5")
              ("0" / "1" / "2" /     / "5")
              1DIGIT
multiline ::= 1*<any character, including ".", CR, and LF,
                but not including (CRLF "." CRLF)>

text      ::= <any character, including bare CR and bare LF,
                but not including CRLF>
```

Figure 4.5: **NNTP Interaction Syntax**

next (last): Advances (or retreats) the pointer for the "current article", and returns the `Message-ID:` header for the new current article, along with the NNTP server's local article number.

article: Returns a multi-line parameter containing the headers and body of the news article indicated by the parameter to this command. If no parameter is present, the current article is indicated; if a `msg-id` is provided, then the news article having that `Message-ID:` header is indicated; otherwise, the news article having the specified local article number is indicated. In the latter case, the pointer of the current article is set to the indicated news article.

head (body): As `article`, but the multi-line parameter returns only the headers (or body) of the indicated news article.

stat: Returns the `Message-ID:` header for the indicated news article, along with the NNTP server's local article number for that news article. If the news article is indicated via a local article number, the pointer of the current article is set to the indicated news article.

ihave: The response indicates whether the NNTP server wants the client to transfer the news article identified by this command's parameter, which specifies a `Message-ID:` value. If so, the client transfers the news article, using the same algorithm as SMTP's `DATA` command.

post: The response indicates whether the NNTP server will allow the client to post a news article. If so, the client transfers the news article, using the same algorithm as SMTP's `DATA` command.

slave: Indicates that the client is providing an NNTP service for a collection of users, and asks that the NNTP server act accordingly. In theory, on some systems, this means that the NNTP session will receive higher priority when multiple NNTP sessions are being serviced at one host.

help: Returns a multi-line parameter describing the NNTP commands available.

quit: terminates the NNTP session.

As can be seen from the breadth of commands available, NNTP can be used either for news propagation by a downstream USENET node, or for news browsing by a remote user.

4.4   Implementation Issues for Message Transfer Agents

As should be expected, there is a lot more to realizing a message transfer agent than simply implementing a relaying protocol such as SMTP. These deal with issues of correctness, performance, and resource utilization. Let's consider some areas which experience has shown to be absolutely critical. (The reader might want to glance back to the observation made on page 18 to understand why issues such as these are important.)

4.4.1   Size Limitations

The SMTP specification defines the minimal sizes of many data structures which an SMTP implementation must manipulate, such as addresses, command lines, and reply lines. As with all Internet technology, implementors are encouraged to produce software which far exceeds these limits, or impose no limits whatsoever.

The SMTP specification does not limit the maximum size of a content. However, the Internet Host Requirements document mandates that electronic mail messages up to 64K bytes must be supported.

4.4.2   Queue Management

A message transfer agent may have several queues containing messages for relaying. Typically, a queue contains messages of a similar priority all destined for a common community. The SMTP service does not have an explicit notion of priority, but this can be determined via local mechanisms, e.g., destination community or perhaps content size.

A message transfer agent often must re-queue a message or recipient for later processing due to a transient problem. In particular, after the first transiency encountered, the Internet Host Requirements document recommends a retry interval of at least 30 minutes, preferably with the interval increasing to two or three hours. In any event, the message transfer agent should retry sending the message for at least four or five days. All of these values should be configurable. Section 2.2.5

starting on page 49 identified several transient errors, as did the SMTP command descriptions starting on page 134.

As an implementation option, when an electronic mail message has been in a queue for several days, but before the message transfer agent decides to give up, it might opt to send an error report indicating that delivery is still pending. This is termed a *soft error report*.[5]

Use of Caching

Earlier it was noted how a DNS resolver could maintain a cache of information. A message transfer agent should maintain two additional caches.

The first cache keeps track of the IP addresses which are known to have SMTP servers available. Whenever a TCP connection is attempted, the message transfer agent updates its cache to reflect whether the connection was established. Similarly, if the TCP connection is established, but the SMTP server indicated that its local MTA was unavailable, this too should be noted in the cache. Later, when the message transfer agent uses the mail routing algorithm based on MX resource records, knowledge of available SMTP servers can be used as a secondary sort key for MX resource records having the same preference value. Hence, it is possible for the sending application to select an MX record with a higher cost, if its associated IP-address is known to be good (and/or the IP-addresses associated with other MX records are known to be bad).

The second cache keeps track of existing SMTP sessions. After completing an SMTP transaction, but before releasing the connection, the message transfer agent looks for other messages in the queue which contain recipients that are serviced by the SMTP server on the other end of that connection. If so, a new SMTP transaction is started for those recipients, even if the envelope being processed still has other recipient addresses present. Normally, only a small number of simultaneous SMTP sessions will be handled by a message transfer agent. This number should be configurable, however.

The rationale for using these caches is to minimize both the number

---

[5]The generation of soft error reports is not necessarily a good idea! See the discussion on "improper explosion" on page 162 for the details.

of attempts to establish a TCP connection and the number of new TCP connections established. When an internet becomes congested, use of this caching knowledge can greatly reduce load on the network. As might be expected, if more than one recipient for a particular electronic mail message is served by a connected SMTP server, then the content should be transferred at most once.

4.4.3   Command Handling

The description of SMTP commands starting on page 134 was quite detailed in that decisions were made based on all three digits of a reply code. The Internet Host Requirements document recommends that decisions be based solely on the first digit of the reply code. The rationale for this is that some SMTP server implementations return incorrect or even invalid reply codes. Regardless, both the Internet Host Requirements document and the author agree that any text associated with a reply should be ignored by the decision-making process in a client.

The Internet Host Requirements document requires that a client implement configurable timeouts for each SMTP command. If a result is not returned within the indicated amount of time, then the client closes the TCP connection and considers this a transient error. The suggested minimum values are:

Command	Timeout
greeting	5 minutes
MAIL FROM	5 minutes
RCPT TO	5 minutes
DATA	2 minutes
data send	3 minutes
data end	10 minutes

The "data send" timeout is how long the SMTP client should wait for each TCP buffer containing a part of the content to be transferred to the SMTP server. The "data end" timeout is how long the SMTP client should wait for a response after sending the final dot-character marking the end of the content.

Similarly, an SMTP server should have a configurable, minimal timeout of 5 minutes while waiting for a command from the client. Further, in order for these timeouts to work well, an SMTP server needs to minimize two activities:

- recipient verification; and,

- content acceptance.

When the `RCPT` command is received, the SMTP server should determine if the argument identifies a local recipient. If so, it should verify that the recipient is able to receive messages; otherwise, if the argument is an alias or mailing list containing at least one recipient reached by a remote message transfer agent, it is probably best to issue a 250 code immediately. Later on, if one or more electronic mail addresses prove faulty, an error report can be generated accordingly. This is largely a resource-tradeoff: if the verification process takes too long, the client will assume that the SMTP server is misbehaving; otherwise, if a blanket verification is given, then the resources associated with an SMTP transaction may be needlessly wasted.

In terms of content acceptance, the server SMTP should immediately write a new `Received:` header before copying the content from the TCP connection to the storage buffer for the new message. The Internet Host Requirements document indicates that a `from` field should be present containing both the client's specified identity and a dotted-quad corresponding to the client's IP address. Once the final dot-character has been received, the SMTP server should secure the storage buffer, placing it into a message queue, and then immediately issue a 250 code. Any additional processing of the message should occur after the reply is issued by the SMTP server. This minimizes the possibility that a transient network problem will break the TCP connection and thereby cause a subsequent attempt to deliver the message, even though the SMTP server has already taken responsibility for it.

```
S: <wait for connection on TCP port 25>
C: <open connection to server>
S: 220 dbc.mtview.ca.us SMTP service ready
C: MAIL FROM: <mrose@dbc.mtview.ca.us>
C: RCPT TO: <nsb@thumper.bellcore.com>
C: RCPT TO: <galvin@tis.com>
C: RCPT TO: <pvm@darpa.mil>
C: RCPT TO: <jromine@ics.uci.edu>
C: RCPT TO: <Stef@nma.com>
C: RCPT TO: <mdz@ssw.com>
C: DATA
S: 250 sender ok
S: 250 recipient ok
S: 250 recipient ok
S: 250 recipient ok
S: 250 recipient ok
S: 250 recipient ok
S: 250 recipient ok
S: 354 Enter mail, end with "." on a line by itself
...
```

Figure 4.6: Example SMTP Pipelining Interaction

4.4.4   Pipelining

One performance enhancing technique which is being used on an experimental basis is called *pipelining*.

An adequate message transfer agent will transfer a message at most once to a given SMTP server. Hence, as noted earlier, if there are multiple recipients serviced by a given SMTP server, the SMTP transaction will contain multiple RCPT commands followed by a single DATA command. Earlier, the example in Figure 4.2 on page 143 gave an example of this. However, a clever message transfer agent will pipeline commands to the SMTP server, as shown in the example in Figure 4.6.

That is, for each message, the client will issue a single TCP send containing the the MAIL FROM:, RCPT TO: and DATA commands. The purpose of this is to minimize both network traffic and latency — the receiving application will process each command, in turn, and the sending application must correlate the responses, as they dribble back,

```
S: <wait for connection on TCP port 25>
C: <open connection to server>
S: 220 dbc.mtview.ca.us SMTP service ready
C: MAIL FROM: <mrose@dbc.mtview.ca.us>
C: RCPT TO: <nsb@thumper.bellcore.com>
C: RCPT TO: <galvin@tis.com>
C: RCPT TO: <pvm@darpa.mil>
C: RCPT TO: <jromine@ics.uci.edu>
C: RCPT TO: <Stef@nma.com>
C: RCPT TO: <mdz@ssw.com>
C: DATA
S: 250 sender ok
S: 550 remote delivery not allowed
S: 550 remote delivery not allowed
S: 550 remote delivery not allowed
S: 550 remote delivery not allowed
S: 550 remote delivery not allowed
S: 550 remote delivery not allowed
S: 354 Enter mail, end with "." on a line by itself
C: .
S: 250 message sent
...
```

Figure 4.7: Example SMTP Pipelining Recovery

to the appropriate command.

Of course, if none of the recipient addresses are accepted, the client must check to see if the DATA command was accepted (it shouldn't have been), and if so, it must send a single dot, as shown in Figure 4.7. Otherwise, if the DATA command failed, then the client simply voids the transaction by using the RSET command.

Note that use of pipelining introduces a new failure mode: if there is a very large number of recipients, then the available TCP window might not be large enough to handle all of the RCPT commands and the DATA command. In this case, the SMTP session will eventually lock up! The solution to this unlikely problem is to send commands in units which are always smaller than the TCP window size (usually 4K octets). To avoid this problem commands should be sent in blocks which are slightly smaller than the underlying window size.

Regrettably, there is a second danger: in violation of the SMTP specification, some SMTP servers may flush their TCP input buffer whenever an SMTP command fails. At the risk of starting a soapbox, such implementations should be fixed, and the implementors responsible should be made to type-in

> *I will write robust software.*

one-thousand times as punishment.

4.4.5   Mailing Lists

Although an extremely useful facility, experience has shown that, by and large, maintenance of mailing lists is quite troublesome. [53] empirically documents the problems encountered by one site which maintains several large mailing lists. For the purpose of discussion in *The Internet Message*, the general problems of mailing list handling fall into several categories:

Improper Explosion

On some mailing lists, error reports are not being sent to the envelope's originator. There are two reasons for this:

- First, there is a lot of code written by people who don't understand the difference between the envelope and the content. Thus, their software looks in the headers of the contents, and sends error reports to the address in the `From:` header. (In fact, there is even software in use that tries to look in the headers to figure out who the recipients are.) The author's advice: fix the software.

- Second, there are other message transport protocols which simply do not have the concept of an envelope, and therefore there is no choice but to use the headers. From a purist perspective, these systems aren't electronic mail systems, because they don't exhibit the qualities of the model for message handling introduced back on page 2. The author's advice: get new software.

One solution employed by the author is to use a special explosion process for mailing lists. This is discussed later on in Section 5.1.2 on page 187.

Designing and implementing electronic mail transport systems is *not* rocket science. It simply should not be that difficult to get even the basics right. After all, the basic model has been available for over 13 years, and reasonable implementations have been in use for even longer. Can we at least try to get the basics right?

soap...

...soap

Soft Error Reports

Message transfer agents servicing a mailing list subscriber cause problems if they generate soft error reports:

- First, a human has to look at an error report to see whether it is soft. If so, the error report can be safely ignored. If not, the mailing list administrator must act upon the error report.

- Second, for mailing lists, who really cares that an electronic mail message is still sitting in a queue waiting for further processing? Perhaps some mailing lists might have a time-sensitive nature, but most don't.

Unfortunately, the author doesn't have a solution for this. Although one can make the argument for soft error reports being desirable, one could counter that it is really acting as a substitute for a confirmation of final delivery. But, the SMTP envelope doesn't allow for selection of either service.

Novice Users

A common problem occurs when novice users in the Internet community confuse the address of the mailing list with the address of the mailing list administrator. A solution is for the mailing list administrator to be one of the subscribers to the mailing list, and then to act accordingly when such a message is received. However, this does not stop administrative traffic from going to all recipients on the list. Of course, better education for neophytes helps to cut down on such traffic.

Nested Mailing Lists

Because an address on a mailing list may in fact be another mailing list, there is the potential for routing loops. In practice, such loops are infrequent. However, as noted earlier in the soapbox on page 141, SMTP's EXPN command can be used to provide invaluable diagnostic information.

A more insidious problem is that the use of nested lists obscures who is responsible for a particular recipient address. For example, an electronic mail message is sent to a mailing list which properly explodes it (as described earlier in Section 4.1.1). One of the new recipients is in fact an alias at a remote site. As a result, when the remote site expands the alias, it doesn't create a new envelope with a different originator. Now suppose that one of the addresses in this second mailing list is incorrect, the error report will go to the administrator of the first mailing list, who has to somehow figure out what went wrong. The solution is simple: the remote site should subscribe once to the first mailing list using an address corresponding to a local mailing list, not a simple alias.

A related problem occurs when a person receiving messages from the mailing list via a local alias wants to change their address or to remove it. If that person sends an electronic mail message to the mailing list administrator, the person's address won't be listed among the subscribers for the mailing list. However, the administrator can find those addresses which go to the person's site and suggest that the PostMaster at that site be contacted.

4.5 Technology Comparison

In MHS, the envelope used by the message transfer service is much richer than that used by SMTP.

To begin, the MHS envelope varies depending on the kind of content being carried:

- a *user message*, submitted by a user agent;

- a *delivery report*, generated by a message transfer agent, at the request of a user agent, when an electronic mail message was delivered, or was unable to be delivered, to a particular recipient; or,

- a *probe message*, generated when a user agent wishes to test whether a recipient's address is reachable.

The MHS envelope for user messages contains information such as:

- a global message identifier, and optionally a user agent message identifier, which allows message transfer agents to coordinate user messages with delivery reports;

- the O/R-name of the originator that submitted the electronic mail message;

- the O/R-names of the recipients, and various per-recipient flags (including whether responsibility should be taken for delivery to this recipient);

- the content type which identifies the messaging protocol being employed by the user agents, along with an indication of the type of information carried in the content;

- the priority of the electronic mail message; and,

- trace information.

The other two kinds of MHS envelopes carry a subset of this information. In addition, the 1988 version of MHS allows cooperating message transfer agents to define extensions to an MHS envelope.

An extension contains three parts:

- a type, which identifies the extension;

- an associated value; and,

- a flag indicating if knowledge of the extension is critical for submission, transfer, or delivery.

If a message transfer agent receives an envelope with an extension that it doesn't recognize, and finds it needs to perform one of the operations listed in the flag (e.g., delivery), the message transfer agent rejects the message with the appropriate report.

As can be seen, the MHS transfer service is richer than the one provided by SMTP. In particular, delivery reports are a desirable feature. However, there are still some surprising deficiencies.

First, there is no standardized address which every MHS message transfer agent must recognize and accept, i.e., there is no "PostMaster" equivalent.

At the risk of starting a soapbox, this shows a shocking naïveté of the difficulty in diagnosing the problems encountered when running a distributed message transfer system in the real-world.

Second, when two message transfer agents relay a message, they do so using a bulk-mode transfer facility, in which the entire envelope and contents are exchanged. Unfortunately the MHS architecture does not provide for next-hop address verification.[6] This means that the next-hop message transfer agent must accept the transfer of the envelope and entire content, before it can determine whether it can deliver to any of the recipient addressees. In the case where none of the recipients are acceptable (which is most likely when there is a single recipient in the envelope), this is wasteful of resources.

In retrospect, it appears that envelope negotiation and content transfer should be done in different network exchanges, and that by using an approach similar to the one suggested earlier in Section 4.4.4,

---

[6]The probe operation is an end-to-end service reporting whether a message will ultimately be accepted or rejected by the recipient's user agent. Of course, it is possible that any message transfer agent in the transfer path could detect an error and return an early notification to the probe. However, there is no way to guarantee that the probe will be evaluated only at the next-hop.

```
Date:     Wed, 19 Feb 92 04:20:36 +0000
From:     "UK.AC.NSF" MTA <postmaster@nsfnet-relay.ac.uk>
To:       pvm
Subject: Delivery Report (failure) for pvm@mil.darpa.vax


---------------------------- Start of body part 1

This report relates to your message: Re: current U...
     of Wed, 19 Feb 1992 04:19:56 +0000

Your message was not delivered to
     pvm@mil.darpa.vax for the following reason:
     Incompatibility between two sites on the route of the
     message (please contact local administrator)
     Authorisation failure at site 'nsfnet-relay.ac.uk' for recip
     '@nsfnet-relay.ac.uk:pvm@vax.darpa.mil' Reason: 'block: imta
     (unset unset) sender (unset unset) omta (unset unset) recip
     (unset unset)'
```

Figure 4.8: Example Delivery Report

---

one can minimize the number of network exchanges necessary for envelope negotiation.

A clear limitation of the current Internet mail system is the lack of a standardized format for error reports. This means that a human must often examine such messages in order to determine what response is appropriate. Although MHS provides a structured delivery report for this purpose, this too usually must be conveyed to a human. Figure 4.8 starting on page 167 shows an example of an actual delivery report generated by an MHS message transfer agent and subsequently received by an Internet user. (Had an MHS user received this delivery report, the body would have been similarly rendered.) Although it is clear that the MHS delivery report contains a wealth of information, it is arguable as to whether the delivery report is useful, as a message which must be interpreted by humans must first be understandable by humans.

In this particular example, the reason for the rejection, as stated in the third to last line of this figure, reads more like a *mantra* than a

```
***** The following information is directed towards the local
***** administrator and is not intended for the end user
*
* DR generated by mta sun2.nsfnet-relay.ac.uk
*     in /PRMD=uk.ac/ADMD= /C=gb/
*     at Wed, 19 Feb 1992 04:20:11 +0000
*
* Converted to RFC 822 at sun2.nsfnet-relay.ac.uk
*     at Wed, 19 Feb 1992 04:20:37 +0000
*
* Delivery Report Contents:
*
* Subject-Submission-Identifier:
*     [/PRMD=uk.ac/ADMD= /C=gb/;<9202190425.AA01280@sun4.darpa.mil>]
* Content-Identifier: Re: current U...
* Subject-Intermediate-Trace-Information:  /PRMD=uk.ac/ADMD= /C=gb/;
*     arrival Wed, 19 Feb 1992 04:19:56 +0000 action Relayed
* Subject-Intermediate-Trace-Information:  /PRMD=uk.ac/ADMD= /C=gb/;
*     arrival Mon, 17 Feb 1992 04:25:11 +0000 action Relayed
* Recipient-Info: pvm@mil.darpa.vax,
/RFC-822=pvm(a)vax.darpa.mil/O=nsfnet-relay/PRMD=uk.ac/ADMD= /C=gb/;
*     FAILURE reason Unable-To-Transfer (1);
*     diagnostic No-Bilateral-Agreement (17);
*     last trace (ia5) Mon, 17 Feb 1992 04:25:11 +0000;
*     supplementary info "Authorisation failure at site
*     'nsfnet-relay.ac.uk' for recip
*     '@nsfnet-relay.ac.uk:pvm@vax.darpa.mil' Reason: 'block: imta
*     (unset unset) sender (unset unset) omta (unset unset) recip
*     (unset unset)'";
****** End of administration information

The Original Message follows:


---------------------------- Start of forwarded message 1

<<in the interests of brevity, the original message has been removed
  in this figure...>>

---------------------------- End of forwarded message 1
```

Figure 4.8: Example Delivery Report (cont.)

diagnostic. i.e.,

> *"block, imta*
> *(unset unset)*
> *sender*
> *(unset unset)*
> *omta*
> *(unset unset)*
> *recip*
> *(unset unset)"*

Presumably the author of the software can make sense of it.

Much of the transport functionality introduced by MHS offers little real value over approaches which are comparatively much simpler and more tractable. However, by providing these functions, implementation of MHS requires an investment to support the full range of features available. Further, although these features are rich, they are not adequate to provide *transparent* mappings to the services offered by the myriad of mail transports already in existence. This combination of high complexity, coupled with low transparency, means that MHS is not well-suited for providing a global message transfer system.

soap...

...soap

Chapter 5

Mailbox Services

Once again, let's return to the model for message handling introduced back on page 2. It's now time to consider the delivery protocol used when a message transfer agent performs final delivery.

In the Internet community, final delivery is a local matter. However, there are actually three different protocols available to provide this functionality, if desired by a recipient. So, we'll begin our discussion by looking at what happens during the final delivery process. Next, we'll look at a simple mailbox access protocol. Finally, we'll briefly introduce two alternatives.

5.1   The Final Delivery Process

Final delivery occurs when a message transfer agent determines that it is logically connected to the recipient's user agent. In the Internet community, the default action in such cases is to deliver the electronic mail message to the user's mailbox or terminal. Prior to final delivery, the message transfer agent writes a `Return-Path:` header at the beginning of the headers of the electronic mail message. This header contains the electronic mail address of the envelope's originator.

From the perspective of the model for message handling, the action of delivery to a mailbox or terminal is a user agent function. However, from an implementation perspective, one can view the message transfer agent as acting on behalf of the user agent as it passes the electronic mail message through the delivery slot and into a mailbox or onto a terminal.

It is important to appreciate that this is not the only way in which final delivery occurs. Depending on the configuration of the message transfer agent, it might actually be able to invoke the user agent allowing for some other action to take place during final delivery. Let's look at the facilities available when MH is the user agent.

5.1.1   Delivery to a User Agent

In MH, an "mhook" is a program that is executed whenever the local message transfer agent is ready to deliver an electronic mail message to the user.[1] Once the local message transfer agent is configured to know that an mhook should be invoked, MH provides a consistent environment for the actual execution. Each time the delivery slot for a user receives an electronic mail message, a user-defined file, termed the user's `maildelivery` file, is consulted to determine what actions the user agent should take. Figure 5.1 shows the syntax of this file.

---

[1] The mhook facility in MH is derived from an earlier facility found in the Multichannel Memo Distribution Facility (MMDF) [54, 55].

```
line       ::= [(comment / directive [WSP])] LF

comment    ::= "#" 1*<any character except LF>

directive ::= matches WSP action WSP result WSP string

matches    ::= "source"  WSP value    ; envelope originator
             / "addr"    WSP value    ; envelope recipient
             / "default" WSP ignore   ; not yet delivered
             / "*"       WSP ignore   ; always matches
             / field     WSP value    ; message header

action     ::=  "destroy"             ; always succeeds
             / ("file"    / ">")      ; appends
             /  "mbox"                ;   ..
             / ("pipe"    / "|")      ; executes
             / ("qpipe"   / "^")      ;   ..

result     ::= "A" / "R" / "?" / "N"

WSP        ::= 1*(SP / TAB / ",")

field      ::= word
value      ::= word
ignore     ::= word

word       ::= <"> *(wtext / escaped-q) <">
wtext      ::= <any character except <">, "\", or LF>
escaped-q ::= "\" <">
```

Figure 5.1: MH Delivery Slot Directives

Here's how the mhook facility works: MH first tries to determine
the envelope information corresponding to the message being delivered.
(Depending on the particular message transfer agent software, this may
not be possible.) Then, the user's `maildelivery` file is examined, line
by line. When a directive is encountered, MH decides if the directive
applies to the electronic mail message which is passing through the
delivery slot. The algorithm depends on the `matches` component of the
directive:

source: If the envelope's originator is identified by the `value`
component, then this directive applies.

addr: If the envelope recipient address which caused this electronic mail message to pass through the user's delivery slot
is identified by the `value` component, this directive applies.
This is useful when an alias for the user appears in the
recipient envelope, since the alias address, and not the user's
address, will be used for the comparison.

default: If the message has not yet been accepted as delivered,
this directive applies.

*: This directive always applies.

field: If the named field appears in the electronic mail message,
and its value matches, in a case-insensitive fashion, the string
contained in the `value` component, then this directive applies.

If the directive is not applicable, MH goes on to the next line. Otherwise, the `result` component of the directive is examined to determine
what action should be taken.

A: The activity associated with this directive is performed. If this
activity succeeds, then the message is considered to have been
accepted for delivery.

R: The activity associated with this directive is performed. The
success of the activity is ignored.

?: If the message has not yet been accepted for delivery, the activity associated with this directive is performed, and if the activity succeeds, then the message is considered to have been accepted for delivery.

N: If the previous directive applied to this message and the message has not yet been accepted for delivery, the activity associated with this directive is performed, and if the activity succeeds, then the message is considered to have been accepted for delivery.

To determine the activity associated with this directive, the `action` component is examined:

destroy: This activity always succeeds.

file/mbox: The electronic mail message is appended to the file named by the `string` component. When the electronic mail message is written, a new header `Delivery-Date:` is added. The value of this header is a date-time specification using the standard RFC-822 syntax. This activity succeeds if the message can be completely appended.

If the `action` component is **file**, then the format used is compatible with the local message transfer agent software; otherwise, if the `action` component is **mbox**, then MH's mailbox format is used instead.

pipe/qpipe: The command named by the `string` component is executed and the electronic mail message is supplied as the input to the command. Commands are given a certain amount of time to execute, based on the size of the electronic mail message. This activity succeeds if the command executes successfully.

The `string` component is interpreted by the UNIX shell (for meta-character evaluation). However, if the **qpipe** directive is used, the shell is bypassed and the command is directly executed. This achieves a small increase in performance.

```
*   -    mbox  R  mhbox/INCOMING
To  mrose pipe  R  "bin/radiomail.sh mrose@radiomail.net"
```

Figure 5.2: **The Author's** maildelivery **file**

If after reading each line in the user's `maildelivery` file, the electronic
mail message has not yet been accepted for delivery, MH will consult
a system-wide `maildelivery` file. If this file doesn't exist or if it too
doesn't consider the message accepted for delivery, then MH will deliver
the message to the user's mailbox.

An Example

To appreciate the power of MH's mhook facility, let's look at a realistic
example. Figure 5.2 shows the author's `maildelivery` file. The first
directive states that all messages are to be appended to the mailbox
named

>   mhbox/INCOMING

in the user's home area. The author uses this mailbox for audit
purposes.[2] Regardless of the outcome of this activity, the message
is not considered accepted for delivery. The second directive states
that if the electronic mail message being delivered has a `To:` header
containing the string "`mrose`", then the command

>   bin/radiomail.sh mrose@radiomail.net

in the user's home area should be executed. Again, regardless of the
outcome of this activity, the message is still not considered accepted for
delivery. As such, when the command completes, MH will deliver the
message to the user's default mailbox. So, this author's `maildelivery`
serves to simply perform one or two tasks for every message received.
Interested readers are probably wondering what this second task accomplishes.

---

[2]Yes, the author has a copy of every message he's received or sent since 1986.
Even using file compression, these audit files take up nearly 250MB of storage.

The author subscribes to an alphanumeric paging service. An alphanumeric pager is a one-way device which receives short textual messages via radio-transmission. Although coverage in the author's service area is largely ubiquitous, the size of each paging message is limited to less than 512 characters. Further, the screen on the pager can display only 80 characters at a time. Hence, information "real estate" is at a premium. This means that the content of the paging message must be concise.

The author also subscribes to a commercial service on the Internet, RadioMail®, which offers a gateway between Internet electronic mail and several paging networks in the United States. When a message directly addressed to the author passes through the delivery slot, the command

```
bin/radiomail.sh mrose@radiomail.net
```

is responsible for determining if the author is out of the office and carrying his pager. If so, this command constructs a "bullet" message to be sent to the author's alphanumeric pager.[3] The bullet message is supposed to concisely describe the information content of the electronic mail message.

We now proceed to the most lengthy, detailed example in *The Internet Message*. Uninterested readers, or readers who aren't fond of UNIX, might wish to skip to page 187. Otherwise, let's examine the UNIX shell script which constructs the bullet message. The shell script is shown in Figure 5.3 which starts on page 178.

First, the shell script checks to make sure that it was invoked with an argument — the address on the gateway which reaches the author's pager. Otherwise, the shell script terminates. Then, the shell script looks for a file called .radiomail.off in the user's home area. If this is present, the shell script terminates (this means that the author is in the office).

When a command runs under MH's mhook facility, it has a limited execution environment, in which only "standard" UNIX commands are

---

[3]The service which offers the gateway between Internet electronic mail and paging networks will automatically construct bullet messages, if so desired. However, the author prefers to construct them according to his own format.

```
: run this script through /bin/sh

RADIOMAIL="$1"
if [ -z "$RADIOMAIL" ]; then
    exit 1
fi
if [ -f .radiomail.off ]; then
    exit 0
fi

GAWK="/usr/local/bin/gawk"
MHL="/usr/local/lib/mh/mhl -nobell"
MHMAIL="/usr/local/bin/mhmail"
MHN="/usr/local/bin/mhn"
SCAN="/usr/local/bin/scan -width 512"

P=/tmp/radiomail$$.prf   C=/tmp/radiomail$$.ctx F=/tmp/radiomail$$
M=1     N=2
trap "rm -rf $P $C $F" 0 1 2 3 13 15

cd /tmp

echo "Path: /tmp" > $P
echo "mhn-show-text/plain: cat" >> $P
MH="$P" export MH

echo "Current-Folder: $F" > $C
MHCONTEXT="$C" export MHCONTEXT

mkdir $F
chmod 700 $F
cat > $F/$M
```

Figure 5.3: Constructing a Bullet Message

normally available. So, several shell variables are defined which name some non-standard commands that this shell script will be using:

GAWK: the GNU variant of the awk text processing language.

MHL: the MH program used to display a message using a superset of the formatting facility described earlier on page 83.

MHMAIL: one of the MH programs used to submit a message for delivery.

MHN: the MH program used to handle multi-media messages. (All of Chapter 6 is devoted to multi-media electronic mail. Wait for it!)

SCAN: the MH program used to generate a scan listing of a message.

As noted earlier, MH maintains an environment so that its commands behave consistently (e.g., to keep track of the current folder, the current message, and so on.) Because the shell script will be using MH commands, it doesn't want them to interfere with any other message handling activities going on for the user. So, it constructs a transient environment which will be used precisely for the duration of the shell script's execution, and then removed. Finally, the last three lines of the figure on page 178 complete initialization of this environment: a uniquely-name folder is created, protected so only the user can access it, and finally the electronic mail message being delivered is copied to it.

Continuing on, the shell script now identifies the party on whose behalf the electronic mail message was sent. The shell variable MBOX is set to the local part of the associated electronic mail address. If the value found appears to be from a message transfer agent administrator or from the author himself, the shell script exits. Otherwise, the shell variable FROM is set to the entire electronic mail address, and the shell variable SUBJECT is set to the value of the Subject: header.

Next, the shell script tries to determine the personal name of the party on whose behalf the electronic mail message is sent. This is a lot more difficult than one might expect. The friendly function in MH's formatting facility knows how to look for personal names appearing either as a phrase or in a comment associated with an address. If it can't find one, it returns the electronic mail address in the usual

    local@domain

format. So, the shell script uses the friendly function, and strips off any bracketing quotation characters, if any. For example, if the address was

    "Marshall T. Rose" <mrose@dbc.mtview.ca.us>

then the friendly function would return

    "Marshall T. Rose"

and the shell script would set the PERSON shell variable to

    Marshall T. Rose

However, when an MHS address appears in an Internet electronic mail message, it might look like this:

    /PN=REGINALD.SIMMONS/O=BSE/PRMD=BIS/ADMD=BELLSOUTH/C=US/@sprint.com

(Readers with a good sense of smell will now appreciate why the soap-box appearing on page 74 is well-deserved.) In this address, the personal name is

    REGINALD.SIMMONS

```
MBOX=`$SCAN -format "%<{from}%(mbox{from})%|%<{reply-to}%(mbox{reply-to})\
%|%<{return-path}%(mbox{return-path})%>%>%>" $M`
case "$MBOX" in
    MAILER|MAILER-DAEMON|SMTP|Postman)
        exit 0
        ;;

    [Pp][Oo][Ss][Tt][Mm][Aa][Ss][Tt][Ee][Rr])
        exit 0
        ;;

    mrose)
        exit 0
        ;;

    *)  ;;
esac

FROM=`$SCAN -format "%<{reply-to}%{reply-to}%|%<{from}%{from}%|%<{sender}%{sender}\
%|%<{return-path}%{return-path}%>%>%>%>" $M`

SUBJECT=`$SCAN -format "%{subject}" $M`
case "$SUBJECT" in
    "MIB for checking")
        exit 0
        ;;

    *)  ;;
esac

PERSON=`$SCAN -format "%(friendly{from})" $M \
    | sed -e 's%^"\(.*\)"$%\1%' \
    | sed -e 's%^.*/PN=\([^/]*\)/.*$%\1%'`
if [ ! -z "$PERSON" ]; then
    PHONE=`grep "^&$PERSON&" $HOME/.phone.tex \
            | awk -F"&" '{ print $4; }' \
            | sed -e 's%.*: \(.*\)\\\\%\1%' \
            | sed -e 's% %-%g'`
    if [ ! -z "$PHONE" ]; then
        PERSON="$PERSON $PHONE"
    fi
fi

$MHL -form $HOME/mhbox/mhl.headers < $F/$M > $F/$N

CONTENT=`$SCAN -format "%{content-type}" $M`
if [ ! -z "$CONTENT" ]; then
    BODY="$MHN -form $HOME/mhbox/mhl.null -show -type text/plain $M"
else
    BODY="$MHL -form mhl.body"
fi
```

Figure 5.3: Constructing a Bullet Message (cont.)

So, a check is made for this as well. Next, the shell script looks in the author's personal phone directory to see if the personal name is listed there. If so, the person's phone number is appended onto the value of the `PERSON` shell variable.

Finally, the shell script begins the creation of an intermediate message by copying interesting headers. This is done by running `mhl` with the filter file `mhl.headers`. Following this, the shell script checks to see if the electronic mail message has a `Content-Type:` header. If present, this indicates that the message is multi-media. If so, a command, `BODY`, is defined which will extract only the textual portions of the message body. If not, the `BODY` command will extract the entire message body.

As shown on the facing page, the `BODY` command is now run and whatever it produces is passed to a `gawk` script, which filters out extraneous information, and then appends the result as the body of the intermediate message. There are two kinds of extraneous information which are filtered out.

- From those messages which are replies, if the reply contains any text from some other message (e.g., the message that was replied to), then that text is removed.

  Unfortunately, there is no Internet-standard, nor dominant convention in the Internet community, as to how a reply should include such text in its body. The goal of the `gawk` script is to filter out any included text. Given the complexity of the script, the reader should appreciate that it isn't easy. For example, some user agents start the body of a reply with:

  ```
  In message <6871.7021977402@dbc.mtview.ca.us> you write:
  >    some text from original message
  >    possibly on multiple lines
  ```

  Others start the body of a reply with the headers from the original message, but indent each one, and so on.

  Obviously, the choice to remove included text is a policy matter. Although many correspondents delight in including some or most of the text of the original message when they reply, the author views this as somewhat wasteful. In fact, even though the author originates some 50 messages per day of personal correspondence,

```
$BODY < $F/$M | $GAWK '
BEGIN    {
             started = 0;
             indented = 0;
             slurping = 0;
         }
/^Excerpts from mail: / {
             if (!started) {
                 slurping = 1;
                 next;
             }
         }
/^MHS:   Source date is:.*$/ || /^.* writes:$/ || /^.* you write:$/ {
             if (!started)
                 next;
         }
/\*\*\* Reply to note of/ || /^[ \t]*From: / || /^[ \t]*Reply to:[ \t]*RE>/ {
             if (!started)
                 next;
         }
/^[ \t]*To: / {
             if (started)
                 exiting = 1;
             next;
         }
/^[ \t]*Date: / {
             if (!started) {
                 indented = 1;
                 next;
             }
         }
/^ *-----/ || /^_____/ || /^%!/ {
             exiting = 1;
         }
/^[ \t]*>[ ]*/ {
             next;
         }
/^[ \t]+[^ \t]/ {
             if (indented)
                 next;
         }
         {
             if (exiting)
                 next;
             if (slurping) {
                 if (NF <= 0)
                     slurping = 0;
                 next;
             }
             if (!started && NF <= 0)
                 next;
             started = 1;
             indented = 0;
             print $0;
         }
' >> $F/$N
```

Figure 5.3: Constructing a Bullet Message (cont.)

he still manages to remember most of what he reads or says in those messages. Given the limited display capacity of a pager, it is critical to construct bullet messages which contain *new* information.

- From those messages which forward other messages, once the beginning of an encapsulated message is encountered, all remaining text is removed.

  Usually a message which forwards others starts with some informative text followed by one or more of the messages. Referring back to the example given on page 105, the `gawk` script will try and keep the text

  ```
  ...here is the message I was referring to.
  ```

  ```
  /mtr
  ```

but ignore the rest.

The way `gawk` works is simple: the commands given in the `BEGIN` pattern are executed, then the body of the original message is processed one line at a time. The patterns in the `gawk` script are examined, in order, for each line. If a line matches the pattern, termed a *regular expression*, the commands associated with that expression are executed. Regardless, the next pattern is examined. Only if a `next` command is executed will the remaining patterns be skipped.

Finally, as shown on the facing page, we come to the last part of the shell script. MH's `scan` command is called to construct the body of the bullet message by looking at the intermediate message which was just constructed. The body of the bullet message starts with the name of the person (and possibly their phone number). Next, depending on how long ago the original message was sent, an indication of the weeks ("w"), days ("d"), hours ("h"), or minutes ("m") is given. Following this is the `Subject:` header and then the body of the intermediate message. The text generated by the `scan` command is limited to 400 characters, and is given to the `mhmail` program to be submitted for delivery to the pager gateway.

```
$SCAN -width 400 -format "\
$PERSON \
%(void(rclock{date})))\
%<(gt 604800)%(void(rclock{date})))%02(divide 604800)w %|\
%<(gt 086400)%(void(rclock{date})))%02(divide 086400)d %|\
%<(gt 003600)%(void(rclock{date})))%02(divide 003600)h %|\
%<(gt 000060)%(void(rclock{date})))%02(divide 000060)m %>%>%>%>\
%<{subject}%{subject} %>\
%<{body}<< %{body}>>%>" $N | \
    $MHMAIL $RADIOMAIL -from "$FROM" -subject "$SUBJECT"

exit 0
```

Figure 5.3: Constructing a Bullet Message (cont.)

So, putting it all together, a message, such as the one shown in Figure 5.4 on page 186, would result in a bullet message being sent with a body of:

> Craig Burton 801-943-1966 05m Re: e-mail test << I got the message. I am now sending you a response. CB >>

When received on the author's pager, he would know that it was likely sent from Craig Burton a little more than five minutes previously.[4]

---

[4]Because it is possible for the bullet message to be detained at a message transfer agent between the author's system and the paging network, this time is a lower-bounds estimate.

```
Return-Path: <CBurton_+a_TBG-HQ_+1Craig_Burton+r%The_Burton_Group@mcimail.com>
Received: from NRI.Reston.VA.US by dbc.mtview.ca.us (4.1/3.1.090690)
            id AA03680; Thu, 16 Apr 92 20:15:43 PDT
Received: from mcimail.com by NRI.Reston.VA.US id ab15695;
            16 Apr 92 23:14 EDT
Date: Fri, 17 Apr 92 03:10 GMT
From: Craig Burton
      <CBurton_+a_TBG-HQ_+1Craig_Burton+r%The_Burton_Group@mcimail.com>
To: Marshall Rose <mrose@dbc.mtview.ca.us>
Subject: Re: e-mail test
Message-ID: <43920417031034/0005174218DC4EM@mcimail.com>

MHS:   Source date is:      16-Apr-92 18:32 MST


I got the message. I am now sending you a response.

CB
```

Figure 5.4: Example Message for Processing into a Bullet Message

Another Example

A popular facility available with most user agents is a *vacation* hook, which sends back a canned reply to the originator of a message, e.g.,

```
Hello, this is an automated response.  Please send as many
messages as desired, as only this one notice will be
generated.  A pre-recorded follows:

I am on travel from April 20-24 and won't be able to read
my mail.  I will be checking voice mail on +1 415 968 1052.

/mtr
```

It is important to determine when such a canned reply should be sent. As implied by this message, the vacation facility maintains a database of mailboxes, keyed by originator, to whom the recording has been sent.

But, there is one other case in which generating a reply would be inappropriate. Suppose the recipient is a subscriber to a mailing list. In this case, the originator of the message probably couldn't care less as to whether a particular subscriber has gone fishing. So, the vacation facility should examine the headers of the incoming message, and if the user's electronic mail address is not listed in the `To:` header, then a reply should not be generated. (Remember, the facility is part of the user agent, so it consults the headers, and not the envelope.)

Sadly, there are many poor implementations of this facility which blindly spew forth a reply. The author, having received such canned replies for over a decade, is not a particularly patient person in this regard. Hence, whenever the author receives an inappropriate vacation message, he invokes a command which sends back a note to the offending party, asking them to fix their user agent.

5.1.2 Delivery to a Mailing List

As noted in the soapbox early on page 163, there are a lot of non-conformant message transfer agents in the world. This is also true of user agents. For example, a lot of them won't honor a `Reply-To:` header when replying; or, sometimes they do not allow the user to indicate that a reply should also go to the `To:` or `cc:` fields in a message, in addition to the originating party. The author maintains a few mailing lists, for small groups engaged in private discussion, and has sought to find a way to avoid a lot of the problems with mailing lists described back in Section 4.4.5.

So, when the author maintains one of these mailing lists, here's what he does. First, he creates three aliases in his local message transfer agent:

```
alias
alias-List
alias-Request
```

where `alias` is the name of the mailing list. When final delivery is performed for the first alias, (i.e., when someone sends to the mailing list), a user agent is activated which will send a synthesized message to the mailing list subscribers.

This synthesized message contains all of the headers from the original message except those containing addresses, trace information, or dates. The `Subject:` header is changed so that it starts with a sequence number. Each time a message is sent to this mailing list, the number is incremented. This is done because, for some sites in the technology backwater, reliability of message delivery also appears to be a problem.

So, when an electronic mail message does get through, the user can check to see if perhaps others didn't. (Since the message transfer system can re-order messages, this isn't foolproof, nor is it automated, but it is adequate.)

Then, these headers are added along with the body of the original message:

```
From:      alias@dbc.mtview.ca.us (originator)
To:        alias-List
Dcc:       membership-addresses
Reply-To:  alias@dbc.mtview.ca.us
Errors-To: alias-List
```

where `membership-addresses` is the collection of electronic mail addresses which make up the mailing list subscribers, and `originator` is the personal name (or electronic mail address) found in the `From:` header of the original message. As for the three cryptic headers:

- The `Reply-To:` header is present because some (non-conformant) user agents generate replies to the `Sender:` field instead of the `From:` field, but sometimes these user agents will honor a `Reply-To:`.

- The `Errors-To:` header is present because some message transfer agents will ignore the information in the envelope and send back error reports to the `From:` address — unless an `Errors-To:` header is present.

- The `Dcc:` header is used locally when the synthesized electronic mail message is submitted by MH. The submission envelope will contain the electronic mail addresses given in this header, but the header will be removed when the message is submitted.

Of course, when the message is submitted to the local message transfer agent by MH, it will add `Message-ID:`, `Date:`, and `Sender:` headers.

If the submission of the synthesized message fails, it is filed into a special folder and a message is sent to the `alias-Request` address. Regardless, the original message is filed into a different folder, and an audit entry is made.

```
Return-Path: <mrose@dbc.mtview.ca.us>
Received: by dbc.mtview.ca.us (4.1/3.1.090690)
            id AA05325; Thu, 16 Apr 92 16:91:34 PDT
To: Untouchables@dbc.mtview.ca.us
Subject: test message
MIME-Version: 1.0
Content-Type: text/plain; charset="us-ascii"
Date: Thu, 16 Apr 1992 16:01:04 -0700
Message-ID: <2913.703465264@dbc.mtview.ca.us>
From: Marshall Rose <mrose@dbc.mtview.ca.us>

hi.  as per last week's action, i've ...

<<in the interests of brevity, the majority of the body of
  this message has been removed in this figure...>>

/mtr
```

Figure 5.5: Example Message for Submission to a Mailing List

Let's look at an example. Figure 5.5 shows a message as it passed through the delivery slot associated with a mailing list, and Figure 5.6 on page 190 shows the synthesized message as it was submitted to the subscribers to the mailing list. Comparing the two, we see that the **MIME-Version:** and **Content-Type:** headers were copied verbatim, and that the **Subject:** header was slightly modified. Following this are the replacement headers.

So, the big question is: what is the value of the second alias, **alias-List**? The answer is: this alias expands to zero addresses. So why have it? Here's the reason: The ideal set of headers for the synthesized message is:

```
To:   list subscribers: membership-addresses;
From: alias@dbc.mtview.ca.us (originator)
```

When submitted to the message transfer system, The **To:** header would look like this:

```
To:   list subscribers: ;
```

```
MIME-Version: 1.0
Content-Type: text/plain; charset="us-ascii"
From: Untouchables@dbc.mtview.ca.us (Marshall Rose)
To: Untouchables-List@dbc.mtview.ca.us
Subject: [1] test message
Reply-to: Untouchables@dbc.mtview.ca.us
Errors-To: Untouchables-Request@dbc.mtview.ca.us
Message-ID: <2913.703465264@dbc.mtview.ca.us>
Date: Thu, 16 Apr 1992 16:01:04 -0700
Sender: daemon@dbc.mtview.ca.us

hi.  as per last week's action, i've ...

<<in the interests of brevity, the majority of the body of
  this message has been removed in this figure...>>

/mtr
```

Figure 5.6: Example Synthesized Message Submitted

Thus, the only electronic mail address in the headers for the synthesized message would be:

```
From: alias@dbc.mtview.ca.us (originator)
```

so that all replies would go back to the mailing list. Unfortunately, some message transfer agents look in the headers to examine the `To:` field. They should **never** do this, but the author already had his tirade back on page 163. Of course, those very same message transfer agents don't understand all of RFC-822's address syntax, so they decide to "fix" the header, by changing it, e.g., to

```
To:    list.subscribers;@domain
```

which isn't syntactically valid. So, the `Dcc:` and null-alias trick is used instead to produce

```
To:    alias-List@dbc.mtview.ca.us
From: alias@dbc.mtview.ca.us (originator)
```

So why is the synthesized message approach allowed to examine the content and manipulate the headers? The answer is simple: this approach is acting as a user agent. The electronic mail message has already passed through the delivery slot and therefore as a user agent, processing of the content is allowed.

Of course, there are other approaches for running "safe" mailing lists. For example, the original electronic mail message could have been forwarded to the mailing list subscribers. However, the disadvantage to that approach is that it is less automatic for recipients. For example, if a forwarding approach is used, then a scan listing of the message will show the address of the forwarding agent. In contrast, with the synthesized approach, the address shown is often the actual originator, since many user agents will pick out personal names in the `From:` field.

There is a drawback of course: the electronic mail address of the originator does not appear in the headers of the synthesized electronic mail message, which makes it impossible to automate a reply which goes back to the originator and no one else. From the author's perspective, he would rather not go to the extremes given here. If only the user agent employed by one of his correspondents would allow replies to both the originator and the `To:` field in a message!

5.2   Post Office Protocol

The Post Office Protocol[5] is used to provide remote access to a mailbox. Depending on one's perspective, it can be viewed as residing in one of two different places in the model for message handling.

From one perspective, the POP service is a part of the local message transfer agent. Electronic mail messages are stored with the service until a user agent accepts delivery. From this perspective, POP provides a user with asynchronous access to the delivery slot.

From another perspective, the POP service is a part of the user agent. Electronic mail messages are passed through the delivery slot to the user's mailbox, which are accepted for delivery by the POP service on the user's behalf. So, "half" of the user agent resides on the same system as the local message transfer agent. Later on, the other "half" of the user agent acts as a client and retrieves the electronic mail messages from the user's mailbox. From this perspective, POP provides the user with a split-user agent facility.

Arguments can be made in favor of either approach. From our perspective, it is important to appreciate only that POP allows a user agent to be network-distant from its local message transfer agent.

5.2.1   Design Criteria

The design goals of the Post Office Protocol are two-fold:

- to minimize complexity on the message transfer agent by supplying only very simple access methods to the electronic mail messages stored in a mailbox; and,

- to reduce the minimal level of intelligence required on the part of a client.

The first goal is to allow POP to scale well: it is reasonable to expect a single message transfer agent to service hundreds of simultaneous

---

[5]There are actually three versions of the Post Office Protocol. *The Internet Message* discusses only version 3 of POP, [7], which as of this writing is the current version.

user agents. In order to achieve this, the POP service will expect a low-latency transport service (e.g., TCP running over a LAN). The second goal is to accommodate a wide range of systems that provide clients. Some may be single-user desktops, whilst others may be more powerful workstations. By taking a minimalist approach, it was hoped that POP would be implemented on a large number of different systems.

From the historical perspective, it is interesting to note that the administrators of many systems often choose not to run a local message transfer agent, even if those systems have more than sufficient resources. The reason is primarily one of convenience: installation, configuration, and maintenance of a message transfer agent can be time-consuming. If a few systems are already providing this facility within an enterprise, and if network connectivity is uniformly good, then there is often little to gain in running additional message transfer agents at such a site. Although in retrospect it shouldn't be surprising, experience has shown that it is a lot easier to bring up a single POP server and dozens or hundreds of clients, than it is to manage more than a few message transfer agents.

5.2.2 Protocol Interactions

A POP interaction is straight-forward: A POP server listens on TCP port 109. A client establishes a TCP connection to the POP server and awaits a greeting. The greeting indicates the status of the POP service. If the status is acceptable to both parties, the client identifies itself and then initiates one or more POP transactions. When the client is finished, it issues a command to release the service, and waits for the POP server to return a response and close the TCP connection. The client then closes the TCP connection.

Figure 5.7 on page 194 shows the syntax of POP interactions, which is in NVT ASCII.

```
            ; case-insensitive matching of string-literals
commands  ::= "USER " mailbox       CRLF
            / "PASS " string        CRLF
            / "STAT"                CRLF
            / "LIST" [" " msg]      CRLF
            / "RETR " msg           CRLF
            / "DELE " msg           CRLF
            / "LAST"                CRLF
            / "RSET"                CRLF
            / "NOOP"                CRLF
            / "QUIT"                CRLF
            / optional
optional  ::= "RPOP " string        CRLF
            / "TOP " msg      " " num CRLF

response  ::= "+OK"   [" " *text]   CRLF
              [multiline CRLF    "." CRLF]
            / "-ERR"  [" " *text]   CRLF
multiline ::= 1*<any character, including ".", CR, and LF,
                but not including (CRLF "." CRLF)>

mailbox   ::= string
string    ::= 1*<any chracter except SP, TAB, or CRLF>
msg       ::= 1*DIGIT
num       ::= 1*DIGIT

text      ::= <any character, including bare CR and bare LF,
                but not including CRLF>
```

Figure 5.7: POP Interaction Syntax

The command syntax is less complex than the syntax used by SMTP. Response codes are simpler: either a command succeeds (+OK) or it fails (-ERR). The former reply code is termed a positive response, whilst the latter reply code is termed a negative response. Some commands will result in a multiline positive response following the response code — as expected, the usual data-stuffing algorithm is employed.

Commands

We now consider the various commands available in POP.

Server Identification

When a client opens a TCP connection to a POP server, the server returns a greeting indicating the status of the POP service. If a positive response is returned, the client proceeds to identify itself; otherwise, the client closes the TCP connection.

Client Identification

The client now identifies the mailbox which it wishes to access by issuing the USER command. If a negative response is returned, the client can either try another mailbox name, or it can release the POP service.

If a positive response is returned, the client uses the PASS command and supplies as its argument the plaintext password associated with the mailbox.[6] If a negative response is returned, the client can either reissue the USER command, or it can release the POP service. Otherwise, if a positive response is returned, the client now initiates one or more POP transactions.

---

[6]This introduces quite a potential for security abuse. Later, on page 201, we'll look at a non-standard extension to POP which removes this problem.

There are three different kinds of POP transactions:

- examination of the status of the mailbox and its component electronic mail messages;

- retrieval of a message, in whole or in part, from the mailbox; and,

- deletion of a message from the mailbox.

In order for the POP service to provide these transactions, it must be able to decompose a mailbox into its component electronic mail messages. The messages in the mailbox are contiguously numbered starting with 1 for the first message. Further, for each electronic mail message contained in the mailbox, the POP server must calculate the size of the message in octets.

Mailbox Examination

The **STAT** command is used to determine the number of electronic mail messages in the mailbox and the total size of the mailbox. The POP server returns a positive response having this syntax:

```
statresp  ::= "+OK " 1*DIGIT " " 1*DIGIT
```

where the first number is the number of messages (which may be zero if the mailbox is empty). The second number is the size of the mailbox in octets.

Once the client has determined the size of the mailbox, at its option it can determine the size of each individual electronic mail message, by using the **LIST** command. If an argument is present, this indicates the message number to be examined. If the message number does not exist (or has been marked for deletion), then a negative response is returned. Otherwise, the response has this syntax:

```
list1resp ::= "+OK " 1*DIGIT " " 1*DIGIT
```

where the first number is the message number, and the second is the size of the electronic mail message in octets.

If no argument is given, then a multiline response is returned. For each message not marked for deletion, a line is returned which identifies a message number and the size of that electronic mail message in octets.

Finally, the client can use the LAST command to find out the highest message number accessed since the POP service was started (or a RSET command was used). When either event occurs, the counter is set to zero.[7] Afterwards, when an electronic mail message is retrieved or marked for deletion, if the number associated with that message is larger than the counter, the counter is updated accordingly.

Message Retrieval

The RETR command is used to retrieve an entire electronic mail message. The argument identifies a message in the mailbox which has not been marked for deletion. If a positive response is returned, it is multiline and contains the entire content: the headers and body.

An optional POP command, TOP can be used to retrieve all the headers of an electronic mail message and then zero or more lines from the body of the message following the initial blank line. If a positive response is returned, it is multiline. For example,

> TOP 1 4   *1st message → 4 lines*

retrieves the headers, the blank line following the headers, and then the first four lines lines from the body of the first message in the mailbox.

Message Deletion

The DELE command is used to mark the named message for deletion. The electronic mail messages remain in the mailbox until the POP service is released. This allows the client to use the RSET command prior to service release and thereby undo the effect of any previous DELE commands.

Service Release

To release the service, the client uses the QUIT command. The POP server is required to remove any electronic mail messages marked for

---

[7]The example of the LAST command on page 9 of [7] is in error when it states that a LAST command used immediately after a RSET will return a value of 1 — the value 0 should be returned.

deletion and then return a positive response. The client will close the TCP connection, and then the POP server does likewise.

Miscellaneous Commands

There is one miscellaneous command, NOOP, which is simply an application-layer "ping" to see if the POP server is still functioning. The POP server is required to return a positive response.

In addition, one command not discussed thus far is RPOP which uses an insecure authentication facility available in some environments.

5.2.3   An Example Interaction

Let's consider a straight-forward example to get the feel for the protocol. In the discussion below, (S) refers to a POP server, and (C) refers to the client.

Figure 5.8 shows an example POP interaction. In this example, note that with the exception of the response to the STAT command, any text in between the response code (+OK or -ERR) and the end of the line is strictly for human informational purposes.

After identifying the desired mailbox, the client issues a STAT command to determine the size of the mailbox. Then it uses a LIST command to find the size of each electronic mail message contained therein.[8] Next, the client asks to see the headers and first four lines of the first message after the blank line which follows the headers. (This is the very same electronic mail message that was shown in the example in Figure 5.4 back on page 186.) Since the body of this message contains only three lines, the TOP command returns only these three lines. Finally, the client releases the service.

This example isn't particularly representative of the way many clients use POP. For example, when an MH user incorporates new mail, the MH program responsible for this employs this algorithm:

---

[8]Presumably the client uses the STAT command in order to allocate some data structure based on the number of messages. Otherwise, the client could calculate the number of messages and size of the mailbox by examining the multiline response to the LIST command.

```
S: <wait for connection on TCP port 109>
C: <open connection to server>
S: +OK POP server ready <11069.703563570@dbc.mtview.ca.us>
C: USER mrose
S: +OK password required for mrose
C: PASS ********
S: +OK maildrop has 4 messages (3455 octets)
C: STAT
S: +OK 4 3455
C: LIST
S: +OK
S: 1 660
S: 2 903
S: 3 709
S: 4 1183
S: .
C: TOP 1 4
S: +OK
S: Return-Path: <CBurton_+a_TBG-HQ_+1Craig_Burton+r%The_Burton_Group@mcimail.com>
S: Received: from NRI.Reston.VA.US by dbc.mtview.ca.us (4.1/3.1.090690)
S:               id AA03680; Thu, 16 Apr 92 20:15:43 PDT
S: Received: from mcimail.com by NRI.Reston.VA.US id ab15695;
S:               16 Apr 92 23:14 EDT
S: Date: Fri, 17 Apr 92 03:10 GMT
S: From: Craig Burton
S:        <CBurton_+a_TBG-HQ_+1Craig_Burton+r%The_Burton_Group@mcimail.com>
S: To: Marshall Rose <mrose@dbc.mtview.ca.us>
S: Subject: Re: e-mail test
S: Message-ID: <43920417031034/0005174218DC4EM@mcimail.com>
S:
S: MHS:    Source date is:       16-Apr-92 18:32 MST
S:
S:
S: I got the message. I am now sending you a response.
S: .
C: QUIT
S: +OK POP server signing off
C: <closes connection>
S: <closes connection>
```

Figure 5.8: Example POP Interaction

- The `STAT` command is used to determine the number of electronic mail messages in the mailbox. If there are no messages, the program releases the service and then terminates.

- For each electronic mail message in the mailbox, the `RETR` command is used to retrieve the message and store it in the folder. Once the message is secured, the `DELE` command is used to mark the message for deletion.

- The `QUIT` command is used to release the service and thereby zero the mailbox.

Of course, other clients in MH have different algorithms. For example, MH can be told to operate upon the POP service as if it were a folder. In this case, MH maintains a cache of electronic mail messages which it has retrieved (either in part or in whole) from the POP service. Then, when an MH command executes, it checks the cache to see if a copy of the message exists, in sufficient detail, for its use. If not, the MH command uses either the `RETR` or the `TOP` command depending on what it requires. For example, to generate a scan listing, only the first few lines of the message body are needed. So, one might speculate that the reason that the `TOP` command was used in Figure 5.8 on page 199 was that the user wanted to see a one-line summary of the message. Once the POP command completed, the MH command might display:

```
 1  04/17 03:10GMT Craig Burton    Re: e-mail test<<MHS: Source date is
```

5.2.4 Non-Standard Facilities

As the number of environments which use POP increase, (at least) two deficiencies have been observed:

- the mailbox authentication scheme is easily susceptible to masquerade attacks; and,

- for environments with high-latency transports, the functional split between user agent and POP client, incurs a high performance penalty.

To address these issues, the author has been experimenting with some modest changes to POP: authentication without plaintext passwords and remote scan listings. It must be emphasized that these are strictly local enhancements to the POP service. At present, they carry no standardization weight, whatsoever, in the Internet community.

Authentication without Plaintext Passwords

Each POP session starts with a USER/PASS exchange. This results in a mailbox password being sent in the clear on the network. For intermittent use of POP, this may not introduce a sizable risk. However, many POP client implementations connect to the POP server on a regular basis — to check for new mail. Further the interval of session initiation may be on the order of five minutes. Hence, the risk of password capture is greatly enhanced. A new method of authentication is required which provides for both origin authentication and replay protection, but which does not involve sending a password in the clear over the network. A new command, APOP, is introduced to provide this functionality.

A POP server which implements the APOP command will include a timestamp in its banner greeting, which corresponds to an RFC-822 msg-id. (Refer back to the figure on page 95 for the syntax of this production.) The timestamp **must** be different each time the POP server returns a greeting. For example, on a UNIX implementation in which a separate UNIX process is used for each instance of a POP server, the syntax of the timestamp might be:

```
<process-ID.clock@hostname>
```

where process-ID is the decimal value of the server's process-identifier, clock is the decimal value of the system clock, and hostname is the fully-qualified domain-name corresponding to the host where the POP server is running.

The POP client makes note of this timestamp, and then uses the APOP command. The syntax of this command is shown in Figure 5.9 on page 202. The digest component is calculated by applying the MD5 message-digest algorithm[56] to a string consisting of the timestamp (including the bracketing < and > characters) followed by a shared

```
            ; case-insensitive matching of string-literals
nonstd    ::= "APOP "          digest                    CRLF
            / "XTND SCAN " width   [" " format] CRLF

scanresp  ::= 1*DIGIT " " 1*DIGIT   " #" *text   CRLF

digest    ::= 32(DIGIT / "A" / "B" / "C" / "D" / "E" / "F"
                      / "a" / "b" / "c" / "d" / "e" / "f")

width     ::= 1*DIGIT
format    ::= <"> *(ftext / escaped-f) <">
ftext     ::= <any character except <">, "\", CR, or LF>
escaped-f ::= "\" <">                      ; literal double-quote
            / "\\"                         ; literal backslash

text      ::= <any character including bare CR and bare LF,
              but not including CRLF>
```

Figure 5.9: Non-Standard additions to POP Syntax

secret.[9] This shared secret is a string known only to the client (which identifies itself with the USER command), and POP server. Great care should be taken to prevent unauthorized disclosure of the secret, as knowledge of the secret will allow any entity to successfully masquerade as the named mailbox. The digest itself is a 16-octet value which is sent in hexadecimal format.

When the POP server receives the APOP command, it verifies the message-digest provided. If the message-digest is correct, the POP server returns a positive response, and the client may initiate one or more POP transactions. Otherwise, the client can either re-issue the USER command, or it can release the POP service.

So, how does this provide a basis for authentication? The answer is simple: it's magic. Actually, security experts conjecture that it is computationally infeasible to calculate any input string to the MD5 message-digest algorithm that will produce a specific output string. Hence, only an entity which knows the shared secret can generate

---

[9]MH uses the MD5 implementation contained in [56], which is hereby identified as "derived from the RSA Data Security, Inc. MD5 Message-Digest Algorithm".

or verify the message-digest supplied as the argument of the `APOP` command.

Consider this exchange:

```
S: <wait for connection on TCP port 109>
C: <open connection to server>
S: +OK POP server ready <1896.697170952@dbc.mtview.ca.us>
C: USER mrose
S: +OK password required for mrose
C: APOP c4c9334bac560ecc979e58001b3e22fb
S: +OK maildrop has 4 messages (3455 octets)
   ...
```

In this example, the shared secret is the string "`tanstaaf`". Hence, the MD5 algorithm is applied to the string

```
<1896.697170952@dbc.mtview.ca.us>tanstaaf
```

which produces a message-digest value of

```
c4c9334bac560ecc979e58001b3e22fb
```

Remote Scan Listings

The current POP design works best when network latency is on the order provided by most LANs. However, when POP is used over low-speed connections (e.g., 2400bps dialup-lines), it does not work well.

Historically, the POP model has been to make only minimal requirements on the POP server. In order to operate more effectively over low-speed connections, this model must be modified somewhat. Implementation experience shows that the largest improvement can be achieved by making one shift: having the POP server generate a scan listing for the client. Instead of using the `TOP` command for this purpose, a new command `XTND SCAN`, is introduced to provide this functionality.

The syntax of this command is shown in Figure 5.9 on page 202. The `width` component is the maximum length for a scan listing. The optional `format` component is a quoted-string with the semantics of MH's format file facility. If the `format` parameter is not given, the POP server uses a locally-defined default value. Note that the format string must not generate a scan listing containing either CR or LF.

When the POP server receives the `XTND SCAN` command and if it implements it, it returns a positive response. Otherwise a negative response is returned. Thereafter, whenever the client uses a `LIST` command, the syntax of a corresponding positive response is of the form shown for `scanresp` in Figure 5.9 on page 202. As usual, the first two fields give the message number and the size of the message in octets. However, any text between the hash-character ("#") and the end of line is the string calculated when the formatting string is applied to the message.

So, if the message shown in Figure 5.8 back on page 199 were the first message in the mailbox, then, one might expect to see:

```
    ...
S: XTND SCAN 80
C: +OK SCAN
S: LIST 1
C: +OK 1 660 #   1  04/17 03:10GMT Craig Burton      Re: e-mail test<<MHS: ...
```

Of course, the greatest performance would be achieved if a `LIST` command were issued without arguments.

5.3   Other Approaches

The POP service is simple, some say too simple. Independently of POP, two other delivery protocols have been developed in the Internet community. These are now briefly introduced.[10]

5.3.1   Interactive Mail Access Protocol

The Interactive Mail Access Protocol (IMAP) [57, 58] is a much more sophisticated protocol than POP.[11]

Communications between the IMAP server and client is asynchronous — that is, once an IMAP session is established, the IMAP server may send unsolicited messages to the client. Further, each transaction is prefixed by a tag for synchronization purposes — when a multiline command completes, this tag will be returned. In addition, this facility allows the client to have a few transactions simultaneously in progress during the IMAP session, if so desired.

The IMAP service associates one or more mailboxes with each user. A property-list (collection of attributes) is associated with each electronic mail message. By fetching a property, its value is transmitted to the client. Similarly, by storing a property, its value is transmitted to the server. Included in the list of properties are: the RFC-822 representation of the message, the headers, the body, individual headers, and so on.

In addition, there are some special properties, such as a collection of flags which indicate the status of the message (seen, deleted, and so on). Hence, to delete an electronic mail message, one selects the

---

[10]The author could easily add 20 pages onto the length of *The Internet Message* by making an in-depth presentation of each. Instead, only POP is given such treatment. This is not meant to slight either protocol. Both are significantly more advanced than POP (with a correspondingly higher cost of implementation). Instead, the author feels that the treatment of POP and the introduction of these two protocols is consistent with the level of detail in *The Internet Message*. On the other hand, it is true that the author did develop POP, but didn't work on the other two protocols. Critics might (justifiably) find this suspicious.

[11]Actually, for historical (some say hysterical) reasons, there are two variants of IMAP. In the context of the high-level discussion presented in *The Internet Message*, there is no point in examining the differences between the two.

desired mailbox and then stores the `deleted` value into the `FLAGS` attribute associated with the desired message. Later on, using the `EXPUNGE` command will result in the expected behavior. Finally, one can use a `SEARCH` command to look for electronic mail messages which satisfy client-defined criteria.

IMAP also supports a *bulletin-board* facility that allows several users to share common access to a collection of "special" mailboxes. This is useful for discussion groups and the like, and is most commonly used to support access to news messages, as described earlier in Section 3.5 starting on page 120.

The power of IMAP lies in its flexibility. Unlike POP, which shifts the balance of computational burden to the client at the expense of network traffic, IMAP shifts the burden to the IMAP server and considerably reduces network traffic.

5.3.2   Distributed Mail System Protocol

A different line of research has produced the Distributed Mail System Protocol (DMSP) [59]. The DMSP is built-around a *repository* model in which multiple message stores for a user are loosely synchronized (i.e., may have transient inconsistencies). The idea is that a person might desire a single centralized mailbox, but be forced to use several computers, e.g., a workstation in the office, a personal computer at home, and a laptop computer on travel.

As with IMAP, the repository associates multiple mailboxes with a user, and also includes a bulletin-board facility. However, unlike IMAP, the repository allows those mailboxes to be partially replicated on one or more clients acting on the user's behalf. When the client establishes a DMSP session, it synchronizes itself with the repository.

The basic message handling operations of DMSP are similar to those of POP. DMSP lacks the flexibility of IMAP, but solves a different problem.

Chapter 6

Multi-media Mail

Thus far, we've seen how the basis for electronic mail messages in the Internet is firmly rooted in NVT ASCII. Further, although the headers are structured, the actual body is plain text. Thus, one might suppose that Internet electronic mail is limited to the exchange of memo-based textual messages among an English-writing constituency. Nothing could be further from the truth!

In this chapter, we introduce the mechanism by which arbitrarily structured content types may be exchanged between two user agents. This work is interesting in that it adds great functionality to the Internet message transfer system, but does so in a way which avoids exercising known problems with non-conformant user agents and message transfer agents. The engineering trade-offs made may be contentious, but it is impertinent to argue with success, and the technology we're about to describe appears to have been received very well by the Internet community.

From a historical perspective, it should be noted that multi-media messaging has existed for a long time in the Internet community (e.g., [60, 61]). What distinguishes this new work is that it provides an implementation-independent mechanism which allows for interoperability between these systems.

6.1   Multi-Media Body

Early in 1992, the author read his mail and was privileged to hear the
voice — not read the words — of Nathaniel S. Borenstein:

> *"Memory is cheap, but bandwidth is cheaper."*

Yes, the author got "voice mail" from one of his colleagues who had
spear-headed the introduction of multi-media mail into the Internet
community.

The technology which makes this possible is termed MIME, or
Multi-purpose Internet Mail Extensions [46]. Actually, this title is
somewhat misleading since MIME defines the structure for Internet
message bodies and is largely orthogonal to RFC-822, which defines
the structure of Internet message headers.[1]

Before going into the details, let's consider an example which illustrates the power MIME offers. On the morning of Wednesday, March
11, the members of the IETF working group which developed MIME
received an electronic mail message containing a body with a scant 3004
octets. The semantics of this message body were as follows:

- If the user agent is able to render:

    1. some richly-formatted text;

    2. an audio snippet;

    3. some plain text;

    4. a bit-mapped image; and,

    5. some more richly-formatted text.

  then display those contents, in sequence, to the user;

- Otherwise, display a different textual content to the user.

Since the author was using a desktop with a grayscale window-system
and an audio-chip, the first alternative was taken.

---

[1]The title was chosen because it had a good acronym — MIME — which might
be thought of as referring to the accurate imitation of some kind of communication.

```
Date:        Wed, 11 Mar 1992 16:27:37 EST
Subject:     Barbershop MIME
From:        Nathaniel Borenstein
To:          ietf-822@dimacs.rutgers.edu,
             info-metamail@thumper.bellcore.com
cc:          John Lamb,
             Michael Littman,
             "David A. Braun"
```

Those of you not running MIME-compliant mail readers won't get a lot
out of this, nor will those without ftp access to the Internet, but
for the lucky few....

Here are the infamous *Telephone Chords*, the world's premier (=only)
all-Bellcore barbershop quartet, singing about *MIME*. Note that
because the "message/external-body" MIME construct is used, this
whole message is only about 3000 bytes -- at least, until you start
reading it.   :-)

Press RETURN to go on

Figure 6.1: An Example of richly-formatted Text

So, the first thing the author saw was the text shown in Figure 6.1.
The first part is simply `mhl` reporting on the headers which the author
finds interesting. The second part shows some text with some words
emphasized.

The author, his interest piqued, gingerly tapped the RETURN key.
His user agent then asked if it could initiate a file transfer to retrieve
the next content:

```
Retrieve quartet.au using anonymous FTP from site thumper.bellcore.com?
```

The author typed "y" and a few minutes later, he heard, in (nearly)
perfect four-part harmony:

> *"Let me send you email, if you have the time.*
> *Let me send you email, now that we have MIME.*
> *You have lots of bandwidth, I have lots of bits.*
> *Let's use MIME for e-mail, plain text is the pits!"*

sung to the tune of a traditional song of U.S. culture.[2] In fact, the harmony may have been perfect, but the audio-chip on the author's desktop is of similar quality to telephone voice-grade service.

Why did it take a few minutes to transfer the audio? The author connects to the Internet with a 9.6K dial-up line and the digitized audio content was nearly 400Kbytes.

The user agent printed a blank line (the raw text mentioned earlier), and then asked the author for permission to initiate a second file transfer:

```
Retrieve quartet.gif using anonymous FTP from site thumper.bellcore.com?
```

The author, now smiling ear-to-ear, typed "y" and a couple of minutes later a new window popped up, as shown in Figure 6.2. (Had the author's desktop had color display capabilities, then this image would have been rendered colorfully rather than in grayscale.)

Finally, the text shown in Figure 6.3 was displayed.

Had the author been using a "dumb" terminal, then instead of this multi-media extravaganza, he would have seen the text shown in Figure 6.4 on page 212.

This example illustrates the range of MIME's power:

- it allows for the electronic mail message body to have nested contents;

- it allows for the user agent to select among alternative representations of contents;

- it allows for a content actually to be a pointer to data stored elsewhere; and,

- each content can contain arbitrary data, binary or textual.

In fact, as we explore the details of MIME, we'll see that there are even more capabilities available.

The MIME specification [46] includes a formal definition of the term *MIME conformant*. Although the precise details are beyond the

---

[2]*Let Me Call You Sweetheart*, words by Beth S. Whitson, music by Leo Friedman, arrangement © 1986 by S.P.E.B.S.Q.S.A., Inc.

Figure 6.2: The Telephone Chords, A Moment Immortalized

Left to right:

> John Lamb, *bass*
> David Braun, *baritone*
> Michael Littman, *lead*
> Nathaniel Borenstein, *tenor*

Press RETURN to go on

Figure 6.3: Another Example of richly-formatted Text

```
Those of you not running MIME-compliant mail readers won't get a lot
out of this, nor will those without ftp access to the Internet, but
for the lucky few....

Here are the infamous Telephone Chords, the world's premier (=only)
all-Bellcore barbershop quartet, singing about MIME.  Note that
because the "message/external-body" MIME construct is used, this
whole message is only about 3000 bytes -- at least, until you start
reading it. :-) [An Andrew ToolKit view (mailobjv) was included
here, but could not be displayed.][An Andrew ToolKit view (mailobjv)
was included here, but could not be displayed.]  Left to right:
                         John Lamb, bass
                       David Braun, baritone
                       Michael Littman, lead
                   Nathaniel Borenstein, tenor
```

Figure 6.4: The Alternative Text

scope of *The Internet Message*, the basic idea is that MIME-capable software will generate electronic mail messages with contents that can be unambiguously recognized; further, when MIME-capable software processes an incoming message, it will be able to process contents information not intended for human consumption and shield the human user from the uninterpreted rendering of those contents.

6.1.1   Content Types

MIME is built around the notion of a *content type*. This is a specification of a particular kind of data. If the headers of an electronic mail message contain the **Content-Type:** header, then its value indicates what kind of content is contained in the body of the electronic mail message. The syntax of this header is shown in Figure 6.5. Observant readers will note that the **tspecials** production rule is a slightly more restricted variant of the **specials** production shown in Figure 3.2 back on page 80. Further, as with the syntax for RFC-822, comments or white-space can be placed in between any two lexemes, although this is not shown in this figure, or any figure which follows.

```
           ; case-insensitive matching of type and subtype
content    ::= "Content-Type" ":" type "/" subtype *(";" parameter)

type       ::= "multipart"
             / "message"
             / "text"
             / "image"
             / "audio"
             / "video"
             / "application"
             / <"X-" immediately followed by token>

subtype    ::= token / <"X-" immediately followed by token>

parameter  ::= attribute "=" value

           ; case-insensitive matching
attribute  ::= token

value      ::= token / quoted-string

token      ::= 1*<any character except SPACE or tspecials>

tspecials  ::= "(" / ")" / "[" / "]" / <"> / "\"
             / "," / "." / ":" / ";" / "@" / "<" / ">"
             / "/" / "?" / "="

quoted-string
           ::= <"> *(qtext / quoted-pair) <">

qtext      ::= <any character except <">, "\", CR,
                  but including LWSP>

LWSP       ::= CRLF 1*SPACE
CRLF       ::= <carriage-return followed by line-feed>
```

Figure 6.5: MIME Content-Type Syntax

So, a *content type* is identified by:

- a type, which gives general guidance as to the resources required in order to process the content;

- a subtype, which refines the content; and,

- zero or more parameters, which allow for customization of the content.

As with the headers defined for RFC-822, there are two extensibility mechanisms defined for content types. First, if a local environment wishes to define its own content types, it can do so, simply by starting the type or subtype with the string "X-". Second, Internet-standards are allowed to define new content types as long as they do not conflict with any other standard content types (and do not start with "X-", of course).

Standard Content Types

Although extensibility is a key aspect of MIME, many suspect that although there will be many new subtypes defined, there will never be more than the seven pre-defined types. The reason for this is that the standard seven cover a lot of ground.

Let's now look at each in turn.

multipart

The `multipart` type is used to convey a content value which contains several subordinate parts. Figure 6.6 on page 216 shows the syntax of this content type, along with its value. (This figure uses the BNF defined in Figure 3.1 on page 77.)

Basically, a `multipart` content, regardless of its subtype, conveys zero or more body parts, each separated by a delimiter. Each of the body parts is structured in a similar fashion to an electronic mail message. Unlike a message however, no header fields need be present. Hence, any of the body parts could start with a blank line. In fact however, there are usually headers present, and they should all be named with a prefix of "Content-". If no `Content-Type:` header is present, then the value `text/plain` is used as a default, which means that the body part contains unstructured text from the NVT ASCII repertoire.

There are four subtypes:

mixed: This indicates that the body parts should be processed sequentially.

parallel: This indicates that body parts should be processed in parallel. However, if more than one body part requires exclusive access to a common resource (e.g., if rendering two or more body parts requires access to the user's keyboard), or if the user agent is incapable of simulating parallel processing, then sequential processing is acceptable.

digest: This indicates that each body part is an electronic mail message. This mechanism completely obsoletes the digest encapsulation scheme in [45] which was described back in Section 3.3.1 on page 102. For reasons which we'll explain in a moment, it's actually a much better way to do encapsulation.

alternative: This indicates that although there are multiple body parts present, they have identical semantic content. As such, only one should be processed. The body parts are ordered in terms of expressive power, with the least

```
            ; case-insensitive matching of string-literals
multipart ::= "multipart" "/" subtype ";" "boundary" "=" boundary
subtype   ::= "mixed"
            / "parallel"
            / "digest"
            / "alternative"

boundary  ::= *69(btext / " ") btext

btext     ::= ALPHA / DIGIT
            / "'" / "(" / ")" / "+" / "_" / "," / "-" / "." / ":"
            / "/" / "?" / "="

mulipart-value
          ::= preamble 1*(delimiter CRLF bodypart)
              delimiter "--"          ; no white-space allowed
              epilogue

premable  ::= *text                   ; ignored

            ; no white-space allowed
delimiter ::= CRLF "--" boundary

            ; no line may start with ("--" boundary)
bodypart  ::= *field *(CRLF *text)

epilogue  ::= *text                   ; ignored

ALPHA     ::= <any alphabetic character, "A" through "Z" and
              "a" through "z">
DIGIT     ::= <any numeric character, "0" through "9">
```

Figure 6.6: Multipart Content-Type Syntax

expressive content being the first, and the most expressive content being the last. (The reason for this is simple: if a user agent which is not MIME-capable comes across a `multipart/alternative` message, the first text that it will display will be from the content type which is the least expressive. This initial part will hopefully be unstructured text, so that a human user can make sense of it.)

The only thing left to describe is how the body parts are separated. To begin, the entire content value is represented using the NVT ASCII repertoire. Each body part is separated by a delimiter string, which consists of a line that starts with two hyphen-characters ("--") and is followed by up to 70 characters. The characters are chosen so that the delimiter string is not used to start any line in any of the body parts. Generation of the delimiter can be done by scanning each body part, or by generating random strings which are unlikely to occur in the body part.[3] Also, note that because the delimiter actually contains the preceding (and following) CR and LF, the body part needn't end in a CR-LF sequence.

So, why use this approach instead of the one described in Section 3.3.1 back on page 102? Although the earlier approach has the advantage of much simpler processing, it is undone by its recursive nature! Suppose an electronic mail message is repeatedly forwarded using the earlier approach. The length of lines with the encapsulation markers will grow steadily by two characters each time. Some implementations of message transfer agents either truncate or wrap long lines. The result, thanks to these non-conformant implementations, is broken encapsulations.

In contrast, using the MIME approach, when one repeatedly forwards electronic messages, the length of lines with the boundaries remains constant. Of course, each time a forwarding occurs, a new delimiter string must be generated. Further, note that the delimiter string must not end in a space. The reason for this is simple: some user agents and message transfer agents remove trailing white-space. The thoughtful reader will note that MIME is carefully engineered

---

[3]The author has difficulty believing in the correctness of the latter approach, though there are those who say it can be done.

to coexist with the existing message transfer system — including the non-conformant software which might be encountered!

Finally, even though the two schemes are incompatible, software which implements the older scheme can usually burst an electronic mail message with a `multipart/digest` content, provided there isn't any nesting of forwarded messages. In fact, the syntax for `multipart` content allows for preamble and epilogue text, which are often found when collections of messages are digestified. Since there is no `Content-Type:` header associated with either textual component, they are ignored by MIME-capable software. However, it may be useful to put text there for the benefit of humans using older user agents. The only disadvantage of this emulation is that an extra CR-LF sequence appears at the end of the body of each message.

Figure 6.7 gives an example of an electronic mail message body which contains a `text/plain` content and a `multipart/mixed` content nested inside a `multipart/alternative` content. There is a preamble for the outer layer, which can only be seen by older user agents. It wisely instructs the human user to read only the first part and to then skip the rest of the message. Although not shown in this figure, the `multipart/mixed` content contains five body parts.

```
Content-Type: multipart/alternative;
        boundary="Interpart.Boundary.Qdjbh920M2Yt4L5uUD"

> THIS IS A MESSAGE IN 'MIME' FORMAT.  Your mail reader does not
> support MIME. Please read the first section, which is plain text,
> and ignore the rest.

--Interpart.Boundary.Qdjbh920M2Yt4L5uUD
Content-type: text/plain; charset=US-ASCII

Those of you not running MIME-compliant mail readers won't get a lot
out of this, nor will those without ftp access to the Internet, but
for the lucky few....

Here are the infamous Telephone Chords, the world's premier (=only)
all-Bellcore barbershop quartet, singing about MIME.  Note that
because the "message/external-body" MIME construct is used, this
whole message is only about 3000 bytes -- at least, until you start
reading it.   :-) [An Andrew ToolKit view (mailobjv) was included
here, but could not be displayed.][An Andrew ToolKit view (mailobjv)
was included here, but could not be displayed.]  Left to right:
                        John Lamb, bass
                     David Braun, baritone
                     Michael Littman, lead
                  Nathaniel Borenstein, tenor

--Interpart.Boundary.Qdjbh920M2Yt4L5uUD
Content-Type: multipart/mixed;
        boundary="Alternative.Boundary.Qdjbh920M2YtQL5uQz"

--Alternative.Boundary.Qdjbh920M2YtQL5uQz

<<in the interests of brevity, the body parts contained in
  the multipart/mixed content have been removed in this figure...>>

--Alternative.Boundary.Qdjbh920M2YtQL5uQz--

--Interpart.Boundary.Qdjbh920M2Yt4L5uUD--
```

Figure 6.7: Multipart Content-Type Example

message

The `message` type is used to convey a content value which is another electronic mail message. Figure 6.8 shows the syntax of this content type. (This figure uses the BNF defined in Figures 6.5, 3.1, and 3.7 on pages 213, 77, and 92, respectively.)

There are three subtypes:

rfc822: This indicates that the content value is simply an electronic mail message. For example, when forwarding messages, the `multipart/digest` content type is used and each subordinate body part is of type `message/rfc822`.

partial: This indicates that the content value is a fragmented message. The `id` parameter is used to coordinate fragments belonging to a single complete message. (Care must be taken in selecting the value for the `id` parameter, as this is the sole means used to identify related message fragments — as a practice, this parameter should have the same semantics as the `Message-ID:` header.) The `number` parameter indicates which fragment this content corresponds to (the first fragment is numbered 1, and so on). The `total` parameter, which needs to be present only on the final fragment, indicates the number of fragments which comprise the complete message.

external-body: This indicates that the content value is a pointer to the content, rather than the actual value itself. The `access-type` parameter indicates the access method which should be used to retrieve the content.

The content values of each of these is represented using the NVT ASCII repertoire.

The `message/rfc822` content type is rather self-explanatory: the content value consists of headers, possibly followed by a blank line and the body. If the electronic mail message contains a structured body, then the headers of the message include a `Content-Type:` header.

```
                  ; case-insensitive matching of string-literals
message   ::= "message" "/" subtype
subtype   ::= "rfc822"
              / "partial"           partial
              / "external-body" ";" external

              ; a plain 'ol RFC-822 message
rfc822-value
          ::= 1*field *(CRLF *text)

partial   ::= ";" "id"      "=" value
              ";" "number" "=" 1*DIGIT
              [";" "total"  "=" 1*DIGIT]

              ; first fragment contains some headers
partial-value
          ::= *(CRLF *text)

external  ::=      "access-type" "=" type
              [";" "expiration"  "=" date-time]
              [";" "size"        "=" 1*DIGIT]
              [";" "permission"  "=" ("read" / "read-write")]

type      ::= ("ftp" / "anon-ftp")    name    site   [dir] [mode]
              / "tftp"                 name    site
              / ("afs" / "local-file") name   [site]
              / "mail-server"          server
              / <"X-" immediately followed by token>

name      ::= ";" "name"       "=" value
site      ::= ";" "site"       "=" value
dir       ::= ";" "directory"  "=" value
mode      ::= ";" "mode"       "=" value
server    ::= ";" "server"     "=" value

              ; not really an RFC-822 message,
              ; but one field must be a "Content-Type:" header
external-value
          ::= 1*field *(CRLF *text)
```

Figure 6.8: Message Content-Type Syntax

The `message/partial` content type is used when an electronic mail message is deemed too large to be conveniently handled. For example, some message transfer agents impose a maximum limit on the size of a message which they will transfer. As noted earlier, the Internet Host Requirements document mandates that electronic mail messages up to 64K bytes must be supported. So, by using MIME, one can fragment a large message and send it in little pieces. A MIME-capable user agent will then automatically re-construct the message.

The fragmentation algorithm for an electronic mail message is simple:

1. Split the message body into n parts.

2. From the original message, remove the `Message-ID:` header along with any headers named with a prefix of "`Content-`".

3. For each of the n parts, construct a message fragment. The headers of each message fragment will be identical to the headers of the original message, except that:

   - A different `Message-ID:` will be present in each message fragment.

   - A `Content-Type:` of `message/partial` will be present in each message fragment. The `id`, `number`, and `total` parameters will be initialized accordingly.

The body of each message fragment will contain the appropriate part from the message body of the original message, except that the body of the first message will contain whatever headers were removed from the original message in Step 2, followed by a blank line.

The reassembly algorithm is also simple:

1. Make sure that all n message fragments have been received.

2. Create a new electronic mail message, copying the headers from the message fragment having a parameter of `number=1`, but not copying the `Message-ID:` header nor any headers named with a prefix of "`Content-`".

```
Message-Id: <9204261204.AA10067@dbc.mtview.ca.us>
To: mrose@dbc.mtview.ca.us
Subject: letter-book archive
Mime-Version: 1.0
Content-Type: message/partial; id="<10018.704289854@dbc.mtview.ca.us>";
       number=1; total=15
Content-Description: part 1 of 15
Date: Sun, 26 Apr 1992 05:04:15 -0700
From: "Marshall T. Rose" <mrose@dbc.mtview.ca.us>

Message-ID: <10018.704289854@dbc.mtview.ca.us>
Content-Type: application/octet-stream; type=tar; conversions=x-compress
       (extract with uncompress | tar xvpf -)
Content-Transfer-Encoding: base64

H52QbMrQoVNGTgsxb96seQGgocOHECNKnEixosWLFUGAkHGjRgOQADSCiEGDBkiRJE2GFMlSIwyN
<<in the interests of brevity, the remainder of the body
 of the message has been removed in this figure...>>
```

Figure 6.9: Message/Partial Content-Type Example

3. For each message fragment, starting with the first and proceeding in ascending order, append the message body to the newly created electronic mail message.

Note that as the message body of the first message fragment contains the **Message-ID:** and "Content-" headers from the original message, these will automatically be appended onto the headers of the newly created message.

These algorithms have been carefully constructed so as to make message fragmentation and reassembly completely transparent. In fact, the fragmentation process can be recursive, if a user wishes to fragment a **message/partial** content, in order to transfer it to some other mailbox.

Figure 6.9 shows the first message fragment of an electronic mail message which has been fragmented into 15 parts. (Don't worry about the headers, other than **Content-Type:**, which are named with a prefix of "Content-", they will be introduced later in Sections 6.1.2 and 6.1.3.) The key thing to note is that the body of the first message fragment contains the key information on the original message: its unique identifier and its content type.

Finally, as shown in Figure 6.8 back on page 221, the content value for the `message/external-body` content type appears to be a message, but only a `Content-Type:` header need be present, which indicates the actual content type. If a body is present, then this contains additional information that may be used to access the content value, according to the particular value associated with the `access-type` parameter. It is important to remember that if a body is present, it is only parameter information and is not part of the actual content value.

The access method used to retrieve the actual content value is one of:

ftp: This indicates that the File Transfer Protocol [62] should be used. The `name` parameter indicates the name of the file, which is stored in the directory named by the `dir` parameter. The `site` parameter is a domain name of a host where the file resides. If the content value isn't NVT ASCII, then the `mode` parameter indicates how FTP should retrieve the file, usually this is `image`.

anon-ftp: This is identical to `ftp` access method, except that instead of asking the user for FTP authentication information, the user agent will automatically supply FTP credentials for the "anonymous" user.

tftp: This indicates that the Trivial File Transfer Protocol [63] should be used. The `name` and `site` parameters have the expected meaning. (TFTP does not use authentication information.)

afs: This indicates that the Andrew File System [64] should be used. The `name` parameter has its expected meaning. The `site` parameter is present only to indicate the scope of machines which might have the file. The left-most domain name of this parameter value may be a wildcard-character ("`*`").

local-file: This indicates that the file containing the content value is actually local. The `name` and `site` parameters have the same meaning as they do for the `afs` access method.

mail-server: This indicates that the content value can be obtained by sending an electronic mail message to the address identified in the `server` parameter. When a message is sent, the body, if any, found in the content value is copied. This allows arbitrary mail server commands to be specified and automatically sent.

As usual, two extensibility mechanisms are possible for access methods: First, if a local environment wishes to define its own access methods, it can do so, simply by starting the `access-type` value with the string "`X-`". Second, Internet-standards are allowed to define new access methods as long as they do not conflict with any other standard access methods (and do not start with "`X-`", of course).

There are also three other parameters that might be used:

expiration: The date and time when the content value is likely to become unavailable.

size: This indicates the number of octets comprising the content value. This may help the recipient to decide whether the user agent should be directed to retrieve the content.

permission: This indicates whether the content value is likely to change. If so, then each time the user agent references the `message/external-body` content type, it should fetch the content value anew.

Figure 6.10 on page 226 shows an example of a `audio/basic` content (which we'll introduce later on in Section 6.1.1), the value of which is stored on a host which allows anonymous FTP access. (Don't worry about the `Content-Description:` header, it will be introduced later in Section 6.1.3.) Note that if the content value was available on multiple hosts, then a `multipart/alternative` content could be used: each subordinate body part would be a `message/external-body` content, and each would use the `site` parameter to name a different host, and perhaps even have different `access-type` parameter values.

```
Content-type: message/external-body;
      access-type="anon-ftp";
      site="thumper.bellcore.com";
      directory="pub/nsb";
      name="quartet.au"
Content-Description:  The Telephone Chords, A Moment Immortalized

Content-type: audio/basic
```

Figure 6.10: Message/External Content-Type Example

```
msg part   type/subtype             size description
    1        multipart/alternative  2913
      1      multipart/mixed        1688
      1.1    text/richtext           481
      1.2    message/external-body    29 Let Me Sing You Email (audio)
             audio/basic
      1.3    text/plain                1
      1.4    message/external-body    27 The Telephone Chords, A Moment
             image/gif
      1.5    text/richtext           217
      2      text/plain              817
```

Figure 6.11: Table of Contents for Example Message

Finally, it should be noted that the `message/external-body` mechanism, like `message/partial`, is meant to be transparent to the end-user. When a user agent encounters such a content, it should automatically retrieve the actual content value, or (in the case of the author's user agent), it should inform the user and ask for permission to perform the retrieval.

So, we now know enough about how MIME structures content types and values to revisit the example message discussed starting on page 208. When MH is asked to produce a "table of contents" for a multi-media electronic mail message, it produces something like the text shown in Figure 6.11.

This indicates that message number 1 has two parts contained within a `multipart/alternative` content. The part numbers printed by MH are not found in the MIME message. Rather they are present simply as an aid to the user to understand the structuring of the message. MH estimates the size of each content value and prints it; however, because MH hasn't been asked to retrieve the external content values, and a `size` parameter wasn't specified, there isn't any size information available on the external content values.

So, we've now looked at the `multipart` and `message` types, now let's look at the other five, namely `text`, `image`, `audio`, `video`, and `application`.

text

The **text** type is used to convey a content value which is textual in nature. Figure 6.12 shows the syntax of this content type. (This figure uses the BNF defined in Figure 6.5 on page 213.) Observant readers will note that the content value needn't conform to the NVT ASCII repertoire. Later on, in Section 6.1.2 starting on page 236 we'll find out how MIME accomplishes this!

There are two subtypes:

plain: This indicates that the content value is unstructured text.

richtext: This indicates that the content value is actually input to a special text formatting language, termed *richtext*.

A requirement on subtypes is that their content be readable by humans, even if formatting directives are embedded. Hence, binary representations of textual documents are not defined using the **text** content type.

The richtext language allows for a least-common denominator text formatting facility. The syntax of a **text/richtext** content value is very simple:

- The "<" character indicates the beginning of a directive, which is either simple or balanced. All other characters are literal text.

- A simple directive is used for one of three purposes:

  - to render a literal "<" character;

  - to render a line-break; or,

  - to render a page-break.

- A balanced directive is used to activate a new formatting environment. As implied by its name, when an environment is activated, later on there must be an indication that the environment is terminated. Of course, balanced directives may be nested.

```
            ; case-insensitive matching of string-literals
text        ::= "text" "/" subtype [";" "charset" "=" charset]
subtype     ::= "plain" / "richtext"

            ; case-insensitive matching of values
charset     ::= "us-ascii"
            / <"iso-8859-" immediatedly followed by 1*DIGIT>
            / <"X-" immediately followed by token>

richtext-value
            ::= *(rtext / directive)

directive ::= simple / balanced

simple      ::= "<lt>"              ; "<"
            / "<nl>"                ; new-line
            / "<np>"                ; new-page

balanced    ::= start richtext-value stop

            ; no embedded white-space allowed
start       ::= "<"  1*40(ALPHA / DIGIT / "-") ">"
stop        ::= "</" 1*40(ALPHA / DIGIT / "-") ">"

            ; CRLF is treated as a single SPACE
rtext       ::= <any octet value other than "<">

ALPHA       ::= <any alphabetic character, "A" through "Z" and
                "a" through "z">
DIGIT       ::= <any numeric character, "0" through "9">
```

Figure 6.12: Text Content-Type Syntax

```
Content-type: text/richtext; charset=us-ascii

Those of you not running MIME-compliant mail readers
won't get a lot out of this,
nor will those without ftp access to the Internet,
but for the lucky few....
<nl>
<nl>Here are the infamous <bold>Telephone Chords</bold>,
the world's premier (=only) all-Bellcore barbershop quartet,
singing about <bold>MIME</bold>.
Note that because the "message/external-body"
MIME construct is used,
this whole message is only about 3000 bytes -- at least,
until you start reading it.   :-)
<nl>
```

Figure 6.13: Text/Richtext Content-Type Example

Key to understanding the success of richtext is the notion that a richtext interpreter needn't perform any action when it encounters an environment which it doesn't implement. This allows richtext to degrade naturally, depending on the rendering capabilities of the user's MIME-capable software.

Figure 6.13 shows an example which corresponds to the rendering shown in Figure 6.1 back on page 209. Note that unless a line-break is forced by the "<nl>" directive, the richtext interpreter breaks lines as it deems appropriate for the user's output device. (In richtext, any white-space or CR-LF sequence encountered has the semantics of a single space.) Similarly, Figure 6.14 shows an example which corresponds to the rendering shown in Figure 6.3 on page 211.

The charset parameter is used to indicate the character set for the textual information. The default value, us-ascii, refers to the NVT ASCII repertoire. As of this writing, the other defined values are based on the ISO 8859 family of character sets. As usual, two extensibility mechanisms are possible for character sets: First, if a local environment wishes to define its own character sets, it can do so, simply by starting the charset value with the string "X-". Second, Internet-standards are allowed to define character sets as long as they do not conflict with any

---

```
Content-type: text/richtext; charset=us-ascii

<nl>
  Left to right:
<nl><center>John Lamb, <italic>bass</italic>
<nl>David Braun, <italic>baritone</italic>
<nl>Michael Littman, <italic>lead</italic>
<nl>Nathaniel Borenstein, <italic>tenor</italic> </center>
<nl>
```

Figure 6.14: Another Text/Richtext Content-Type Example

---

other standard access methods (and do not start with "X-", of course).

By way of illustration, Internet-conformant electronic mail messages which lack a **Content-Type:** header have this content value:

Content-Type: text/plain; charset=us-ascii

Note that the value of a **text/richtext** content may contain characters from different character sets. The **charset** parameter value specifies the default character set, and a balanced directive may be used to activate interpretations of different repertoires.

Actually, the issue of character sets in MIME is worthy of a soapbox. | soap... | The author longs for the good ol' days of the Internet community, where, although technical discussions were heated, the people developing technology would pull together for the sake of the community.[4] Unfortunately, there are a few individuals out there who seem more interested in safe-guarding their own little piece of the Internet than in developing competent solutions for the Internet community. Sadly, the work on MIME fell victim to this, which delayed community consensus for about half a year. The author regrets that he is not empowered by the *Great Internet God* to sentence these people to an extended term of community service. There were two issues that were particularly contentious, and the character set issue is one of them. It is a strict requirement that documents placed on the standards-track must cite only stable, publicly-available, documents. However, there are

---

[4]The author suspects that the word "community" had some higher meaning back then.

some enclaves which use non-standard character sets in electronic mail messages. This led to a confrontation in which one of the more vocal inhabitants of a European enclave, went non-linear when his locally-defined character set wouldn't be included in the MIME specification. He didn't care that he could document his character set, submit it for Internet publication, and then have the IANA add it to the list of standard MIME character sets later on. He wanted *his* character set to be a part of the MIME specification. This individual was shouted down (via electronic mail of course), by one of the most vocal US members of the Internet community. The amusing part was that the US member wanted a non-standard Japanese character-set added, but decided to pursue the correct course for having it added later on. Although some might view Internet technology as being US-centric, there are many

`...soap` examples where this simply isn't true.

```
            ; case-insensitive matching of string-literals
            ; the  values for each is a string of octets
image       ::= "image" "/" ("gif" / "jpeg")

audio       ::= "audio" "/" "basic"

video       ::= "video" "/" "mpeg"
```

Figure 6.15: Image, Audio, and Video Content-Type Syntax

image, audio, and video

The **image** type is used to convey a content value corresponding to a still-image picture; the **audio** type is used to convey a content value corresponding to digitized sound; and, the **video** type is used to convey a content value containing moving pictures perhaps with a sound-track. Figure 6.15 shows the syntax of these content types.

The subtypes for these various contents all refer to industry standards for the exchange of image, audio, or video data:

image/gif: Image data encoded using Compuserve's *Graphics Interchange Format* (GIF).

image/jpeg: Image data encoded using the ISO/IEC 10918 specification, which as of this writing is a Committee Draft. JPEG is useful for encoding full-color and gray-scale images from real-world scenes. It uses a variable-loss compression algorithm so that images may be compactly encoded and exchanged, usually with little degradation visible to the human eye.

audio/basic: Audio data encoded in the 8–bit ISDN μ-law format, sampled at 8KHz, and having a single channel.

video/mpeg: Video data encoded using the ISO/IEC 11172 specification, which as of this writing is a Committee Draft.

```
                ; case-insensitive matching of string-literals
application
            ::= "application" "/" subtype
subtype     ::= "octet-stream" stream
              / "oda"            oda
              / "postscript"

stream      ::= [";" "name"          "=" value]
                [";" "type"          "=" value]
                [";" "conversions" "=  conversion]
                [";" "padding"       "=" padding]
conversion
            ::= 1#<"X-" immediately followed by token>
padding     ::= "0" / "1" / "2" / "3" / "4" / "5" / "6" / "7"

oda         ::= ";" "profile" "=" value
```

Figure 6.16: Application Content-Type Syntax

application

Finally, the `application` type is used to convey a content value which is meant for a mail-enabled application. Figure 6.16 shows the syntax of this content type. (This figure uses the BNF defined in Figure 6.5 on page 213.)

There are three subtypes:

octet-stream: This indicates that the content value is arbitrary binary data. The `name` parameter suggests a file name to be used when storing the content value locally. Similarly, the `type` parameter gives the human user a hint as to the typing of the data. (This parameter value isn't standardized.)

The `conversions` parameter is a comma-separated list of operations which have been performed on the data, in order, prior to inclusion in the content value. Hence, to return to the original data, the reverse operations must be performed, from right-to-left. At present, no standard conversions are defined.[5]

---

[5]Although one might consider the UNIX *compress* facility an ideal candidate,

Finally, the `padding` parameter indicates how much padding (from 0 to 7 bits) was appended onto the stream of bits composing the content value. This parameter need be present only if the content value isn't an integral number of octets in length.

oda: This indicates that the content value is a document encoded using the *Open Document Interchange Format* (ODIF), as specified in ISO/IEC standard 8613. The `profile` parameter indicates which document application profile should be used when processing the content value.

postscript: This indicates that the content value is a PostScript program. As with many of the possible `application` types, the execution of this content value has the potential for considerable system mischief. The MIME specification takes great care to outline the relevant security issues.

As might be imagined, the `application/octet-stream` content, combined with message fragmentation, is useful for implementing a file transfer facility using electronic mail messages.

---

there appears to be some question as to the intellectual property rights of the coding scheme which it uses.

```
                    ; case-insensitive matching of type and subtype
encoding   ::= "Content-Transfer-Encoding" ":" mechanism

mechanism ::= "7bit"
              / "quoted-printable"
              / "base64"
              / "8bit"
              / "binary"
              / <"X-" immediately followed by token>
```

Figure 6.17: MIME Content-Transfer-Encoding Syntax

6.1.2   Content Transfer Encoding

Thus far, discussion in *The Internet Message* has postponed mention of how arbitrary binary data may be used for a content value. When a content value contains information from outside the NVT ASCII repertoire, the `Content-Transfer-Encoding:` header is used to indicate how the content value has been encoded. Figure 6.17 shows the syntax of this header.

Standard Transfer Encodings

In addition to providing the usual extensibility mechanisms, there are three useful encoding schemes, and two other schemes provided for non-standard environments. It is important to appreciate a few things about transfer encodings:

- The `multipart` and `message` content types specifically disallow the use of any encoding scheme other than `7bit`. This requirement has the (desired) effect of eliminating nested transfer encodings, which would unnecessarily complicate user agents.

- Otherwise, there is no *a priori* binding between a content type and the mechanism used to encode its value. Although some content values may lend themselves towards a particular encoding, these are independent issues.

- One should view the encoding and decoding of a content value as completely separate activities from processing the value. Hence, when processing an incoming message, the value is decoded to its native form prior to being processed as a particular content type.

- Although MIME allows for extensibility of transfer encodings, the definition of new mechanisms is almost certainly a bad thing, as it introduces a significant reduction in interoperability.

7bit

This is the default encoding mechanism. The 7bit encoding means that the content value conforms to the NVT ASCII repertoire.

quoted-printable

This encoding scheme is used when the content value is mostly (or entirely) from the NVT ASCII repertoire. It is useful when only a small percentage of the characters have the 8th bit set, or when it is possible that an intervening mail transfer agent might transform some of the non-alphanumeric characters present. Figure 6.18 on page 238 shows the syntax for the quoted-printable encoding.

The rules are fairly simple: any character which has the 8th bit set, the equals-character ("="), and any trailing spaces or tabs on a line, must be encoded using a three-character sequence, which starts with the equals-character and is followed by the hexadecimal representation of the character's value. In addition, any other character can be so encoded, at the discretion of the encoding user agent. Further, note that if a line ends with the three-character sequence which consists of a "=" followed by CR-LF, then these three characters are ignored. In fact, each line of a quoted-printable encoding must be less than or equal to 78 characters, including the trailing CR-LF sequence. This allows MIME-capable software to transparently fold long lines into units which are more easily digestible by some message transfer agents.

The only rule which is non-intuitive deals with how lines with trailing white-space are handled. The reason for this was introduced earlier: some user agents and message transfer agents remove trailing white-space, and others may actually add white-space. So, when decoding a quoted-printable encoding, any trailing white-space is ignored. Once

```
                    ; maximum line length (including CRLF) is 78 characters
quoted-printable
              ::= *([*(ptext / SPACE / TAB) ptext] ["="] CRLF)

ptext         ::= octet / <any character except "=", SPACE, or TAB>

                    ; must be used when 8th-bit is set, "=", and for trailing
                    ;    SPACEs and TABs
                    ; may be used for any other character
octet         ::= "=" 2(DIGIT / "A" / "B" / "C" / "D" / "E" / "F")

                    ; although not necessary, these are good candidates for
                    ; octet encoding
recommended
              ::= "[" / "]" / <"> / "\" / "@" / "!" / "#"
                    / "$" / "^" / "'" / "{" / "|" / "}" / "~"
```

Figure 6.18: Quoted-Printable Encoding Syntax

again, the thoughtful reader will note that MIME is carefully engineered to coexist with the existing message transfer system — including the non-conformant software which might be encountered!

Finally, it is important to appreciate that the quoted-printable encoding does include the hyphen-character ("-") which is also used by the delimiter strings in multipart contents. In order to streamline generation of delimiter strings, they should include the two character sequence "=_", a sequence of characters which can never occur in a quoted-printable encoding.

base64

This encoding scheme is used when the content value is a string of octets. Every 24 bits are "exploded" into a four-character sequence taken from a special subset of the NVT ASCII repertoire. Although the encoded value is one-third larger, it is immune to diddling by all known character set translation software (i.e., the characters chosen have identical representation in all currently standardized character sets).

6-bit	b64	6-bit	b64	6-bit	b64
0	A	26	a	52	0
1	B	27	b	53	1
2	C	28	c	54	2
3	D	29	d	55	3
4	E	30	e	56	4
5	F	31	f	57	5
6	G	32	g	58	6
7	H	33	h	59	7
8	I	34	i	60	8
9	J	35	j	61	9
10	K	36	k	62	+
11	L	37	l	63	/
12	M	38	m		
13	N	39	n		
14	O	40	o		
15	P	41	p		
16	Q	42	q		
17	R	43	r		
18	S	44	s		
19	T	45	t		
20	U	46	u		
21	V	47	v		
22	W	48	w		
23	X	49	x		
24	Y	50	y		
25	Z	51	z		

Table 6.1: Translating 6-bit to Base64

The rules are fairly simple: three octets are taken from the input stream and viewed as a 24–bit quantity, which is subsequently divided into four six-bit quantities. Each six-bit value is then indexed into a table of 64 characters, as shown in Table 6.1. If the input stream is not an integral number of 24–bit quantities, then an equals-character ("=") is used as a pad character for each 8–bit quantity trailing. Hence, a **base64** encoding will end with zero, one, or two equal-characters. Finally, each line of a **base64** encoding must be less than or equal to 78 characters, including the trailing CR-LF sequence. This means that at most an encoding line represents 19 octets from the content value.

When decoding a **base64** encoding, any character encountered which is not in the coding repertoire is ignored. It is an implementation option as to whether the user agent considers this a fatal error, a warning situation, or simply ignores the extraneous characters.

So looking back to Figure 6.9 on page 223, we see the first line of a `base64` encoding. The first four characters is the sequence "H52Q", which has six-bit values 7, 57, 54, and 16, and therefore represents the 24–bit quantity:

$$(7 << 18) \mid (57 << 12) \mid (54 << 6) \mid 16)$$

or `0x1f9d90`.

The only tricky thing about using `base64` is to make sure that textual data uses the CR-LF sequence for line-termination prior to applying the `base64`. Hence, if the local system uses some other sequence for line-termination, then conversion to the CR-LF sequence should occur prior to applying the `base64` encoding. Similarly, when storing a content value in local form, after applying the `base64` decoding, any CR-LF sequences should be mapped to the local line-termination sequence.

Finally, it should be noted that the `base64` encoding has three significant advantages over other encoding schemes (e.g., the UNIX `uuencode` scheme) which are commonly in use:

- its repertoire does not include the hyphen-character ("-") which is used by the delimiter strings in `multipart` contents;

- it is empirically safe from message transfer agent interference (the transformations will survive all known gateways and broken message transfer agents); and,

- it is used by other Internet electronic mail technologies, such as Privacy-Enhanced Mail, discussed in the next chapter.

8bit and binary

The `8bit` and `binary` encodings are used by enclaves which claim to use Internet mail but do not conform to Internet-standards. Both support an 8–bit character repertoire. The `8bit` encoding is used where the content value has a line concept which matches the NVT ASCII notion of CR-LF. In contrast, the `binary` encoding is used where there is no line concept in the content value.

The reason why these two encoding schemes are present is worthy $\boxed{\text{soap}\ldots}$ of a long soapbox, but since this chapter is running a bit long, the author will "cut to the chase". As might be guessed, someone got the idea that it was okay to ship around 8–bit data in Internet electronic mail messages, and started doing so. Of course, none of the Internet-standards on electronic mail allow this, and the practice does cause degenerate behavior with some software. When the work on MIME began, it was necessary to broker a compromise which would allow these non-conformant enclaves to continue their misbehaving ways. Naturally, this still wasn't enough of a *doggie-biscuit* to keep that particular someone from delaying the process, and numerous confrontations over many months were necessary to beat his position into irrelevance. $\boxed{\ldots\text{soap}}$

```
miscellany
           ::= "MIME-Version"         ":" 1*text
             / "Content-ID"           ":" msg-id
             / "Content-Description" ":" *text

msg-id     ::= "<" addr-spec ">"
```

Figure 6.19: MIME-Version, Content-ID, and Content-Description Syntax

6.1.3   Miscellaneous Information

Finally, there are three other headers used with multi-media electronic mail messages which have been alluded to throughout this chapter. Figure 6.19 shows the syntax of these headers. (This figure uses the BNF defined in Figures 3.2 and 3.6 on pages 80 and 90, respectively.)

Let's consider each of these headers in turn.

MIME-Version: This identifies the version of MIME in use. All multi-media electronic mail messages in the Internet must have this header. The current value is "1.0".

Content-ID: This contains a unique identifier for this content, with semantics equivalent to the `Message-ID:` header.

Content-Description: This allows an arbitrary textual comment to be attached to the content. Looking back at the example in Figure 6.10 on page 226, one can see where MH gets the description information shown in Figure 6.11 on page 226.

6.1.4   A MIME-capable User Agent

Appendix B starting on page 317 contains information on three openly-available MIME implementations. For now, we'll look at one, *multi-media MH*.

To modify MH to use MIME, three changes were made:

- the display facility was modified to look for a `Content-Type:` header, and if something other than a `text/plain` content is present (or if the content is transfer-encoded), then a special program, `mhn`, is invoked to display the electronic mail message;

- the composition facility was modified to automatically fragment large messages, as a user option; and,

- a simple multi-media composition editor was created.

In addition, a facility to transfer directory hierarchies was added. Let's now consider each of these in turn.

The `mhn` program is used to manipulate a multi-media electronic mail message. On the author's desktop,

```
% mhn -help
```

yields the output shown in Figure 6.20 on page 244.

This is not nearly as daunting as one might suspect, particularly since MH programs often automatically invoke `mhn` on the user's behalf.

`mhn` has three modes: `list` (generate a table of contents), `show` (render content values), and `store` (write content values in native format). Although `show` is the default mode, the user can select any combinations of the modes. The `+folder` and `msgs` arguments have the usual MH meaning: they select the electronic mail messages to be processed.

Normally `mhn` will operate on the content of each of the named messages. However, by using the `-part number` and `-type content` switches, the scope of `mhn`'s operation can be focused on particular components (of a `multipart` content) and/or particular content types.

A part specification consists of a series of numbers separated by dots. For example, in a `multipart` content containing three parts,these

```
% mhn -help
syntax: mhn [+folder] [msgs] [switches]
  switches are:
  -[no]auto
  -[no]ebcdicsafe
  -(form) formfile
  -[no]headers
  -[no]list
  -part number
  -[no]realsize
  -[no]rfc934mode
  -[no]serialonly
  -[no]show
  -[no]store
  -type content
  -[no]verbose
  -(help)

version: MH 6.7.4a #7[UCI] (dbc) of Fri Mar 27 07:57:55 PST 1992
options: [APOP='"/etc/pop.auth"'] [BIND] [BPOP] [BSD42] [BSD43]
        [MHE] [POP] [POPSERVICE='"pop3"'] [RPATHS] [SENDMTS]
        [SMTP] [SUN40] [TYPESIG=void] [UCI] [WHATNOW] [ZMAILER]
```

Figure 6.20: Getting Help from MH's mhn

would be named as 1, 2, and 3, respectively. If part 2 was also a `multipart` content containing two parts, these would be named as 2.1 and 2.2, respectively. (Take a look at Figure 6.11 back on page 226 for an example.) Note that the `-part` switch is effective only for messages containing a `multipart` content. If a message has some other kind of content, or if the part is itself another `multipart` content, the `-part` switch will not prevent the content from being acted upon.

A content specification is given using the standard MIME notation; i.e., the type and subtype are separated by a solidus-character ("/"). Although in MIME, subtypes are mandatory, this needn't be true for a content specification. To specify a content, regardless of its subtype, we just use the name of the content, e.g., `audio`. Note that regardless of the values given to the `-type` switch, a `multipart` content is always acted upon. Further note that if the `-type` switch is used, and it is desirable to act on a `message/external-body` content, then the `-type` switch must be used twice: both for the content which is being externally referenced and for the `message/external-body` content.

Recall from Section 3.2.1 that each user of MH maintains a profile which contains default values for each MH command. Because the display environment in which `mhn` operates may vary for a user, `mhn` will look for the environment variable `$MHN`. If present, this specifies the name of an additional user profile which should be read. Hence, when a user logs in on a particular display device, this environment variable should be set to refer to a file containing definitions useful for that display device. Normally, only entries controlling the rendering of content values need be present. Finally, `mhn` will attempt to consult one additional user profile, which is created by the system-administrator.

Generating a Table of Contents

The `-list` switch tells `mhn` to list the table of contents associated with the named messages. The `-headers` switch indicates that a one-line banner should be displayed above the listing. The `-realsize` switch tells `mhn` to evaluate the "native" (decoded) format of each content prior to listing. This provides an accurate count at the expense of a (hopefully) small delay.

```
msg part  type/subtype           size description
     2     multipart/mixed        61K The Simple Times
        1  multipart/mixed       1678 Issue Information
      1.1  text/plain             314 Masthead
      1.2  text/plain             373 READ-ME
      1.3  text/plain             668 Disclaimer
        2  multipart/mixed        56K Issue Contents
      2.1  text/plain             13K Technical Article
      2.2  text/plain            6045 Industry Comment
      2.3  multipart/mixed        35K Featured Columns
    2.3.1  text/plain            7556 Applications and Directions
    2.3.2  text/plain            4037 Ask Dr. SNMP
    2.3.3  text/plain            7006 Security and Protocols
    2.3.4  text/plain            9163 Standards
    2.3.5  text/plain            7773 Working Group Synopses
      2.4  multipart/mixed       1749 Miscellany
    2.4.1  text/plain            1199 Recent Publications
    2.4.2  text/plain             306 Activities Calendar
        3  multipart/mixed       3046 Administrative Information
      3.1  text/plain            1071 Publication Information
      3.2  text/plain            1138 Submissions
      3.3  text/plain             481 Subscriptions Information
```

Figure 6.21: Table of Contents for an issue of *The Simple Times*

Actually, this facility is more useful than it might seem. For example, the author is the coordinating editor of an openly-available publication on Internet network management, *The Simple Times* [65], which is available both via hard-copy and electronic mail. The latter is available in two editions: either **PostScript** or MIME. The vast majority of each issue of the newsletter is simple text, but it is still worthwhile to use the `multipart` content in order to provide structure. Figure 6.21 shows an example of the table of contents for the first issue.

One could easily imagine writing a **UNIX** shell script which prints the table of contents and then asks the user which parts should be displayed. Figure 6.22 starting on page 247 shows the script that the author uses.

```
: run this script through /bin/sh

C=/tmp/st$$.ctx L=/tmp/st$$.lst P=/tmp/st$$.prf

trap "rm -f $C $L $P" 0 1 2 3 13 15

echo "MH-Sequences:" > $P
cat ${MH-$HOME/.mh_profile} >> $P
MH="$P" export MH
cp ${MHCONTEXT-`mhpath +`/context} $C
MHCONTEXT="$C" export MHCONTEXT

F= M= N=
for A in $*
do
    case "$A" in
        -file)  if [ ! -z "$F" -o ! -z "$M" ]; then
                    echo "showtimes: do not mix files and messages" 1>&2
                    exit 1
                fi
                F="-file" N="file "
                ;;

        +*|@*)  if [ ! -z "$F" ]; then
                    echo "showtimes: only one folder at a time" 1>&2
                    exit 1
                fi
                F="$A" N="$F:"
                ;;

        *)      if [ ! -z "$M" ]; then
                    echo "showtimes: only one message at a time" 1>&2
                    exit 1
                fi
                M="$A"
                ;;
    esac
done

if mhn -list $F $M > $L; then
    if [ -z "$F" ]; then
        N="+`folder -fast`:"
    fi
    if [ -z "$M" ]; then
        M="`mhpath cur`"
        M="`basename $M`"
    fi
else
    exit 1;
fi

cat $L
```

Figure 6.22: The "showtimes" Script

```
X=0 Y=0
Z=`xdpyinfo | fgrep 'dimensions:'| awk '{ print $2; }'`
XX="`echo $Z | sed -e 's%\(.*\)x.*%\1%'`"
YY="`echo $Z | sed -e 's%.*x\(.*\)%\1%'`"
XX="`expr \( $XX \* 5 \) / 12`"
YY="`expr \( $YY \* 2 \) / 3`"

echo -n "st> "
while read A; do
    case "$A" in
        [123456789]*|0)
                O="`fgrep \ $A\  $L | \
sed -e 's%.......................................\(.*\)%\1%'`"
                if [ -z "$O" ]; then
                    echo "no such part number"
                else
                    xterm -geometry =80x20+$X+$Y \
                        -title "$O (part $A of $N$M)" -e \
                        mhn -nolist -show -part "$A" $F $M &

                    X=`expr $X + 90` Y=`expr $Y + 60`
                    if [ $X -gt $XX ]; then
                        X=0
                    fi
                    if [ $Y -gt $YY ]; then
                        Y=0
                    fi
                fi
                ;;

        list|"")
                cat $L
                ;;

        *)      echo "enter part number to display"
                ;;
    esac
    echo -n "st> "
done
echo ""

exit 0
```

Figure 6.22: The "showtimes" Script (cont.)

The invocation of the script is:

```
% showtimes [+folder] [msg]
```

The script begins by setting up a transient MH environment for the user. It then looks at any arguments supplied by the user. Following this, at the end of the figure on page 247, `mhn` is invoked to generate a table of contents for the message, and this is displayed to the user.

On the next page, the script, which expects to be running on an **X Window System** desktop, finds out how large the screen is. The script now enters an input loop, prompting with:

```
st>
```

If the user enters a part number, then a new window will be created, and positioned on a different portion of the screen. Otherwise, the table of contents is listed again. This continues until the user enters the end-of-file character, at which point the script exits.

Whenever a new window is displayed, its title bar is initialized accordingly. For example, if the user enters:

```
st> 2.3.2
```

then the title of window would be:

```
Ask Dr. SNMP (part 2.3.2 of +inbox:2)
```

Rendering Content Values

The `-show` switch tells `mhn` to display the contents of the named messages. The headers of the message are displayed with `mhl` (introduced back on page 3.3.2), using a format file which will show only the headers of the message. (The choice of format file can be overridden by the `-form formfile` switch.)

`mhn` actually knows very little about rendering content values. In fact, the only content type it explicitly deals with is `multipart`. For the rest, `mhn` will look for information in the user's profile to determine how the different contents should be displayed. This is accomplished by consulting a display string, and executing it under the **UNIX** shell,

with the command's input set to the content value. The display string
may contain these escapes:

%-escape	action
%a	insert content parameter list
%e	exclusive execution
%f	insert filename containing content value
%F	%e, %f, and command reads from user's terminal
%l	display table of contents prior to displaying content value
%p	%l, and ask for confirmation
%s	insert content subtype

For those display strings containing the %e or %F escapes, mhn will
execute at most one of these at any given time. Although the %F-escape
expands to be the filename containing the content value, the %e-escape
has no expansion as far as the shell is concerned.

First, mhn will look for an entry of the form:

```
mhn-show-<type>/<subtype>
```

to determine the command to use to display the content. If this isn't
found, mhn will look for an entry of the form:

```
mhn-show-<type>
```

to determine the display command. If this isn't found, mhn has two
default values:

```
mhn-show-text/plain: %pmoreproc %F
mhn-show-message/rfc822: %pshow -file %F
```

which are standard MH commands. If neither applies, mhn will check
to see if the message has an application/octet-stream content with
parameter type=tar. If so, mhn will use an appropriate command. If
not, mhn will complain.

Example entries might be:

```
mhn-show-application/PostScript: lpr -Pps
mhn-show-audio/basic: raw2audio 2>/dev/null | play
mhn-show-image: xv %f
mhn-show-text/richtext: richtext -p %F
```

Finally, `mhn` will process each message serially — it won't start showing the next message until all the commands executed to display the current message have terminated. In the case of a content type of `multipart/parallel`, parallel rendering might cause confusion, particularly on uni-window displays. The `-serialonly` switch can be given to tell `mhn` to always display parts in serial.

Storing Content Values

The `-store` switch tells `mhn` to store the contents of the named messages in "native" (decoded) format. Two things must be determined: the directory to store the content, and the filenames. Files are written in the directory given by the **mhn-storage** profile entry, e.g.,

```
mhn-storage: /tmp
```

If this entry isn't present, the user's current directory is used.

    `mhn` will look for information in the user's profile to determine how the different contents should be stored. This is achieved through the use of a formatting string, which may contain these escapes:

%-escape	action
%m	insert message number
%P	insert "." followed by part number
%p	insert part number
%s	insert content subtype

If the content isn't part of a multipart content, the %p-escapes are ignored. Note that if the formatting string starts with a "+" character, then these escapes are ignored, and the content is stored in the named folder. (A formatting string consisting solely of a "+" character indicates the current folder.)

First, mhn will look for an entry of the form:

```
mhn-store-<type>/<subtype>
```

to determine the formatting string. If this isn't found, mhn will look for an entry of the form:

```
mhn-store-<type>
```

to determine the formatting string. If this isn't found, mhn will check to see if the content is application/octet-stream with parameter type=tar. If so, mhn will choose an appropriate filename. If the content is not application/octet-stream, then mhn will check to see if the content is a message. If so, mhn will use the value "+". If not, mhn will use the value "%m%P.%s".

Note that if the formatting string starts with a "/", then content will be stored in the full path given (rather than using the value of mhn-storage or the user's current directory.) Similarly, if the formatting string starts with a "|", then mhn will execute a command which should ultimately store the content. Note that before executing the command, mhn will change to the appropriate directory. Also note that if the formatting string starts with the "|" character, then mhn will also honor the %a-escape when processing the formatting string.

Example entries might be:

```
mhn-store-text: %m%P.txt
mhn-store-audio/basic: |raw2audio -e ulaw -s 8000 -c 1 > %m%P.au
mhn-store-application/PostScript: %m%P.ps
```

Further note that when asked to store a content containing a partial message, mhn will try to locate all of the fragments and combine them accordingly. Thus, when all of the fragments are collected, they could all be put in their own folder and the command:

```
% mhn all -store
```

would be issued. This will store exactly one message, containing the sum of the fragments. Note that if mhn cannot locate each fragment, it will not store anything. Finally, if the -auto switch is given and the content type contains a name parameter (and if the parameter value doesn't begin with a "/"), then the content value will be stored according to the parameter value.

```
body        ::= 1*(content / LF)

content     ::= directive / plaintext

directive ::= "#"  type "/" subtype 0*(";" parameter)
                 comment description [filename]              LF
            / "#@" type "/" subtype 0*(";" parameter)
                 comment description external                LF
            / "#forw"  description ["+"folder] [0*msg]        LF
            / "#begin" description ["alternative" / "parallel"] LF
              1*body
              "#end" LF

comment     ::= ["(" comment ")"]
description
            ::= ["[" description "]"]

plaintext ::= ["Content-Description:" *text LF LF]
              1*line
              ["#" LF]

line        ::= "##" *text LF          ; interpreted as ("#" *text LF)
            / *text LF

text        ::= <any character excluding LF>
```

Figure 6.23: mhn Composition Syntax

Composing Multi-Media Messages

The **mhn** program can also be used as a simple editor to aid in composing multi-media messages. The syntax of an **mhn** composition file is shown in Figure 6.23. (This figure uses the BNF defined in Figures 6.5 and 6.8 on pages 213 and 221, respectively.)

Basically, the body contains one or more contents. A content consists of either a directive, indicated with a "#" as the first character of a line; or, plaintext (one or more lines of text). Plaintext is gathered, until a directive is found or the composition file is exhausted, and this is made to form a **text/plain** content. If the plaintext must contain a "#" at the beginning of a line, the usual byte-stuffing technique is used, e.g.,

```
##when sent, this line will start with only one #
```

To have two plaintext contents adjacent, a line containing a single "#" is used as a separator, e.g.,

```
this is the first content
#
and this is the second
```

Finally, if the plaintext starts with a line of the form:

```
Content-Description: text
```

followed by a blank line, then this will be used to construct the obvious header.

There are four kinds of directives:

- *type* directives, which name the type and subtype of the content;

- *external-type* directives, which also name the type and subtype of the content, but are used to form a `message/external-body` content;

- the *forw* directive, which is used to forward a digest of messages as a `multipart/digest` content; and,

- the *begin* directive, which is used to create a `multipart` content.

For each of these directives, text encapsulated between the "[" and "]" characters will be used to form a `Content-Description:` header. Similarly, text encapsulated between the "(" and ")" characters will be used to form a comment string which is appended to the `Content-Type:` header.

For the *type* directives, the user may optionally specify the name of a file containing the contents in "native" format. (If the filename starts with the "|" character, then this gives a command whose output is captured accordingly.) If a filename is not given, `mhn` will look for information in the user's profile to determine how the different contents should be composed. This is accomplished by consulting a composition

string, and executing it under the UNIX shell with the command's input
set to the content. The composition string may contain these escapes:

%-escape	action
%a	insert content parameter list
%f	insert filename containing content value
%F	%f, and command reads from user's terminal
%s	insert content subtype

First, **mhn** will look for an entry of the form:

```
mhn-compose-<type>/<subtype>
```

to determine the command to use to compose the content. If this isn't
found, **mhn** will look for an entry of the form:

```
mhn-compose-<type>
```

to determine the composition command. If this isn't found, **mhn** will
complain.

An example entry might be:

```
mhn-compose-audio/basic: record | raw2audio -F
```

Because commands like these will vary, depending on the display environment used for login, composition strings for different contents should
probably be put in the file specified by the $MHN environment variable,
instead of directly in the user profile.

The *external-type* directives are used to provide a reference to a
content, rather than enclosing the contents itself. Hence, instead of
providing a filename as with the type directives, external-parameters
are supplied. These look like regular parameters, so they must be
separated accordingly, e.g.,

```
#@application/octet-stream; type=tar [] access-type=ftp; ...
```

By specifying "[]", an empty description string is given, and the start
of the external parameters is identified.

For the *forw* directive, the user may optionally specify the name of
the folder and which messages are to be forwarded. If a folder is not
given, it defaults to the current folder. Similarly, if a message is not

given, it defaults to the current message. Usage of the -rfc934mode
switch indicates whether mhn should attempt to utilize the encapsulation rules in such a way that it appears as if the older mechanism
specified in [45] (and discussed earlier on page 102) is being used.

For the *begin* directive, the user must specify at least one content
between the begin and end pairs.

After mhn reads the composition file, it constructs the equivalent
MIME message. mhn selects a Content-Transfer-Encoding: value
based on the content:

- if the content is multipart or message, then 7bit is used;

- if the content is text/plain with a charset parameter value of
  us-ascii, then 7bit is used;

- if the content is any other kind of text, then quoted-printable
  is used;

- if the content isn't application/postscript, then base64 is
  used;

- if the repertoire is NVT ASCII and each line is less than or equal
  to 78 characters in length, then 7bit is used; otherwise,

- quoted-printable is used.

For the quoted-printable encoding, the -ebcdicsafe switch indicates
whether the recommended characters listed in Figure 6.18 back on
page 238 should be quoted.

Figure 6.24 shows an example of an mhn composition file that might
have produced the electronic mail message which corresponds to the
table of contents shown in the figure on page 226.[6] One might imagine
that the file preamble.rt contained the content value shown in the
figure on page 230, and that the file epilogue.rt contained the content
value shown in the figure on page 231.

---

[6]Truth in advertising requires that the author disclose two facts: first, the
message was not generated using this method — this is only an example; and,
second, this figure isn't even syntactically correct: the author had to wrap the two
lines containing the *external-type* directives in order to render them properly in the
book.

```
#begin alternative
#begin
#text/richtext [] preamble.rt
#@audio/basic [Let Me Sing You Email (audio)] \
    access-type="anon-ftp"; site="thumper.bellcore.com"; \
    directory="pub/nsb"; name="quartet.au"

#@image/gif [The Telephone Chords, A Moment Immortalized] \
    access-type="anon-ftp"; site="thumper.bellcore.com"; \
    directory="pub/nsb"; name="quartet.gif"
#text/richtext [] epilogue.rt
#end
Those of you not running MIME-compliant mail readers won't get a lot
out of this, nor will those without ftp access to the Internet, but
for the lucky few....

Here are the infamous Telephone Chords, the world's premier (=only)
all-Bellcore barbershop quartet, singing about MIME.  Note that
because the "message/external-body" MIME construct is used, this
whole message is only about 3000 bytes -- at least, until you start
reading it. :-) [An Andrew ToolKit view (mailobjv) was included
here, but could not be displayed.][An Andrew ToolKit view (mailobjv)
was included here, but could not be displayed.]  Left to right:
                        John Lamb, bass
                      David Braun, baritone
                      Michael Littman, lead
                   Nathaniel Borenstein, tenor
#end
```

Figure 6.24: Example mhn Composition File

It must be emphasized that this composition format needn't be understood by humans. Rather, a higher-level program could accept input from the user in a friendlier fashion and construct a `mhn` composition file accordingly.

For the author's desktop, MH is configured so that each and every message is sent out as a MIME message. If only plain text is present, then the default headers:

```
MIME-Version: 1.0
Content-Type: text/plain; charset=us-ascii
```

are used.

6.1.5 Relationship of MIME to Other RFCs

Earlier we noted that MIME is orthogonal to RFC-822, as the former describes the structure of the bodies of electronic mail messages in the Internet community, and the latter describes the structure of the headers. Because MIME provides a comprehensive framework for message bodies, it renders obsolete three RFCs:

RFC 934: "Proposed Standard for Message Encapsulation"

> MIME's `multipart` content type provides superior functionality and robustness, with only a slight increase in complexity for the originator of a message.

RFC 1049: "A Content-Type Header Field for Internet Messages"

> MIME's `Content-Type:` header is a largely compatible extension to this original work.

RFC 1154: "Encoding Header Field for Internet Messages"

> MIME's `Content-Transfer-Encoding:` header provides superior functionality and robustness, with only a modest increase in the encoding of content values.

It should be noted that only the second of these was ever on the Internet standards-track. The first is informational, and the third is experimental.

6.1.6 Message Transfer Agent use of MIME

With the introduction of MIME into the Internet community, there is renewed interest in working on message transfer agents. For example, use of MIME could provide a framework for:

- providing a well-structured format for error reports, by defining a new content type, e.g., `multipart/error-report`;

- automatic fragmentation of an electronic mail message when it reaches a message transfer agent which limits the size of the messages it carries;

- automatic translation of content types likely to be more useful to a recipient; and,

- automatic storage of content types likely to be of interest to a group of recipients.

Although the author is somewhat skeptical of some of these ideas, as of this writing, only initial discussions of these topics are underway. Perhaps some might bear fruit.

6.2   Non-NVT ASCII Headers

In addition to the work on multi-media message bodies, a specification has been developed to allow for the inclusion of characters in electronic mail message headers which are not part of the NVT ASCII repertoire [66]. As with MIME, the specification encodes the characters in such a way that they appear to be NVT ASCII from the perspective of naive message transfer agents and user agents.

The syntax used to encode non-NVT ASCII headers is shown in Figure 6.25. (The definition of `charset` comes from Figure 6.12 on page 229, and many other definitions come from Figure 3.2 on page 80.)

The impact on the headers of an electronic mail message is as follows:

- The syntax of the `Subject:` and `Comment:` headers, defined in Figure 3.9 on page 95, has been updated, along with the syntax of the `Content-Description:` header defined in Figure 6.19 on page 242.

  In general, any header with a syntax of `*text` can now use `encoded-words` instead.

- The definition of the `comment` production supersedes that in Figure 3.2 on page 80.

- Similarly, the definition of the `phrase` production, used as a commentary name for electronic mailbox addresses, supersedes that in Figure 3.6 on page 90. This production is used for headers like `To:`, `From:`, and the like. (Consult page 91 for a discussion of this production.)

The rules are fairly simple: An `encoded-word` refers to a collection of characters which encodes text from a particular character set. An `encoded-word` is limited to 75 characters in length, so if the text to be encoded is longer than that, multiple `encoded-word`s are used, separated by `LWSP`. When rendered, two or more adjacent `encoded-word`s are displayed without any separating white-space.

```
headers    ::= "Subject"             ":" *text / encoded-words
             / "Comment"             ":" *text / encoded-words
             / "Content-Description" ":" *text / encoded-words

comment    ::= "(" *(ctext / quoted-pair / comment
                         / encoded-words) ")"

phrase     ::= 1*(word / encoded-phrases)


           ; when rendered, LWSP is ignored
encoded-words
           ::= encoded-word *(LWSP encoded-word)
encoded-phrases
           ::= encoded-phrases *(LWSP encoded-phrases)


           ; no embedded white-space allowed
           ; maximum length is 75 characters from "=?" to "?="
encoded-word
           ::= "=?" charset "?" ("B" / "Q") "?"
               (*base64 /      *quoted) "?="
encoded-phrase
           ::= "=?" charset "?" ("B" / "Q") "?"
               (*base64 / *more-quoted) "?="

quoted     ::= octet
             / <any character except "=", "?", "_", SPACE, or TAB>


more-quoted
           ::= octet / mtext
mtext      ::= ALPHA / DIGIT / "!" / "+" / "-" / "/"


           ; must be used when 8th-bit is set, "=", "?", "_", SPACE,
           ;   or TAB
           ; for quoted, may be used for any other character
           ; for more-quoted, must be used for anything other than
           ;   mtext
octet      ::= "=" 2(DIGIT / "A" / "B" / "C" / "D" / "E" / "F")

base64     ::= ALPHA / DIGIT / "+" / "/"
```

Figure 6.25: Encoding non-NVT ASCII Headers Syntax

```
To: =?ISO-8859-1?Q?Keld_J=F8rn_Simonsen?= <keld@dkuug.dk>
cc: =?ISO-8859-1?Q?Andr=E9_?= Pirard <PIRARD@vm1.ulg.ac.be>
Subject: =?ISO-8859-1?B?SWYgeW91IGNhbiByZWFkIHRoaXMgeW8=?=
         =?ISO-8859-2?B?dSB1bmRlcnN0YW5kIHRoZSBleGFtcGxlLg==?=
From: =?US-ASCII?Q?Keith_Moore?= <moore@cs.utk.edu>
```

Figure 6.26: An Example of Encoded Headers

Each **encode-word** contains three components:

charset: which indicates the character set being used, such as
   `iso-8859-1`;

B / Q: which indicates whether `base64` or `quoted-printable`
   encoding is used; and,

an encoding: which is the collection of encoded characters.

There are two tricky parts when using the `quoted-printable` encoding:

- first, spaces are always encoded, either as an underscore-character
  ("_") or as "=20"; and,

- second, if the `encoded-word` occurs as a **phrase** within an address
  specification, then virtually all non-alphanumeric characters must
  be expressed in `octet` notation.

The reason for the first part is to enhance readability; the reason for the
second is to minimize the likelihood of problems with non-conformant
message transfer agents.

Figure 6.26 shows an example of some encoded headers, whilst
Figure 6.27 shows how they would be displayed to the user.

To: Keld Jørn Simonsen <keld@dkuug.dk>
cc: André Pirard <PIRARD@vm1.ulg.ac.be>
Subject: If you can read this you understand the example.
From: Keith Moore <moore@cs.utk.edu>

Figure 6.27: An Example of Displaying Encoded Headers

6.3   Technology Comparison

In MHS, the message transfer service is designed to handle multiple kinds of *contents*, each corresponding to a particular kind of electronic messaging activity. Each content is effectively a messaging protocol. Of these, the *interpersonal message service* (IPMS) (either P_2 or P_{22} depending on whether one is referring to the 1984 or 1988 version) is used for the general exchange of electronic mail. In theory, IPMS is more capable than its Internet counterpart, RFC-822, because MHS messages are defined using a formal language and are unambiguously encoded.

An IPMS content consists of a *heading* and one or more *body parts*. The heading contains such information as:

- a message identifier, which is used by the UA when processing the message;

- the MHS address of the originator;

- a list of primary (To:) recipients;

- a list of copy (cc:) recipients;

- a list of blind copy (Bcc:) recipients, whose addresses do not appear in the heading when it is submitted, but who nevertheless appear as recipients in the submission envelope;

- a textual subject field;

- a list of addresses that should receive any reply; and,

- cross-referencing information, such as the identifier of the message to which this is a reply.

The body parts provide for a range of different kinds of information, such as text, voice, facsimile, forwarded messages, and so on. In addition, the IPM service allows user-definable body parts. This contains information identifying the body part type and then contains the actual contents.

Despite the theoretical advantages of using highly-structured mech- | soap... |
anisms for defining and representing electronic mail messages, IPMS
has few, if any, real advantages over Internet electronic mail messages.
Here's why:

To begin with, the definitions of the various pre-defined body parts
are insufficent for interoperable behavior. Look at the voice body
part for example; its definition contains no information whatsoever
regarding the digitization scheme being used. As a result, any given
implementation of the voice body part will almost certainly not be able
to interoperate with any other independent implementation. In fact,
if you go down the list of pre-defined body parts, there are only three
which are sufficiently well-defined for interoperable behavior: ASCII
text, forwarded messages, and (perhaps) Group 3 facsimile.

Second, very few MHS user agents have facilities to display or
compose body parts other than those containing text or forwarded
messages. Perhaps this is due to the lack of well-defined body parts.
More likely, the answer lies in the fact that it is easily an order of
magnitude harder to implement an MHS user agent because of all the
structuring and the like. Certainly all the MHS user agents that the
author has seen are tremendously immature compared to their Internet
counterparts.

Third, remember the soapbox on MHS addressing back on page 74?
Well, MHS addresses have another flaw: the syntax of virtually every
attribute you can put in an MHS address is derived from either a
string of digits (the numeric string repertoire), or the printable string
repertoire (which is a subset of ASCII). So, an MHS address can't have
national character sets in things like surname, firstname, and so on.
(Remember, MHS is an "International" Standard.)

So, what we end up with is an IPMS that is less functional, capable,
and useful than the creaky old RFC-822. In fact, with the introduction
of MIME and the ability to encode non-NVT ASCII headers, Internet
mail has considerable more multi-media capability than MHS (e.g.,
there is no recursive `multipart` capability in IPMS, other than forwarding IPMS contents). Further, this capability was introduced in a
way which does not perturb the installed base — unlike MHS which
pretty much requires that you scrap your existing message transfer
system and install something else.

A few years ago, whenever the author would press a proponent of MHS as to why MHS was a good thing, they would inevitably find themselves limited to two reasons: MHS is multi-media, and MHS is an *International Standard.* Well, the last eight years of experience with MHS has shown that it doesn't deliver multi-media. As for the second reason, the author's response is to note that the Internet-standards are far more responsive to the International community than International Standards are.

The sad part is that the MIME effort will probably prolong the still-born delivery of MHS. Here's why: in the market,

> *the living evolve, the intransient die*

Despite their ever-shrinking numbers, there are still some "OSI intransients" out there who firmly believe that MHS is the way, the truth, and the one true light. With MIME available, it's going to be a lot easier to build near-transparent gateways between the Internet mail and MHS. This means that the intransients have gotten some breathing room. But, every dark cloud has its silver lining: outside of the dubious argument dealing with administrative fiat, proponents of Internet mail now have greater functionality to offer their users, functionality which is clearly superior to MHS, and yet which doesn't interfere with the

`...soap` installed base!

Chapter 7

Privacy-Enhanced Mail

Thus far, we've seen how electronic mail messages in the Internet are exchanged as plaintext or "in the clear". That is, when a message is sent, it is possible for a third-party, either an intermediate message transfer agent, or an eavesdropper, to observe the message as it transits the message transfer system.

In this chapter, we introduce the mechanism, *Privacy-Enhanced Mail* (PEM), by which Internet electronic mail messages may be exchanged so that third-parties are unable to observe, alter, or forge messages.

Unfortunately, these mechanisms are currently undergoing revision. Although the current revisions are fairly stable, as of this writing, they have not yet been published as RFCs. Further, the current RFCs describing PEM have been re-labeled as historical. Hence, the author runs the risk of being highly topical if he writes in detail about either the current, obsolete RFCs or the revised, but not-yet RFCs. Therefore, *The Internet Message* can present only a high-level discussion.

7.1   Overview

There are many security environments that one could imagine for a message handling system. For example, one could attempt to secure the entire message transfer system by securing each message transfer agent and the links between them. However, such an approach has three problems:

- the bootstrapping problem would be horrendous, owing to the large number of existing message transfer agents;

- depending on the security measures required, scaling could be problematic; and,

- such an approach would not necessarily provide protection once an electronic mail message left the message transfer system, as the link between a user agent and its local message transfer agent might be insecure.

This has led many to believe that a more pragmatic security environment is one in which the user agents are solely responsible for providing security-related facilities. Of course, such an approach has its limits, e.g., user agents cannot control routing within the message transfer system. But, experience has shown in situations where it's

some now or all later

that the former approach always wins out.

7.1.1   Design Criteria

With this in mind, let's ask ourselves what security facilities may be available if the user agents are solely responsible. There are four:

message privacy: preventing a third-party from being able to examine the body of an electronic mail message.

originator authenticity: preventing a third-party from being able to forge some other party's identity in an electronic mail message.

message integrity: preventing a third-party from altering an electronic mail message in transit.

originator non-repudiation: preventing the originator of an electronic mail message from falsely denying having it.

The latter service may not be available, depending on the kind of cryptographic mechanisms used.

However, there are also a number of other desirable facilities that are not likely to be obtainable:

sequenced message delivery: preventing a third-party from inserting, replaying, or deleting electronic mail messages from the message exchange between two user agents.

message receipt assurance: ensuring that an electronic mail message is ultimately delivered to its recipient and that a confirmation message is returned to the originator.

denial of service: preventing an unauthorized third-party from congesting the message transfer system so that user agents are unable to communicate.

access control: ensuring that only authorized pairs of user agents are allowed to communicate using the message transfer system.

routing control: preventing an unauthorized third-party from altering the path which electronic mail messages transit through the message transfer system, including changing the recipient which ultimately receives the message. (Of course, if encrypted, the actual recipient will be unable to decipher the message.)

traffic flow confidentiality: preventing a third-party from learning the identities of communicating user agents, along with the amount, frequency, and duration of traffic between them.

Note that even if the message transfer agents were to participate in providing security-related facilities, it isn't clear whether all of these services could be provided.

7.2   Writing Privacy Enhanced Messages

The top-level BNF specification of a privacy-enhanced electronic mail
message is shown in Figure 7.1.[1] A privacy-enhanced message is placed
in the body of an electronic mail message, using the encapsulation
scheme introduced earlier in Section 3.3.1 on page 102.

A privacy-enhanced message consists of headers, possibly followed
by another body. When a user sends an electronic mail message using
privacy-enhancement, there are actually three nested messages:

exterior message: This is the message which is submitted to
the local message transfer agent. The body of this message
consists of a privacy-enhanced message, corresponding to the
pem production in Figure 7.1.

privacy-enhanced message: This is the message which contains
the information that provides privacy-enhanced services.
The body of this message, if present, is termed by the
author the *interior message*.

interior message: This is the message which is available to the
originator before privacy-enhanced services are invoked, and
is available to the recipient after these services have been
completed.

---

[1]This definition is derived from an (as yet) unpublished revision of the current
PEM RFCs. Although this revision appears to be stable, readers should consult
the current RFCs for the actual definition.

```
pem        ::= "-----BEGIN PRIVACY-ENHANCED MESSAGE-----"        CRLF
               (encrypted / miconly / micclear / crl)
               "-----BEGIN PRIVACY-ENHANCED MESSAGE-----"        CRLF

encrypted ::=      "Proc-Type"                    ":" "4" ","
                                                      "ENCRYPTED"  CRLF
                   "DEK-Info"                     ":" dekalg ","
                                                      16HEX        CRLF
                   (symmetric / asymmetric)
                   [CRLF *(1*16base64 CRLF)]

miconly    ::=     "Proc-Type"                    ":" "4" ","
                                                      "MIC-ONLY"   CRLF
                   (symmetric / asymmetric)
                   [CRLF *(1*16base64 CRLF)]


micclear ::=       "Proc-Type"                    ":" "4" ","
                                                      "MIC-CLEAR"  CRLF
                   (symmetric / asymmetric)
                   [CRLF *(*text CRLF)]

crl        ::=     "Proc-Type"                    ":" "4" "," "CRL" CRLF
               1*( "CRL"                          ":" btext         CRLF
                   ["Originator-Certificate" ":" btext         CRLF]
                   *("Issuer-Certificate"    ":" btext         CRLF))
```

Figure 7.1: Privacy-Enhanced Message Top-level Syntax

7.2.1   Privacy-Enhanced Messages

All privacy-enhanced messages start with the `Proc-Type:` header which identifies the privacy-enhancement version in use ("4") and the kind of message. (The first part of the `Proc-Type:` value is analogous to the value of the `MIME-Version:` header introduced earlier in Section 6.1.3 on page 242.)

There are four kinds of messages:

encrypted: the body contains an electronic mail message, in which all four facilities described earlier in Section 7.1.1, are provided.

mic-only: the body contains an electronic mail message, in which originator authenticity and message integrity are provided, however only user agents which are PEM-capable will be able to automatically view the message.

mic-clear: the body contains an electronic mail message, in which originator authenticity and message integrity are provided; any user agent will be able to view the message, but only PEM-capable user agents will be able to verify the authenticity and integrity of the message.

certificate revocation: this tells a user agent that a certification authority has revoked one or more certificates which the user agent might have knowledge of.

Syntax of PEM Headers

The headers of a privacy-enhanced message follow the `LWSP` convention from RFC-822. This means that lengthy header fields can be split onto multiple lines, provided that each subsequent line starts with whitespace.

Before delving into how the services are provided by privacy-enhanced messaging, we need to consider briefly how the exterior and interior messages are viewed.

7.2.2 Exterior Messages

The exterior message must be transmitted in plaintext form to minimize the impact on message transfer agents. Any information of a confidential nature, such as a `Subject:` header, should be placed in the interior message. Hence, the headers of the exterior message will usually be quite minimal.

7.2.3 Interior Messages

The interior message is simply an Internet message, formatted according to RFC-822. This means that before the privacy-enhanced functions in the user agent can be invoked, the message must be represented using the NVT ASCII repertoire (just as if the message were being transmitted using SMTP or POP). If message privacy is desired, then the interior message is transformed into a ciphertext form, which is a string of octets. In this case, the `base64` encoding introduced back on page 238 is used to represent the ciphertext form using the NVT ASCII repertoire. Even if message privacy is not desired, it may be useful to represent the interior message using the `base64` encodings — doing so will make the interior message immune from translation.

Looking back at Figure 7.1 on page 271, we can intuit the different transformations which occur when an interior message is processed:

encrypted: ciphertext form represented using `base64`;

mic-only: plaintext form represented using `base64`; and,

mic-clear: plaintext form represented using NVT ASCII.

7.2.4   PEM and MIME

As an aside, one might wonder why Privacy-Enhanced Mail doesn't use MIME. After all, if one were to define an `application/pem` content type which contained a privacy-enhanced content, then some of this structuring simply would be "free".

As might be imagined, the definition of such a content type is straight-forward: it resembles an RFC-822 message, except that only two kinds of headers are present:

- privacy-enhanced headers; and,

- content-type headers, identifying the form of the interior message (probably `message/rfc822`), and the content transfer encoding, (probably `base64`).

Such an approach has the advantage of allowing Privacy-Enhanced Mail to transfer arbitrary content-types, not just RFC-822 messages.

The reason for this lack of synchronization appears to be historical, and may perhaps even be corrected by the time before you read *The Internet Message*!

7.3   PEM Concepts

The security facilities of Privacy-Enhanced Mail are based on the judicious application of cryptographic algorithms and the management of the keys used as parameters to those algorithms.

The author is a messaging user, not a security professional, and desires to minimize his involvement with security technology. So, for the purposes of discussion in *The Internet Message*, only very minimal treatment of these topics will be given.

7.3.1   Algorithms

In the context of Privacy-Enhanced Mail, cryptographic algorithms are used for three purposes, data encryption, message integrity, and key encryption.

Because cryptographic algorithms are constantly being scrutinized, it is important that Privacy-Enhanced Mail be extensible in its ability to support different algorithms. We now consider the various algorithms currently defined.

Data Encryption

If the message privacy service is desired, the NVT ASCII representation of the interior message is passed through a data encryption algorithm.

At present, only a single algorithm, `DES-CBC` is defined for this purpose. This uses the *cipher block chaining* (CBC) mode of the U.S. Federal Data Encryption Standard (DES) [67, 68]. Because the input to this algorithm is expected to be an integral number of 8 octets in length, a padding convention is defined when this algorithm is used.

The parameters to this algorithm are a *data-encrypting key* (DEK) and an *initialization-vector* (IV); both are 8 octets in length.

Message Integrity

If originator identification and message integrity services are desired, the NVT ASCII representation of the interior message is used as the input to a message-digest algorithm, which produces a *message integrity check* (MIC).

At present, three algorithms are defined:

RSA-MD5: this corresponds to the MD5 message-digest algorithm introduced earlier in Section 5.2.4 starting on page 201.

RSA-MD2: defined in [69], this message-digest algorithm is similar to MD5, but is conjectured to be harder to break.

MAC: defined in [70], this message authentication code is calculated using the CBC mode of the DES.

Key Encryption

When data-encrypting keys and message integrity checks are generated, they are sent as a part of the privacy-enhanced message. A special key management algorithm is used to encrypt these quantities, the parameter to which is termed an *interchange key* (IK).

At present, three algorithms are defined:

DES-ECB: the *electronic codebook* (ECB) mode of the U.S. Federal Data Encryption Standard (DES) [67, 68].

DES-EDE: the *encrypt-decrypt-encrypt* (EDE) mode of the U.S. Federal Data Encryption Standard (DES) [67, 71].

RSA: the RSA public-key encryption algorithm [72].

Of these, the first two are *symmetric* encryption algorithms, as a single key is used for encryption and decryption. In contrast, the last algorithm is *asymmetric*, as the originator uses a recipient's *public* key for encryption, and the recipient uses a *private* key for decryption.

7.3.2 Key Management

Each PEM-capable user agent must manage relationships between correspondents and the keys used for parameters to the cryptographic algorithms.

Each time a privacy-enhanced message is generated, a pseudo-random DEK is generated, and the MIC for the interior message is calculated. So, how do the IK relationships affect what happens next? To find out, we need to look at the rest of the syntax of a privacy-enhanced message, as shown in Figure 7.2 starting on page 278.[2]

---

[2]The syntax shown here is a slight simplification of the full PEM syntax. This was necessary in order to provide for a more straight-forward explanation.

```
symmetric ::= 1*(origsyminfo *rcptsyminfo)
origsyminfo
         ::=       "Originator-ID-Symmetric"   ":" symid        CRLF
rcptsyminfo
         ::=       "Recipient-ID-Symmetric"    ":" symid        CRLF
                   "Key-Info"                  ":" ikalg  ","
                                                   micalg ","
                                                   cryptedek   ","
                                                   cryptedmic  CRLF
symid    ::= useragent "," [iaentity] "," [version]
useragent ::= 1*itext              ; local@domain
iaentity ::= 1*itext               ; any string
version  ::= 1*itext               ;    ..
cryptedek ::= 1*HEX
cryptedmic
         ::= 1*HEX


asymmetric
         ::= 1*origasyminfo *rcptasyminfo
origasyminfo
         ::=       "Originator-Certificate"    ":" btext        CRLF
                 *("Issuer-Certificate"        ":" btext        CRLF)
                   "MIC-Info"                  ":" micalg ","
                                                   micencalg ","
                                                   btext        CRLF
rcptasyminfo
         ::=       "Recipient-ID-Asymmetric"   ":" asymid       CRLF
                   "Key-Info"                  ":" ikalg  ","
                                                   btext        CRLF
asymid   ::= issuer "," [serial]
issuer   ::= btext                 ; issuer's OSI DN
serial   ::= 1*HEX                 ; certificate serial number

dekalg   ::= "DES-CBC"
micalg   ::= "RSA-MD5" / "RSA-MD2" / "MAC"
ikalg    ::= "DES-ECB" / "DES-EDE" / "RSA"
micencalg ::= "RSA"
```

Figure 7.2: Privacy-Enhanced Message Detailed Syntax

```
btext      ::= 1*base64 *(LWSP 1*base64)
base64     ::= 2(ALPHA / DIGIT / "+" / "/")
               2(ALPHA / DIGIT / "+" / "/" / "=")

itext      ::= ALPHA / DIGIT / "(" / ")" / <"> / "." / "@"
               / "<"  / ">"  / "!" / "%" / "'" / "+" / "-"
               / "/"  / "="  / "?" / "_"

text       ::= <any character, including bare CR and bare LF,
                   but not including CRLF>

LWSP       ::= CRLF 1*SP
CRLF       ::= <carriage-return followed by line-feed>
SP         ::= <any SPACE or TAB character>
ALPHA      ::= <any alphabetic character, "A" through "Z" and
                "a" through "z">
HEX        ::= (DIGIT / "A" / "B" / "C" / "D" / "E" / "F")
DIGIT      ::= <any numeric character, "0" through "9">
```

Figure 7.2: Privacy-Enhanced Message Detailed Syntax (cont.)

Symmetric Relationships

If the correspondents use a symmetric encryption algorithm, then they share a common IK. This means that an originating user agent must share a (different) IK with each and every recipient user agent with which it wishes private communications.

Looking back to Figure 7.2 on page 278, the **symid** production is used to capture the semantics of an IK used with a symmetric relationship between two user agents. There are three fields:

- the user agent identification (**useragent**), which corresponds to a mailbox address, e.g.,

  local@domain

  with the usual semantics;

- the *issuing authority* (IA) identification (**iaentity**); and,

- a version number (**version**) for the IK.

Hence, when a privacy-enhanced message is generated, the originating
user agent identifies itself using the

    Originator-ID-Symmetric:

header.
    Then, each recipient is identified using the

    Recipient-ID-Symmetric:

header. Following each instance of this header, the originating user
agent generates a `Key-Info`: header which contains:

- the identity of the key-encryption algorithm used (`ikalg`);

- the identity of the message-digest algorithm used (`micalg`);

- the DEK encrypted using the named key-encryption algorithm
  (`cryptedek`); and,

- the MIC encrypted using the named key-encryption algorithm
  (`cryptedmic`).

Because a user agent might be known under different names, an originating user agent might use more than one

    Originator-ID-Symmetric:

header. As such, interpretation of a `Recipient-ID-Symmetric`: header
requires finding the closest previous

    Originator-ID-Symmetric:

header. In other words, recipient identifiers are grouped after originator
identifiers.

Asymmetric Relationships

If the correspondents use an asymmetric encryption algorithm, then the originator uses the public key of the recipient as the IK.

The originating user agent identifies itself using the

> `Originator-Certificate:`

header. In theory, only the user agent's identity need be transferred, and the corresponding certificate could be retrieved from a Directory service. However, such a Directory infrastructure does not currently exist. Thus, the certificate is placed in the headers of the privacy-enhanced message.

A certificate is a complex structure which contains:

- a version number, so that even more complex structures for certificates can be defined in the future;

- the identity of the entity which uses this certificate;

- the public key associated with that entity;

- the identity of the signature algorithm which signed the certificate;

- the identity of the entity which issued the certificate;

- a serial number, which increases each time that issuing authority creates a new certificate (for any entity) to allow for certificates to be re-issued; and,

- the creation and expiration dates of the certificate;

This structure is encoded using a compact binary representation and then transformed into the NVT ASCII repertoire by using the `base64` coding scheme.

In order to establish a chain of trust for the purposes of authenticating the certificate, multiple occurrences of the

> `Issuer-Certificate:`

may be present. Each occurrence identifies a *certification authority* which issued the certificate to the entity identified in the previous header.

As with the

> `Originator-Certificate:`

header, this header not only identifies an entity, but also includes that entity's certificate.

Following this is the `MIC-Info:` header, which contains three components:

- the identity of the message-digest algorithm used (`micalg`);

- the identity of the key-encryption algorithm used to encrypt the MIC (`micencalg`); and,

- the MIC encrypted using the originator's private key.

Then, each recipient is identified using the

> `Recipient-ID-Asymmetric:`

header. This is done by retrieving the certificate associated with a recipient. Every certificate issued is uniquely identified by the combination of the identity of the issuing authority and the serial number assigned by that authority. So, looking back to page 278, the `asymid` production is used to identify a recipient user agent in an asymmetric relationship. There are two fields:

- the OSI *Distinguished Name* (DN) of the issuing authority; and,

- the serial number of the certificate issued by that authority.

The DN is encoded using a compact binary representation and then transformed into the NVT ASCII repertoire by using the `base64` coding scheme. Following each instance of this header, the originating user agent generates a `Key-Info:` header containing:

- the identity of the key-encryption algorithm used (`ikalg`); and,

- the DEK encrypted using the named key-encryption algorithm.

As with symmetric recipient identifiers, there is an implied grouping between asymmetric recipient identifiers and asymmetric originator identifiers.

Well, believe it or not, we've introduced all the headers found in a privacy-enhanced message. So, let's put them to use.

7.4   PEM Services

A user with a PEM-capable user agent composes a message and asks for either message privacy or message integrity services. In the former case, a DEK is generated, along with whatever other parameters are needed by the desired data encryption algorithm.

Going back to Figure 7.1 on page 271, the first header generated is `Proc-Type:` which identifies whether:

- privacy, originator authenticity, and message integrity are being used (`ENCRYPTED`); or,

- originator authenticity and message integrity are being used (`MIC-ONLY` or `MIC-CLEAR`).

Then, if a DEK was generated, a `DEK-Info:` header is generated identifying the algorithm used to encrypt the interior message, along with the initialization vector used as a parameter to the algorithm.

Processing now varies depending on whether a symmetric or asymmetric IK relationship is used.

In the symmetric case, an `Originator-ID-Symmetric:` header is generated, followed by any number of pairs of

```
Recipient-ID-Symmetric:
Key-Info:
```

pairs. The IK used to generate the information in the latter header is the shared secret between the originator and recipient.

In the asymmetric case, an `Originator-Certificate:` header is generated, followed by any number of `Issuer-Certificate:` headers, and the `MIC-Info:` header. Next follow any number of

```
Recipient-ID-Asymmetric:
Key-Info:
```

pairs. The IK used to generate the information in the latter header is the public key for the recipient.

Finally, if message privacy was desired, the interior message is encrypted using the data encryption algorithm and the DEK. The ciphertext is then represented in NVT ASCII by using the `base64` encoding.

Otherwise, the interior message is output, either using the `base64` encoding (if the `Proc-Type:` header is `MIC-ONLY`), or directly (if the `Proc-Type:` header is `MIC-CLEAR`).

When a privacy-enhanced message is received, a user agent finds the `Recipient-` header which corresponds to it, and applies the inverse transformations. When it recomputes the message-digest, if a mismatch occurs, the user is so informed.

7.5 PEM Infrastructure

Although Privacy-Enhanced Mail is an important advancement in message handling, it must be emphasized that it requires an underlying infrastructure, beyond that of the message transfer system, in order to function.

If symmetric key relationships are used, there must be a secure mechanism for IKs to be communicated between originators and recipients. Obviously, the use of such relationships will not scale to large communities.

On the other hand, if asymmetric key relationships are used, then there must be a mechanism for retrieving the certificate associated with a user agent. The OSI Directory is intended for this purpose. However, the current Directory infrastructure in the Internet is infinitesimal in comparison to the reach of Internet electronic mail. To complicate matters, there must be a means of creating and revoking certificates, which means there must be a well-defined human infrastructure as well, which at present doesn't exist.

It will be interesting to see if Privacy-Enhanced Mail can act as a stimulus to develop both infrastructures. If not, the community which enjoys these enhancements regrettably will be quite limited.

Finally, one reviewer of *The Internet Message* felt that the author should include a soapbox asking why the PEM effort was taking over five years to actually produce working technology for the Internet community. Although the author admits that this topic provides a target-rich environment, in a rare display of restraint, he declines this opportunity. (However, if PEM isn't deployed by 1996, when the second edition of *The Internet Message* is likely to be published, the author will probably write "the mother of all soapboxes" on this topic.)

7.6   For Further Reading

On page 315 in Appendix A, the historical RFCs which deal with
Privacy-Enhanced Mail are listed, namely [73, 74, 75]. Because these
are designated as historical RFCs, they are no longer on the standards-
track. As such, the reader should check with the index of RFCs to
determine if newer documents are available, before consulting these
RFCs.

Chapter 8

Mail Gatewaying

As *The Internet Message* draws to a close, we examine how different message transfer systems interact. This is through a process termed "mail gatewaying". A *mail gateway* is a special entity which sits at the boundary of two message transfer systems. Its job is to provide both connectivity and interoperability services for the user agents on both sides.

In this chapter, we begin by looking at the theoretical basis for mail gateways. This is followed by an examination of current practices.

8.1   Theory of Mail Gateways

The author's very first RFC was published nearly ten years ago in late 1983. It dealt with electronic mail gateways [76]. The document was written in the days before MX resource records — indeed the first publication about the Domain Name System had been issued only a month earlier. Fortunately for the author, although the examples are amusingly dated, the basic principles remain more or less intact.

A mail gateway is more properly termed an *application-gateway*, a device which interconnects the message transfer services offered by two different protocol suites. Because of the store-and-forward nature of electronic mail, mail gateways are particularly well suited for translating between the services and contents available in the mail domains which they interconnect.

8.1.1   Basic Principles

The basic principle for mail gatewaying lies in the observation that the envelope, headers, and body are distinct objects. As such, in a perfect world, a mail gateway translates

- the envelope from one mail domain to another;

- the headers from one mail domain to another; and,

- the body from one mail domain to another.

and never allows information to commingle among these three objects.

For each kind of object, the mail gateway must be able to apply a mapping function which, in a perfect world, will be reversible without loss of information. Because mail gateways are able to access both envelope and content information, they are really neither message transfer agents nor user agents, they are somehow both simultaneously higher and lower in the message handling model. Perhaps it is this strange duality that causes so much confusion in the implementation of mail gateways.

Let's start by taking a high-level look at the three kinds of mappings, and then we'll revisit this issue with some cold pragmatism. Before we begin, let's introduce one last principle: *only* gateways should do translation, "normal" message transfer agents should, under no circumstances, manipulate the headers or body, unless it is to add trace information to the headers. Quite a few problems have been caused by message transfer agents which violate the opaqueness principle of the message handling system.

Above all, a message transfer agent should avoid gratuitous transformations. At one site, for example, all outgoing mail is funneled through a message transfer agent which re-writes local mailbox addresses to incorporate the user's name as listed in their personnel records! Yes, both the `phrase` and `route-addr` components are re-written. Any useful information in the `phrase`, which might be placed there by a sophisticated user, is lost. Because the message transfer agent is not translating between mail domains, this behavior is wholly inappropriate.

Envelope Mappings

The services offered by the message transfer service are largely carried in the envelope. In the Internet world, envelopes are simple: they contain an originator address, a delivery mode, and one or more recipient addresses. In contrast, in the MHS world, the envelope is much more complex, and provides (in theory) a wider range of services.

At a minimum, envelope mapping involves being able to translate between electronic mail names and addresses. To translate other services, a loss of information will almost certainly occur, e.g., there is no delivery-notification service in the Internet message transfer system.

Name and address translation is far from simple, however. There are usually two parts to the process. First, a set of re-writing rules are applied to the address to map it into a canonical address form for the new mail domain. Second, the address is usually "rooted" at the mail gateway, so that any replies will go back to the mail gateway which can then reverse the re-writing. Of course, it is desirable that all mail gateways connecting two particular mail domains use the same rules. If possible, the "rooting" should be dynamic, so that the best mail gateway will be selected in the future.

To understand the notion of "rooting" consider the following question:

"What is your electronic mailbox address?"

The only correct response to such a question is to first ask which mail domain should be used to provide the context for the answer. That is, a response might start with:

"In the Internet community, my mailbox address is ..."

Header Mappings

The headers contain four basic kinds of information:

- electronic mail addresses;

- time-stamps (dates and times);

- electronic mail message pointers; and,

- textual information.

The same address translation facilities used for the envelope must also be employed for those found in the headers. This is critical if user agent functionality such as forwarding and replying is going to work across mail domain boundaries. However, the form of translated addresses may cause problems for later message transfer agents or the recipient's user agent. So, even if a loss of information does not occur, depending on the robustness of the downstream software, anomalies or human user confusion may result.

Translation of time-stamps (e.g., the value of a `Date:` field) is probably straight-forward, so we needn't spend much time on this topic.

However, translation of message pointers (e.g., the value of a `Message-ID:` field) may be problematic unless a deterministic algorithm can be deployed. Obviously the larger the similarity between the syntaxes used in the two mail domains, or the less structured the syntax, the better.

Finally, translation of textual information (e.g., the value of a `Subject:` field) is straight-forward, unless different character repertoires are mandated.

Body Mappings

In each mail domain, the body may be structured, unstructured, or pseudo-structured.

If both are structured or unstructured, then mapping is fairly easy (again assuming the same character repertoires can be used). Similarly, if one is structured and the other unstructured, then mapping should also be straight-forward.

The problem arises when one or both of the mail domains allow for pseudo-structured bodies. For example, in the days before MIME, the format used for message forwarding was pseudo-structured. This meant that the mail gateway had to apply a heuristic (i.e., non-deterministic) algorithm to decide if a message body contained a forwarded message. The problem, of course, is that in this case, the translation process is recursive: if one or more forwarded messages were encountered inside a message body, then the header and body mappings must be applied to them as well.

8.1.2 Imprecise Mappings

It should be clear, even from the preceding high-level discussion, that the mapping functions are not going to be without information loss. All we need argue about is how much loss is acceptable to the end-user. And herein lies the rub: when the mail gateway performs its translations, it does not have any idea as to the user's wishes about what is important and what isn't.

For example, suppose a mail gateway encounters an Internet electronic mail message containing an `audio/basic` content, and this message is to be delivered to an MHS electronic mail address. As of this writing, there is no IPMS body part that corresponds to MIME's `audio/basic` content. What is the mail gateway to do?

It could:

- discard the content and continue processing the message; or,

- reject the message and generate an error report; or,

- attempt some translation to a different representation (in this example, this is rather doubtful).

What is the right choice? The answer is: there is no right choice. The reason is that different users have different requirements, and no matter which policy the mail gateway chooses, it is bound to choose the wrong one sooner or later (probably sooner).

Even with unstructured textual body parts, loss of information may be inevitable. For example, mappings between repertoires (e.g., NVT ASCII and EBCDIC) may cause one-way translation of character representations. Further, variations in line-termination sequences and white-space conventions may also cause problems.

For example, although the CR-LF sequence is used for interchange purposes, the system on which a mail gateway resides may use a different convention. Depending on the particular choice, if a body part contains a CR not followed by an LF, or an LF not preceded by a CR, then confusion may very well ensue. Similarly, on some systems, lines longer than 76 characters are wrapped or truncated; on others, lines may be padded to a particular length; on still others, lines with trailing white-space may be trimmed. Of course, none of these are conformant practices, but a message transfer agent may not have adequate control over its system environment and will simply have to make do as best it can.

Finally, all of the problems thus far have been in the realm of dealing with two mail domains. Suppose there are three. This is known as *Stefferud's three body problem*, which is concisely stated as:

$$G_{2,3}(G_{1,2}(m)) \neq G_{1,3}(m)$$

By way of explanation, suppose one has three mail domains all interconnected. Now suppose an electronic mail message, m, originates from domain D_1, goes through $G_{1,2}$, traverses domain D_2, goes through $G_{2,3}$, and then is delivered in domain D_3. Now suppose an identical message, m', originates from domain D_1, goes through $G_{1,3}$, and then is delivered in domain D_3. Stefferud claims (and the author agrees) that the nature of imprecise mappings means that upon final delivery, m and m' will have entirely different semantics in the header and probably even body.

Why is this a problem? The message transfer agents operating within a mail domain may select different mail gateways, depending on availability, cost, and so on. If m and m' have suffered a different set of transformations, then user agent functionality will greatly suffer.

8.1.3 For Interested Readers

Defining the set of mappings between two mail domains is difficult, tedious, and generally a dirty business. For example, the author could easily add 50 pages onto the length of *The Internet Message* by discussing the mappings between Internet mail and MHS. Instead, the interested reader should consult [77], which defines these mappings. To give the reader an idea of the complexity of such mappings, this document is over 110 pages long and discusses only envelope and header mappings! A supplemental work effort is just beginning in the IETF to define mappings between message bodies for the two mail domains.

8.2   Mail Gateways in Practice

In practice, mail gatewaying is an absolute mess. We'll look at five examples of mail gateways which are broken in various ways and then try to identify the underlying causes.

8.2.1   Example 1: Envelope Fixation

Suppose we have an SMTP envelope that contains several addresses for the same, foreign mail domain. An SMTP connection is established to the mail gateway which interconnects the Internet message transfer service to this other mail domain. Now let's say that some of the addresses given in the `RCPT` commands are rejected, but others are not. The mail gateway in question will refuse the `DATA` command which follows. That is, if it can't deliver to all of the recipient addresses, then it refuses to delivery to any of them.

If this gateway does accept the electronic mail message, it keeps the `From:` and `Subject:` headers, and discards the rest of the message headers. It then constructs a new message header consisting of:

- a translated `From:` header;

- the old `Subject:` header;

- a `Date:` header set to the time when the mail gateway received the message;

- a `To:` header consisting of the addresses given as recipients during the SMTP transaction.

Of course, since the headers of the electronic mail message may have contained addresses from other mail domains, this information is lost, and the user agent's reply functionality does not work as it should.

8.2.2   Example 2: Header Examination

For a second example, suppose we have an RFC-822 message. The minimal set of headers present is:

```
Date:
From:
```

and either a `To:` header or a `Bcc:` header. Note that no recipient addresses need be present. For example, according to RFC-822:

- the `Bcc:` header needn't contain any addresses; and,

- the `To:` header could have an address group which contains no addresses, e.g.,

```
To: Reviewers: ;
```

is perfectly valid.

One of the alleged selling points of MHS is that it is supposed to have been developed for commercial providers of electronic mail services. And, as we all know, commercial providers take these things seriously and offer robust production services. So, let's see what happens when we take an electronic mail message with these minimal headers and try to pass it through an 822/MHS gateway operated by a commercial service provider. In one case, the message was accepted for delivery and then silently discarded. In fact, there wasn't even a log entry indicating that the message had been accepted. In a case dealing with a different service provider, an error report was returned, in which the message body consisted solely of the original message, and buried in the message headers was the "reason" for the problem:

```
Not-Delivered-To: !anybody due to 10 Invalid Parameters
         Message header has unacceptable format
```

Now isn't that informative? It's a good thing that the recipient of this error report wasn't using a header filter when displaying this message. Otherwise, he never would have even seen this extremely helpful diagnostic. (The author is being sarcastic here, but is not soap-boxing — yet!)

The next part of the story is somewhat amusing. Someone started
sending electronic mail to the `PostMaster` for the mail gateway asking
for an explanation. Over the next few months, several messages went
unanswered, until one day, a reply was received, which appeared to
have been automatically generated. Paraphrasing, the text of the reply
went something like this:

> *Thank-you for your message. It has been entered into our*
> *trouble-ticket tracking system as report #1729.*

Further investigation, to the author's knowledge, never occurred, and
the problem remains to this day. Perhaps the last line of the reply was
missing, e.g.,

> *Now serving #3.*

8.2.3   Example 3: Uniformity of Translation

For another example, the author regularly receives messages from a
client whose mailbox is in a different mail domain. The mail gateway
between the two domains has an interesting property: it will translate
the addresses in the `From:` and `To:` headers, but not the `cc:` headers.
As a result, when the author wants to reply to such a message, the reply
will reach only the author of the original message, the `cc:` recipients
are unreachable.

8.2.4   Example 4: Header Mapping

For the fourth example, there are some mail domains which support
only a subset of headers found in an Internet message. When a message
crosses into this domain, the gateway takes any headers it doesn't
recognize and appends them to the body of the message. As a result,
if the body contains any kind of structured object, then it is likely to
be corrupted. In this example, the gateway considers preserving the
body of the message to be less important than losing the information
contained in the headers. Of course, such behavior assumes that a
human user will be making use of the body, rather than some kind of
program, as these trailing headers won't be directly interpreted by the
user agent.

8.2.5   Example 5: Message Body Translation

As the final example, there are some enclaves in the Internet which, for historical reasons, write the domain name part of an electronic mail address in reverse order, e.g.,

```
local@us.ca.mtview.dbc
```

instead of

```
local@dbc.mtview.ca.us
```

Their mail gateways perform the necessary reversal. Alas, these gateways do not check to see if the message body contains forwarded messages. As a result, when an electronic mail message passes through the mail gateway and is subsequently burst, the interior messages have unusable addresses.

8.2.6   The Common Theme

The common theme is that these examples all result in the same problem: user agent functionality is compromised. The underlying cause is that the mail gateways in question do not honor the boundaries between envelope, headers, and body:

- in the first example, the mail gateway throws away information in the headers, only to (incorrectly) regenerate it later on from information in the envelope;

- in the second example, the mail gateway is likely scrutinizing the headers looking for addresses that it might service, instead of looking in the envelope where the recipient addresses truly reside;

- in the third example, the mail gateway should be examining all the headers, but looks instead at an incorrect subset;

- in the fourth example, the mail gateway copies some headers to the body, in order to avoid losing information; and,

- in the fifth example, the mail gateway should look in the body of the electronic mail message, but doesn't.

What can be done?

Some argue that we need to connect the various mail domains using a single mail transit backbone which implements a superset technology. Without going into a soapbox, the author disagrees. Using a superset technology doesn't guarantee mappings which are free of information loss. Keep in mind that although entry into the superset backbone may not result in a loss of information, exit from the superset backbone certainly might, particularly if there isn't an obvious service mapping between the originating and destination mail domains.

This suggests the only practical solution is one in which:

- only minimal services are supported across the backbone; and,

- gateway "rooting" occurs dynamically.

This may seem counter-intuitive, but the author suspects that the solution to our problems lies in choosing the correct subset technology for an interconnected mesh, rather than choosing a superset technology for a ubiquitous backbone.

8.3   Technology Comparison

soap... The soapbox on page 169 explained why MHS makes a poor basis for a global message transfer system. As such, one could argue that it also makes a poor basis for building mail gateways. Rather than delve into this argument, let's deal with the extremely obvious.

By now, the reader is probably firmly convinced that the author absolutely hates MHS. Nothing could be further from the truth! After all, MHS has provided the author and many other veterans of the electronic mail age with so many hours of amusement. For example, in 1984, the CCITT issues its Recommendations on MHS. Four years later, a joint committee of CCITT and ISO/IEC issued the 1988 version of MHS. Naturally, the two versions are incompatible. Regardless as to whether this incompatibility was necessary, the key thing to note is that the committee felt that it was inappropriate to standardize interworking between the 1984 variant and the 1988 variant of MHS. In other words, it was outside of their scope to fix the problem they had just created. When someone talks about an "MHS gatewaying problem", they are talking about gatewaying between incompatible versions of MHS. The author, and anyone else who lives in the real world, finds such behavior and attitudes to be right up there with the comedy one might find in an excellent film such as *Duck Soup*. The difference, of course, is that the Marx Bros. were paid to be funny. The author isn't sure what the members of the International Standards community are being paid for, but let's face it, if their job is to produce usable technology, then *Wrong* is Right.

...soap

Chapter 9

On the Horizon

In closing *The Internet Message*, let's look at the problems which face $\boxed{\text{soap}\ldots}$
us, and then speculate as to where things might be going. Since
this chapter is entirely opinion and conjecture, it is enclosed within
a soapbox.

Historically, the last chapter of each of my books has started with
a great diatribe on the folly of open systems. In this book, we break
with that tradition. (Check out Appendix C starting on page 321 for
that soapbox!) Instead, we'll proceed directly to the topic at hand.

9.1   Lessons Learned

It is clear that for any technology to be successfully deployed it must be *tractable*. In comparing the Internet mail and MHS communities, we have seen how the equivalent services can be offered by two technological thrusts, one an order of magnitude more complex than the other. Although both technologies were "released" at roughly the same time, the result has been that the simpler technology (Internet mail) is now providing production service across the globe whilst its competitor (MHS) is still the subject of pilot projects, ponderous commercial offerings, and continued refinement.

Perhaps the most telling difference between the technical complexities of the two is how data structures are described. MHS pioneered the use of Abstract Syntax Notation One (ASN.1) a formal language for describing data structures in a machine-independent fashion. In contrast, RFC-822 formalized the notion of augmented BNF. Although this latter form is not directly machine processable, it is easily understood by the humans who have to program computers. More importantly, the richness of the ASN.1 language actually introduces problems by making it easier for standards writers to define procrustean data structures. Remember the discussion of MHS addresses (O/R-addresses) which started back on page 71? ASN.1 made it downright easy to define that structure. Perhaps had it been harder to define something so baroque, the standards committee would have given more thought to the consequences of the definition they selected.

It is difficult to over-emphasize how silly MHS addresses really are, but perhaps this (true) story will bring the point home. While the author attended the INTEROP® 92 Spring conference and exhibition, he observed various people meeting each other for the first time — an interaction which typically involved the exchange of business cards which contain electronic mail addresses. Whenever two people who use Internet mail met, one person could initiate a future correspondence simply by typing in the electronic mailbox address of the other. However, when one person uses Internet mail and the other uses MHS, a problem would invariably arise as the Internet person could not decipher the MHS address. In this case, to initiate a future correspondence, the MHS correspondent would have to send a message to the person with an

Internet mailbox, who in turn would reply to the message and then hope for the best. There were actually a few cases when both persons used MHS. Again, a problem would arise since neither could decipher the other's address. In this case, to initiate a future correspondence, the parties decided it would be best to use the telephone!

However, the Internet community is also not without blame. Perhaps the most common used implementation of a message transfer agent in the Internet is `sendmail`. It is a tribute to the Internet mail system that it works so well given that `sendmail` behaves so poorly. To understand `sendmail` one must really view it more as a mail gateway than a message transfer agent. Consider, although it performs the relaying functions of an MTA, `sendmail` re-writes the headers of each and every message it encounters. If a message lacks a `Date:` or `Message-ID:`, `sendmail` will add them. Unfortunately, `sendmail` doesn't understand RFC-822 very well, which, when combined with its re-writing behavior, makes for an absolutely deadly combination.

For example, `sendmail` doesn't understand that a message needn't have any address fields; i.e., a message could use the addressing group construct or an empty `Bcc:` header. But `sendmail` thinks it knows better. Hence, when it encounters the address grouping construct, e.g.,

```
To: Reviewers: ;
```

`sendmail` re-writes this as

```
To: Reviewers:;@local-domain
```

Similarly, if it finds only an empty `Bcc:` header, `sendmail` dutifully adds an `Apparently-To:` header containing the addresses from the envelope, thereby nullifying the originator's intent.

Even ignoring these violations of protocol, `sendmail` is still a lousy message transfer agent. For example, when sending a message to multiple recipients, `sendmail` usually manages to open a new SMTP connection for each recipient, thereby managing to transmit the message once for each recipient, even if multiple recipients are served by the same SMTP server.

Clearly `sendmail` is an excellent example of how to do a lot of things wrong. But, since `sendmail` is shipped with Berkeley UNIX, most sites just put up with it. The irony is that there is a competing, competent implementation, in the Multi-channel Memo Distribution Facility (MMDF) [54, 55]. Although MMDF is much closer toward being a correct implementation of a message transfer agent for Internet mail, it suffers from a tyranny of complexity. The `sendmail` package provides a single program and configuration file. In contrast, MMDF consists of over a dozen programs and several configuration files. As such, one really has to be motivated to want electronic mail to work correctly in order to justify the intellectual investment required to understand how to generate, install, and configure MMDF. In contrast, people just sort of stumble along with a canned `sendmail` configuration, poking at it from time to time if problems arise.

To compound matters, the most commonly used implementation of the Domain Name System, `BIND` is just as poorly implemented as `sendmail`. (Interested readers should consult the soapbox starting on page 53 of *The Little Black Book* [31] for further details.)

The lesson learned is that even with simple, straight-forward technology, it is difficult to produce excellent, or even correct, implementations.

9.2 New Directions

Finally, let's consider where things might be heading with naming and messaging.

The Domain Name System

The Domain Name System is perhaps the world's most distributed database. As such, it is interesting to note that a recent study [78] has observed that DNS traffic is sometimes twenty times greater than necessary. This likely means that considerable tuning is still required in DNS implementations. Further, the study suggests that domain name servers should take a more defensive posture, recognizing certain kinds of aberrant behavior and responding appropriately.

In terms of new functionality, some researchers have begun to ask what additions could be made to the DNS so that it could provide directory service in addition to name service. (A *name service* is one in which the primary operation is read-like; in contrast, a *directory service* relies more heavily on a searching operation.) The trick, of course, is to determine the minimal set of extensions needed to provide a useful directory service.

MIME

MIME appears to have been well received by the Internet community. Hence, future work on multi-media mail in the Internet will almost certainly be based on the MIME framework.

The author suspects that the MIME/RFC-822 combination pretty much spells the death for the global dominance of MHS. Although there will be islands of MHS in the future, we've already seen several soap-boxes discussing why MHS is flawed as the basis for a global message transfer system; some might view the author as being somewhat biased, particularly since he played a small role in the development of MIME. In response, the author merely notes that he's spent nearly a decade waiting for MHS to take off, and is simply tired of waiting for it to deliver the promises which have already been fulfilled in the Internet community.

However, more work must still be done in the Internet community. Earlier, Section 6.1.6 on page 259 outlined how MIME could be used to extend the functionality of the Internet message transfer system. However, such extensions must not reduce interoperability nor unduly increase complexity as they increase the richness of the Internet envelope.

In terms of transfer encodings, one deficiency in MIME is the lack of a checksum or digest computation. Although this must be addressed soon, it should be noted that Privacy-Enhanced Mail may also provide some help in this area. In addition, it is also clear that MIME needs some kind of compression option when applying the `base64` content transfer encoding.

The most exciting development is that we are likely to see an explosion of new content types being registered, as MIME-capable software finds its way into various enterprises. In particular, with MIME as a framework, it is now possible to develop active mailboxes to better support so-called *mail-enabled* applications. As a part of this, computational mail technologies such as ATOMICMAIL [79] are likely to become widespread throughout large portions of the Internet community.

⸻[...soap]⸻ And with that, *The Internet Message* draws to a close.

Appendix A

Relevant Internet Documents

The *Request for Comments* (RFC) document series provides for the dissemination of information about the Internet suite of protocols. Not all RFCs are standards, quite the reverse: relatively few RFCs enjoy any level of standardization. Rather, the majority of RFCs are research notes intended for discussion.

RFCs are available in both printed and electronic form. The printed copies are available, for a modest fee, from the DDN Network Information Center:

> Postal: DDN Network Information Center
> 14200 Park Meadow Drive
> Suite 200
> Chantilly, VA 22021
> US
>
> Phone: +1 800–365–3642
> +1 703–802–4535
>
> Mail: nic@nic.ddn.mil

In electronic form, users may use "anonymous" FTP to the host
`nic.ddn.mil` (residing at [192.112.36.5]) and retrieve files from the
directory "`rfc/`", e.g.,

```
% ftp nic.ddn.mil
Connected to nic.ddn.mil
220-*****Welcome to the Network Information Center*****
     *****Login with username "anonymous" and password "guest"
     *****You may change directories to the following:
        ddn-news            - DDN Management Bulletins
        domain              - Root Domain Zone Files
        ien                 - Internet Engineering Notes
        iesg                - IETF Steering Group
        ietf                - Internet Engineering Task Force
        internet-drafts     - Internet Drafts
        netinfo             - NIC Information Files
        netprog             - Guest Software (ex. whois.c)
        protocols           - TCP-IP & OSI Documents
        rfc                 - RFC Repository
        scc                 - DDN Security Bulletins
220 And more.
Name (nic.ddn.mil:mrose): anonymous
331 Guest login ok, send "guest" as password.
Password (nic.ddn.mil:anonymous): guest
230 Guest login ok, access restrictions apply.
ftp> cd rfc
250 CWD command successful.
ftp> ascii
220 Type A ok.
ftp>
```

Certainly the first RFC to retrieve is the Index of RFCs:

```
ftp> get rfc-index.txt
200 PORT command successful.
150 Opening ASCII mode data connection for rfc-index.txt.
226 Transfer complete.
167512 bytes received in 1.1e+02 seconds (1.4 Kbytes/s)
ftp> quit
%
```

Other sites, also maintain copies of RFCs, e.g.,

>ftp.nisc.sri.com
>venera.isi.edu
>wuarchive.wustl.edu
>ftp.concert.net
>nis.nsf.net
>nisc.jvnc.net
>src.doc.ic.ac.uk

Of course, this list might change, but it's a good place to start.

If your site does not have IP-connectivity to the Internet community, but does have electronic mail access, then you can send an electronic mail message to the electronic mail address

```
mail-server@nisc.sri.com
```

and in the subject field indicate the RFC number, e.g.,

```
Subject: SEND rfcs/rfc1130.txt
```

A reply to your electronic mail message will contain the desired RFC.

If your site has electronic mail access to the Internet community, and you desire notification when new RFCs are published, send a note to the electronic mail address

```
rfc-request@nic.ddn.mil
```

and ask to be added to the **RFC** notification list.

Internet Drafts

Internet Drafts are available only in electronic form. Use "anonymous" FTP to the host `nnsc.nsf.net` (residing at [`192.31.103.6`]) and retrieve files from the directory `internet-drafts/`, e.g.,

```
% ftp nnsc.nsf.net
Connected to nnsc.nsf.net
220 nnsc.nsf.net FTP server
Name (nnsc.nsf.net:mrose): anonymous
331 guest login ok, send ident as password.
Password (nnsc.nsf.net:anonymous): guest
230 Guest login ok, access restrictions apply.
ftp> cd internet-drafts
250 CWD command successful.
ftp> ascii
220 Type set to A.
ftp>
```

Other sites also maintain copies of Internet Drafts, e.g.,

```
munnari.oz.au
ftp.nisc.sri.com
nic.nordu.net
nic.ddn.mil
```

Of course, this list might also change, but it's a good place to start.

If your site does not have IP-connectivity to the Internet community, but does have electronic mail access, then you can send an electronic mail message to the electronic mail address

```
mail-server@nisc.sri.com
```

and in the subject field indicate the name of the draft, e.g.,

```
Subject: SEND internet-drafts/draft-ietf-foo-bar-00.txt
```

A reply to your electronic mail message will contain the desired draft.

If your site has electronic mail access to the Internet community, and you desire notification when new Internet Drafts are published, send a note to the electronic mail address

```
ietf-request@venera.isi.edu
```

and ask to be added to the `ietf` list.

A.1 Administrative RFCs

The key administrative RFCs are:

RFC	Name	Status
1280	IAB Official Protocol Standards	Required
1060	Assigned Numbers	Required
1009	Gateway Requirements	Required
1122	Host Requirements — Communications	Required
1123	Host Requirements — Applications	Required

Note that these RFCs are periodically updated. As with the rest of the RFC series, the most recent document always takes precedence. In particular, note that the IAB Official Protocol standards document is (in theory) updated quarterly.

The information which follows is taken from the IAB Official Standards RFC [15], published in March, 1992. By the time of this reading, a new version of this RFC will no doubt have been published.

A.2   Electronic Mail RFCs

Here are the RFCs which (somehow) deal with electronic mail.
    The RFCs on the standards-track are:

RFC	Name	Status
821	Simple Mail Transfer Protocol	Recommended
822	Format of Electronic Mail Messages	Recommended
954	NICNAME/WHOIS	Elective
974	Mail Routing and the Domain System	Recommended
977	Network News Transfer Protocol	Elective
987	Mapping between X.400 and 822	Elective
1026	Addendum to RFC-987	Elective
1034	Domain Names — Concepts and Facilities	Recommended
1035	Domain Names — Implementation and Specification	Recommended
1049	Content Type Header Field	Recommended
1056	Distributed Mail System Protocol	Elective
1225	Post Office Protocol: Version 3	Elective
1288	Finger User Information Protocol	Elective

Consult the current edition of the Official Protocols RFC to determine
the standardization state (proposed, draft, or full) of each RFC listed
here.

Here are the non-standard, experimental RFCs which (somehow) deal with electronic mail:

RFC	Name	Status
1137	Mapping between 822 and restricted 822	Elective
1148	Mapping between X.400(88) and 822	Elective
1153	Digest Message Format for Mail	Elective
1154	Encoding Header Field for Mail	Elective
1183	New DNS RR Definitions	Limited use
1203	Interactive Mail Access Protocol: Version 3	Limited use
1204	Message Posting Protocol	Limited use

Here are the non-standard, informational RFCs which (somehow) deal with electronic mail:

RFC	Name
886	Message Header Munging
934	Message Encapsulation
976	UUCP mail interface format
1036	Interchange of USNET Messages
1047	Duplicate Messages and SMTP
1082	Post Office Protocol: Extended Service Offerings
1090	SMTP on X.25
1211	Problems with the Maintenance of Large Mailing Lists

Here are the draft RFCs which deal with Privacy-Enhanced Mail:

RFC	Name
1113	Message Encipherment and Authentication Procedures
1114	Certificate-based Key Management
1115	Algorithms, Modes, and Identifiers
1319	The MD2 Message-Digest Algorithm
1321	The MD5 Message-Digest Algorithm

Note that the first three of these have been designated as historical, and are no longer on the standards-track. As such, consult the index of RFCs to determine the identities of the current documents.

A.3   Contact Information

The RFC Editor can be reached at:

> Postal: Jonathan B. Postel
> RFC Editor
> USC/Information Sciences Institute
> 4676 Admiralty Way
> Marina del Rey, CA 90292-6695
> US
>
> Phone: +1 310–822–1511
>
> Mail: rfc-editor@isi.edu

The Internet Assigned Numbers Authority can be reached at:

> Postal: Joyce K. Reynolds
> Internet Assigned Numbers Authority
> USC/Information Sciences Institute
> 4676 Admiralty Way
> Marina del Rey, CA 90292-6695
> US
>
> Phone: +1 310–822–1511
>
> Mail: iana@isi.edu

Appendix B

How to get MIME Software

Although standardized in mid-1992, as of this writing, there are already three independent, openly available implementations of MIME.[1] In addition, several commercial implementations are either under development or have been released. This appendix contains ordering information for the openly available implementations. Turn the page to find out more!

---

[1]This situation bodes well for MIME. In the author's experience, one sign of a successful technology is the availability of multiple independent reference implementations.

MetaMail

The *MetaMail* implementation, written by Nathaniel S. Borenstein of Bellcore, is available via "anonymous" FTP:

host	`thumper.bellcore.com`
directory	`pub/nsb`
file	`mm.tar.Z`
mode	`binary`

The distribution runs on nearly all UNIX variants, MS-DOS, and even more obscure systems, and contains:

- a configurable program used to view MIME messages, along with several shell scripts and programs used to generate non-text messages;

- a set of patches which, when applied, will turn an extensive set of user agents into MIME-capable software (e.g., Berkeley Mail, `elm`, MH, Andrew, Mush, GNU Emacs, etc.);

- a program to display `text/richtext` messages on a dumb terminal;

- a program to display message headers which contain non-ASCII message character sets; and,

- a program which converts Andrew-formatted multi-media messages to plain text.

There is a discussion group for MetaMail; send a message to the electronic mail address

`info-mm-request@thumper.bellcore.com`

and ask to be added to the

`info-mm@thumper.bellcore.com`

mailing list.

Multi-Media MH

The *multi-media MH* implementation, written by the author, is available via "anonymous" FTP as a part of the MH release:

host	`ics.uci.edu`
directory	`mh`
file	`mh-6.7.tar.Z`
mode	`binary`

MH runs on just about every variant of UNIX, and contains:

- a configurable program used to compose, examine, display, or store MIME messages; and,

- modifications to MH's composition commands so that electronic mail messages will be automatically fragmented.

Look in the file `miscellany/multi-media/READ-ME` for installation and configuration instructions.

There is a discussion group for (multi-media) MH; send a message to the electronic mail address

`mh-users-request@ics.uci.edu`

and ask to be added to the

`mh-users@ics.uci.edu`

mailing list.

The author obviously prefers this distribution since it has the best integration with MH. On the other hand, the author uses the program supplied with the MetaMail release when displaying `text/richtext` content values!

C-Client

The C-client distribution written by Mark R. Crispin of the University of Washington, contains MIME support. The distribution is actually an implementation of an API for user agents that access different mailbox services, such as the IMAP variant specified in [57], and so on. The distribution also contains the Pine user agent for UNIX.

host	`ftphost.cac.washington.edu`
directory	`mail`
file	`imap.tar.Z`
mode	`binary`

The distribution runs on many different kinds of platforms, including several UNIX variants, MS-DOS, the Macintosh®, and even Tops20.

Appendix C

The Future of OSI:
A Modest Prediction

Following is a reprint of an invited paper [80] presented at the 1992 IFIP
International Conference on Upper Layer Protocols, Architectures and
Applications, held in Vancouver, Canada from May 27–29. The paper
is reprinted by permission.

It has been included here as the author's final words on the subject
of OSI, OSI standardization, and OSI non-implementation.

C.1 Introduction

"Before Political Correctness there was the concept of Open Systems."

– Internet Proverb (undated)

Readers of these proceedings should be well-versed in the need for solutions that provide vendor-independent, interoperable computer-communications. Indeed, *open systems* (as embodied by either the Internet or OSI suite of protocols) have risen to the forefront of networking. In the interest of brevity, this introduction omits any discussion of the history of networking, open systems, or the protocol suites which compose open systems.

Readers of these proceedings are likely well-versed also in the politics of open systems. Indeed, for numerous reasons, discussions on open systems are fraught with unending arguments given with religious-like zeal. Further, although there is little consensus as to exactly what an open system is, everyone agrees that open systems are "good things".

The purpose of this paper is to examine where OSI now stands, to consider what has led to this situation, and finally to predict the future of OSI.

C.2 Where We Are Now

To evaluate the success of the OSI effort, this section looks at two representative areas: the lower-layer infrastructure, by focusing primarily on the network layer; and, the upper-layer infrastructure, by focusing primarily on the flagship application, MHS.

C.2.1 The Network Layer

> *"The hours are good ... though most of the actual minutes are pretty lousy."*
> – Douglas Adams, *"The Hitchhikers Guide to the Galaxy"*
> *(1979)*

In order for a protocol suite to be widely deployed, it must provide for a ubiquitous lower-layer infrastructure. For example, in the IP-connected Internet, IP provides the single, universal service that allows a global, multi-administration internet to be constructed over a variety of transmission media. Unfortunately, OSI ended up with *two* incompatible network services, one connection-oriented (CO) and the other connection-less (CL).

From the historical perspective, one might argue that in the mid-'80s there simply wasn't any consensus as to which approach was superior. Continuing in an apologist vein, one might then go on to argue that the committee had no choice but to put forth both approaches. Unfortunately, the committee only did half the job: they standardized both approaches, but they did not put forth an approach which allows for interworking between the two. This lack of compatibility has led to the development of OSI environments which do not interoperate.

To date, all solutions which provide for interworking between these two network services either exist outside the model (e.g., the transport-relay approach), or require an invasive change to the transport protocol (e.g., the source routing option for TP4).

Of course, different network services inevitably led to different transport protocols (five different ones, to be precise). This only exacerbates the problems of implementation, interoperability, and interworking.

In contrast, take note of the widespread and seemingly unstoppable deployment of IP-based infrastructure over the last five years. Because there is but a single network service in the Internet suite of protocols, there is simply no such thing as a TCP/IP interworking problem. By using a single network protocol and a dominant transport protocol, the Internet suite of protocols has achieved unprecedented success.

The sad part is that the OSI suite of protocols could have had similar results. Regardless of witty repartee concerning the merits of either the CL or CO approach, the author believes that *either* approach could be made to work well. However, one and exactly one must be chosen. The two approaches are simply too different to be joined together without a catastrophic increase in complexity and loss of transparency.

C.2.2 The Flagship Application

> *"What do you get when you cross a mobster with an*
> *international standard?*
> *You get someone who makes you an offer that you can't*
> *understand."*
> *– Paul V. Mockapetris, quoted in "The Open Book" (1989)*

Experience has shown that exchange of electronic-mail is a popular application for networks. Indeed, with few exceptions, everyone touts the OSI Message Handling System (MHS) as the flagship application of the OSI suite of protocols.

Unfortunately, MHS doesn't seem to be doing too well. To the author's eye there are at least three reasons, as evidenced in the 1984 CCITT Recommendations on MHS:

First, O/R-addresses, the means by which a user identifies another user, are simply incomprehensible. An O/R-address consists of several keyword/value pairs of which there are a dozen or so keywords and four different allowable configurations. Since there is no Directory service (X.500 came four years later and still does not enjoy wide deployment), users must type-in these addresses by hand, at least once. Further, since there is no official textual syntax for an address, formats vary between systems, making it difficult to enter addresses even when they are placed on business cards. Further, to administrators and software, O/R-addresses are supposed to (somehow) convey routing information. Of course, expecting a mailbox to somehow contain embedded routing hints is not particularly scalable or trustworthy. Further, not all software supports routing based on all four configurations, making the job of the administrator even more difficult.

Of course, the all-pain/no-gain situation resulting from O/R-addressing is but one of many fundamental technical problems in MHS. Use of RTS, a bulk-mode transfer facility, for MTA-MTA transactions is another example. While the use of a bulk-mode facility looks good on paper, it is not possible to do address verification with such an approach. This means that an MTA must accept delivery of a message even if it cannot deliver to any of the addressees. A more appropriate approach is to perform verification optionally followed by transfer. (A modestly clever implementation of such an approach will minimize network latency by gathering the verification requests into the smallest number of network exchanges.)

Second, although MHS claims to support multi-media, what it really allows for is multiple body-parts in the same message. MHS simply does not specify enough information to allow for interoperable exchanges of multi-media contents. In practical terms, this means that MHS does not provide a suitable backbone technology for many messaging environments.

Finally, MHS has no gateway methodology. Hence, MHS cannot be used as the basis for some kind of mail transit backbone: whenever it is introduced for such a purpose, addresses, headers, and contents do not cross transparently.

To the continuing amazement of many in the Internet community, MHS(84) is difficult to implement correctly, even in 1992. Commercial products are still flaky (nearly eight years after release of the standard), as evidenced by user complaints that messages going through MHS are dropped with some frequency. Consider the surprise of the author in late 1991 when messages to a commercial MHS user were constantly being lost. After a week of investigation by the commercial provider, the problem was solved. Why did it take so long? Well, it appears that the problem in the MHS implementation was such that the message was "cleanly" dropped, without leaving any log entries! At the risk of stating the obvious: the Internet community has been shipping mail around the globe for over a decade, and while there are occasional problems, the simple fact is that getting the job done is not that difficult — at least not when you use a rational technology.

C.2.3   The Flagship Application (cont.)

> *"Why are Communists preferable to Standards Committees?*
> *Because Communists make 5 year plans."*
> *– Paul V. Mockapetris, quoted in "The Little Black Book"*
> *(1991)*

Of course, the standards community got a chance to fix things in 1988, with mixed results.

To begin, nearly four years after the release of MHS(88), the new standard is having considerable trouble displacing even the modest use of MHS(84)! Why? First, it cost a lot to build, buy, and deploy MHS(84). MHS(88) is a much more complicated technology. Second, there are few commercial implementations of MHS(88). Third, there is no guidance from the standards community as to how to make the transition between MHS(84) and MHS(88). It is almost as if the committee which produced MHS(88) did not wish to even acknowledge the existence of MHS(84).

Next, there are still quite a few things missing from MHS(88). Most notable is the lack of automated routing capabilities. This means that administrators must maintain and manually distribute hand-crafted tables. (The Internet suite of protocols has been using an automated protocol for message routing since 1986.) Second, there is no standardized support for a "Postmaster" address associated with a domain or site. Experience managing large production facilities shows that such facilities are critical.

Finally, addressing is still the source of much amusement or consternation. The latest *megillah* deals with the use of a wildcard ADMD component in an O/R-address. Briefly, three of the different addressing configurations include an ADMD component identifying the public-carrier associated with the mailbox. Of course, not all mailboxes will be provided by public-carriers and some private-carriers may have connections to multiple public-carriers. So, a simplistic model of doing MHS routing based on the

```
<country, admd, prmd>
```

triple cannot be used. One solution is to allow a wildcard value (e.g., a single space-character) for the ADMD component. The real problem is the inclusion of any carrier information in the O/R-address — this information is really routing information and is unnatural for electronic mail addresses.

Finally, use of ADMD routing components is not the only problem with MHS addressing. MHS limits the size of the PRMD component to 16 characters, making it difficult to assign values containing "natural" names.

C.2.4   Other Applications

> *"Did he smile, his work to see? Did he who made the Lamb,*
> *make thee?"*
>
> *– William Blake, "The Tyger"*

OSI has produced other applications. Each of these has achieved even less than MHS, but two deserve at least some minor comment:

- FTAM — file service

  Even with the modest number of document types currently defined, it is difficult to find products from different vendors which implement the same document types. The result — and this is an all too familiar refrain — is that OSI-conformant products simply do not interoperate. Further, outside of the realm of file transfer, FTAM has far too much overhead to be used for file access. This leaves FTAM as the worst of both possibilities, unable to displace either FTP or NFS.

- CMIP — network management

  The author simply cannot find words to adequately describe the incoherence of the OSI approach to network management. Instead, for the grisly details, take a look at *Network Management is Simple: You just need the "Right" Framework*, appearing in the Proceedings of the IFIP 6.6 Workshop held in April of 1991. ("Integrated Network Management, II" published by North-Holland.)

In brief, OSI applications, presumably the things which were supposed to sell OSI to the end-users, don't appear to be very attractive.

C.2.5   The Proof of the Pudding

"We wanted to implement it using OSI so it would look good on our resumes."
  – Graduate student, University of Tennessee/Knoxville (1990)

"A research network based on OSI will be a true production network."
  – Advertisement in "Communications Week" (1991)

So, after fifteen years, what does the International Standards community have to show for its diligent work? The results are not good.

Deployment of OSI systems is still largely limited to pilot systems. Organizations might claim that they are planning to introduce OSI to their enterprises, but the plain fact is that OSI technology simply isn't selling. Of course, this shouldn't be particularly surprising considering that OSI products are relatively immature and interoperability is limited.

Further, there are still a number of infrastructural issues which have yet to be resolved. Of these, perhaps name registration is the most critical. For example, despite the pioneering work of the North American Directory Forum, it's still not clear who "owns" the Directory namespace for either c=US or c=CA. For a more extreme example, consider the fact that it is now nearly eight years after the release of MHS(84) and there is still no agency operating as a registrar of ADMD or PRMD names.

This brings us to an important observation:

> The non-OSI base is *growing* at a faster rate than the OSI market.

Keep this in mind. This observation is crucial for understanding the severity of the problem.

In brief, while OSI still has market awareness, it is enjoying a decline in consumer confidence. This is hardly inspiring.

C.3   What is Wrong?

Is there a fundamental flaw in OSI? I claim there is, and I claim that the problem is in the way OSI standards are produced.

C.3.1   The Process

"When the going gets weird, the weird turn pro."
    – Hunter S. Thompson, "Fear and Loathing in Las Vegas"
        (1971)

". . . there are about 5,000 people who are part of that committee. These guys have a hard time sorting out what day to meet, and whether to eat croissants or doughnuts for breakfast — let alone how to define how all these complex layers are going to be agreed upon."
    – Craig Burton, quoted in "Network World" (1987)

The standards which are produced are so large that no one could possibly implement them fully. This is done in the name of generality and extensibility, though the author suspects that it's done this way because it allows international consensus to be achieved.

Then, several regional groups create profiles of these standards. This is supposedly done to make the standards easier to implement and to foster interoperability, but the author suspects that this simply adds regional differences.

Next, conformance tests are created for profiles. Supposedly, this is done to give the end-user some confidence that the implementations will interoperate. Of course, conformance testing does no such thing! When an implementation passes such a test, all that is proven is that the implementation under test can interoperate with the testing software; however, this testing software probably isn't a part of the end-user environment. There is only one way to prove interoperability between two products, and that is to deploy them in a real-life environment and put them into production use.

Finally, governments make mandates for OSI, to jump-start the market. Of course, this has the opposite effect. Here's why: In a robust market, competition between products is an important catalyst.

If OSI is to survive and prosper, it should do so on the merit of the products which implement its services. By arbitrarily requiring that enterprises procure OSI products, there is less incentive for vendors to offer products which are truly competitive with other open systems technologies. Indeed, in the long-term, it is likely that these mandates will do more harm than good, by prolonging the "childhood" of the OSI market. In a strange way, these mandates for OSI do little more than motivate vendors of the Internet suite of protocols to strive harder to maintain superiority over their OSI competitors.

C.3.2 Other Approaches

> *"Everyone wants results but no one is willing to do what it takes to get them."*
>
> *– Sudden Impact, Warner Bros. (1983)*

By now it must be painfully clear, even to the most callous reader, that the OSI standardization process is tragically and inherently flawed. Fortunately, there is an example of an Open Systems technology which does work, namely the Internet suite of protocols.

Although the Internet standardization process is far from optimal, it does have the advantage of standardizing technology which actually works. Initially a document which defines some technology is produced. When the document has a constituency, it undergoes technical review. During this review process, early experience with implementation is considered important. If the document passes the review, it is declared as defining a "proposed" standard. Proponents of the document are then given a six-to-nine month deadline to demonstrate implementability and usefulness.

When the deadline has expired, there must be significant experience with implementation, including an openly-available reference implementation. Further, there must be some degree of both deployment and interoperability experience. If these criteria are not met, the document is removed from the standards-track. Otherwise, the document advances, and is declared as defining a "draft" standard.

Another six-to-nine month deadline is set, and once again the document undergoes a review based on all this experience. If there is consensus that the document describes a technology which has several independent implementations, along with extensive deployment, and considerable interoperability experience, the document is declared as defining a (full) Internet-standard. Otherwise, the document is modified to reflect the experiences. Depending on the severity of the changes, the document is re-issued as either a "draft" standard or a "proposed" standard, and the appropriate deadline is set once again.

It is critical to observe that implementation, deployment, and interoperability are all important criteria that are considered as a document progresses through the Internet standardization process. Further, note that an openly-available reference implementation is also required in order to foster understanding and availability.

Sadly, all these criteria are lacking in the OSI standardization process. As such, it must be emphasized that the only real things produced during OSI standardization are paper products, which needn't bear any relationship to what is implementable or useful in the real world. In brief, as they do not standardize fielded technologies, the committees which produce OSI standards effectively do "research".[1] As a result, this requires that researchers end up doing the actual implementation. This role-reversal is hardly advantageous (at least to those people who want OSI to succeed).

C.3.3   Does it have to be that complicated?

> *"Skalat madr rúnar rísta nema ráda vel kunni."*
>
> *– Egill Skalla Grimsson*

Experience has shown that a large number of problems have excellent 90% solutions. In brief, when engineering a solution, it is important to balance the benefits and costs of each component of the solution. During this process, it may simply be too expensive to solve certain parts of the problem. For example, the addition of one capability might significantly reduce overall performance. Of course, being able to accurately examine a design and then make the cost/benefit analysis is difficult.

---

[1]The author, being polite, will not comment on the quality of the so-called "research".

Unfortunately, as evidenced by the plethora of voluminous paper standards which is generated, the committees which produce OSI standards never know when to say NO. Rather, meeting user requirements by providing extensibility seems to be the grail. An anecdote will illustrate the folly of the OSI approach.

Over a particularly *fine* lunch, a colleague and I were discussing the computer-communications industry. This particular colleague is in senior technical management in one of the world's leading manufacturers of workstations. In other words, he is responsible for dozens of projects involving computer-communications. The topic of multi-media mail came up, and my colleague volunteered that his company had scrapped their approach of using MHS as the enabling (baseline) technology for multi-media mail. This project had been ongoing for three years involving eight engineers. Their reason was shockingly simple: MHS is simply too broad, too complicated, and too complex for a single lead engineer to bring to reality or to guide its implementation in totality.

Here's why: because product delivery cycles mandate rapid development — the problem is how to reduce multi-media mail development into manageable projects. But, by using MHS as the base technology, everything is so intertwined, that this decomposition cannot be done — a senior engineer cannot perform the separation. Since the enabling technology takes all the effort, the value-added portions of the system are never developed. But, without any value-added, any MHS product is quickly written off by the market as another "me too" offering. Further, without any value-added, ISVs aren't interested in doing portations, and in the final analysis, there are no real OSI application solutions. Finally, even the base technology doesn't solve anyone's particular problem, as it is too general! In brief, the complexity of MHS makes it impractical to use as an enabling technology. (And, of course, every four years things just get more and more complicated.)

Returning to our anecdote, whilst engineers could work on the individual parts, no one person could assume the role of a lead engineer being responsible for tying together the whole system across the network, operating system, file system, protocol and API components. Any student of large software projects will tell you that without such a lead engineer, a large project will invariably fail. In fairness to my colleague, I should note that he has scores of bright people working for him, and his groups have successfully delivered many other complex technologies to market.

Now consider how multi-media mail functionality was introduced into the Internet suite of protocols. The technology providing for the exchange of textual memo-based electronic mail was standardized in 1979. In early 1991, a working group was formed to develop multi-media extensions, Almost twelve months later, the working group completed its primary work, MIME, and the document describing that technology was undergoing review for declaration as a "proposed" standard. During the review process, three independent, interoperable, and openly-available implementations were released. At that time, at least nine commercial implementations were known to be under development. This is the sign of healthy technology. Further, being familiar with both MHS and MIME, the MIME approach to multi-media mail is simpler than, and yet as powerful as, the approach used in MHS(88).

Of course, there are numerous other examples which contrast the successes of the Internet and OSI approaches toward producing technology: the former has proven successful in delivering solutions, and the latter is successful in delivering international agreements on paper.

C.4 Conclusions

"In Hell, sinners get exactly what they ask for."
> *– Internet Proverb (undated)*

OSI is designed as a displacement technology. In fact, the committees that produce OSI standards are very careful neither to reference nor accommodate any non-OSI technology (i.e., the installed base). Thus, two topics are purposefully outside the scope of OSI:

- coexistence between OSI and the installed base; and,

- transition from the installed base to OSI.

In fact, transition and coexistence from one generation of OSI protocols to the next seems to be outside the scope of OSI. For example, the committee which produced MHS in 1988 didn't see fit to standardize how their version of MHS would interwork with the 1984 version of MHS.

So, in the context of the installed base, "coexistence with OSI" means "ignoring OSI", and transition is very painful. This begs the question: could OSI actually be a threat to the installed base?

C.4.1 In Closing

"A solution encompasses a product. A product embraces a technology. A technology implements a standard. They're different."
> *– Michael D. Zisman,* Soft•Switch *(1991)*

The answer, of course, is that OSI is hardly a threat. Because OSI is so hostile toward the installed base, it is extremely difficult for the owner of an installed base to justify the purchase of OSI technology. Further, let's face it: OSI technology is second-rate, the products aren't credible, and there are no real OSI solutions — despite the heroic efforts of researchers such as S.E. Kille and C. Huitema, who both architect and implement lots of OSI code.

So, what is the future of OSI? Recall the earlier observation that:

> The non-OSI base is *growing* at a faster rate than the OSI market.

For a displacement technology that has supposedly been delivering solutions for nearly eight years, this observation sounds like a funeral dirge. The only question remaining is can the International Standards community learn from the failures outlined in this paper before the inertia presently carrying the OSI effort falters. Looking at the number of computer-communications companies which are curtailing or eliminating their OSI development staffs, we may see the answer soon.

Acknowledgements

The author gratefully acknowledges the insights and comments of Keith McCloghrie of Hughes LAN Systems and Einar A. Stefferud of Network Management Associates.

Glossary

abstract syntax: a description of a data type that is independent of machine-oriented structures and restrictions.

Abstract Syntax Notation One: the OSI language for describing abstract syntax; (imprecise usage) both the OSI language and the Basic Encoding Rules.

ACK: the *acknowledgement* bit in a TCP segment.

ACSE: see *Association Control Service Element.*

active open: the sequence events of occurring when an application entity directs TCP to establish a connection.

address: a location associated with an entity of some kind. In the context of an IP network, an address is a numeric identifier for a topological location. In the context of a mail network, an address is a textual identifier of a user of the message transfer system.

address class: a method used to determine the boundary between the network and host portions of an IP address.

address mask: a 32–bit quantity indicating which bits in an IP address refer to the network portion.

ADMD: see *Administrative Management Domain.*

Administrative Directory Management Domain: a Directory management domain run by a PTT authority. See *DMD* and *PRDMD*.

Administrative Management Domain: a MHS management domain run by a PTT authority. Each ADMD must contain MHS routing information to all other ADMDs.

Advanced Research Projects Agency: see *Defense Advanced Research Projects Agency.*

AE: see *application entity.*

AET: see *application entity title.*

AM: an *amendment* to an International Standard.

American National Standards Institute: the U.S. national standardization body. ANSI is a member of ISO.

ANSI: see *American National Standards Institute.*

AP: see *application process.*

APDU: *application protocol data unit*

API: see *Application Programmer's Interface.*

application context: the collection of application service elements (ASEs) which comprises an application entity (AE) along with the rules defining the interactions between the ASEs.

application entity: the OSI portion of an application process (AP).

application entity title: the authoritative name of an OSI application entity, usually a Distinguished Name from the Directory.

application layer: that portion of an OSI system ultimately responsible for managing communication between application processes (APs).

application process: an object executing in a real system.

Application Programmer's Interface: a set of calling conventions defining how a service is invoked through a software package.

application protocol: see *application context.*

application service element: the building block of an application entity (AE). Each AE consists of one or more of these service elements, as defined by its application context.

application services: the services collectively offered by the upper four layers of the OSI model.

ARP: see *Address Resolution Protocol.*

ARPA: see *Defense Advanced Research Projects Agency.*

ASDU: *application service data unit*

ASE: see *application service element.*

ASN.1: see *Abstract Syntax Notation One.*

association: a presentation layer connection augmented with application layer semantics (e.g., application layer naming).

Association Control Service Element: The application service element responsible for association establishment and release.

attribute: an attribute type along with one or more associated values.

attribute set: a collection of attributes, useful in some context, e.g., postal-addressing.

attribute type: a definition of the properties of some information, including its abstract syntax, constraints on that syntax, and what kinds of comparisons can be made between two values belonging to the type.

attribute value: an instance of the syntax associated with an attribute type.

base64: A MIME encoding language which provides invariant mappings across most message transfer agents. See also *quoted-printable.*

Basic Encoding Rules: the OSI language for describing transfer syntax.

BER: see *Basic Encoding Rules.*

bridge: (imprecise usage) an entity responsible for simple mappings at a single layer.

broadcast address: a media-specific or IP address referring to all stations on a media.

broadcasting: the act of sending to the broadcast address.

C: the *C* programming language.

caching: a form of replication in which information learned during a previous transaction is used to process later transactions.

catenet: (historical usage) a collection of interconnected networks, with each network containing one or more hosts.

CCITT: see *International Telephone and Telegraph Consultative Committee.*

CD: a Committee Draft. If ratified, the Committee Draft advances to Draft International Standard (DIS) status.

Charlie-Foxtrot: (colloquial usage) *seriously* beyond all hope.

checksum: an arithmetic sum used to verify data integrity.

CL-mode: see *connection-less mode.*

CLNS: *connectionless-mode network service*

CLTS: *connectionless-mode transport service*

CO-mode: see *connection-oriented mode.*

connection: a logical binding between two or more users of a service.

connection-less mode: a service that has a single phase involving control mechanisms such as addressing in addition to data transfer.

connection-oriented mode: a service that has three distinct phases: *establishment,* in which two or more users are bound to a connection; *data transfer,* in which data is exchanged between the users; and, *release,* in which the binding is terminated.

CONS: *connection-oriented network service*

COR: a *confirmation of receipt* in the network service.

COTS: *connection-oriented transport service*

DAM: a *Draft Amendment* to an International Standard. If ratified, the Draft Amendment advances to Amendment (AD) status.

DAP: see *Directory Access Protocol.*

DARPA: see *Defense Advanced Research Projects Agency.*

DARPA Internet: see *Internet.*

data: (imprecise usage) see *user-data.*

data link layer: that portion of an OSI system responsible for transmission, framing, and error control, over a single communications link.

datagram: a self-contained unit of data transmitted independently of other datagrams.

DCS: see *defined context set.*

Defense Advanced Research Projects Agency: an agency of the U.S. Department of Defense that sponsors high-risk, high-payoff research. The Internet suite of protocols was developed under DARPA auspices. DARPA was previously known as ARPA, the Advanced Research Projects Agency, when the ARPANET was built.

defined context set: the set of defined presentation contexts for a presentation connection.

device: a network element of some kind.

DIB: see *Directory Information Base.*

direct routing: the process of sending an IP datagram when the destination resides on the same IP network (or IP subnet) as the sender.

Directory Access Protocol: the protocol used between a Directory User Agent (DUA) and a Directory System Agent (DSA).

Directory Information Base: the collection of information objects in the Directory.

Directory Information Tree: the global tree of entries corresponding to information objects in the Directory.

Directory Management Domain: a collection of DSAs that holds a portion of the DIT. For political reasons, there are two kinds of DMDs: ADDMDs and PRDMDs. This distinction is largely artificial.

Directory System Agent: an application entity that offers the Directory service.

Directory System Protocol: the protocol used between two Directory System Agents (DSAs).

Directory User Agent: an application entity that makes the Directory service available to the user.

DIS: a *Draft* International Standard. If ratified, the Draft advances to International Standard (IS) status.

Distinguished Name: the global, authoritative name of an entry in the OSI Directory.

Distributed Mail System Protocol: an application protocol offering mailbox retrieval in the Internet suite of protocols.

DIT: see *Directory Information Tree.*

DMD: see *Directory Management Domain.*

DMSP: see *Distributed Mail System Protocol.*

DN: see *Distinguished Name.*

DNS: see *Domain Name System.*

DNS-connected: the subset of the Internet community which can exchange electronic-mail.

domain: an administrative entity responsible for naming entities.

domain name: an administratively assigned name identifying a domain.

Domain Name System: the application protocol offering naming service in the Internet suite of protocols.

dotted quad notation: a convention for writing IP addresses in textual format, e.g., "`192.103.140.1`".

DSA: see *Directory System Agent.*

DSP: see *Directory System Protocol.*

DUA: see *Directory User Agent.*

ECMA: see *European Computer Manufacturers Association.*

end-system: a network device performing functions from all layers of the OSI model. End-systems are commonly thought of as hosting applications.

End-System to Intermediate-System Protocol: the ISO protocol used for gateway detection and address resolution.

end-to-end services: the services collectively offered by the lower three layers of the OSI model.

ES: see *end-system.*

ES-IS: see *End-System to Intermediate-System Protocol.*

European Computer Manufacturers Association: a group of computer vendors that have performed substantive pre-standardization work for OSI.

External Data Representation: a transfer syntax defined by Sun Microsystems, Inc.

Federal Research Internet: see *Internet.*

File Transfer Protocol: the application protocol offering file service in the Internet suite of protocols.

File Transfer, Access and Management: the OSI file service.

FIN: the *finish* bit in a TCP segment.

flow control: the mechanism whereby a receiver informs a sender how much data it is willing to accept.

fragment: an IP datagram containing only a portion of the user-data from a larger IP datagram.

fragmentation: the process of breaking an IP datagram into smaller parts, such that each fragment can be transmitted in whole on a given physical medium.

FTAM: see *File Transfer, Access and Management.*

FTP: see *File Transfer Protocol.*

FU: see *functional unit.*

fully-qualified domain name: a domain name containing the complete path of labels to the root of the naming tree.

functional unit: a grouping of one or more elements of a service that are functionally related. The elements of this group can be enabled or disabled as a unit, by enabling or disabling use of the corresponding functional unit.

gateway: (Internet usage) a router; also, (imprecise usage) an entity responsible for complex mappings, usually at the application layer.

hardware address: see *media address.*

header: (imprecise usage) see *protocol control information.*

host-identifier: that portion of an IP address corresponding to the host on the IP network.

host-number: that portion of a subnetted IP address corresponding to the host-number on the subnet.

host: (Internet usage) an end-system.

IAB: see *Internet Activities Board.*

IANA: see *Internet Assigned Numbers Authority.*

ICMP: see *Internet Control Message Protocol.*

IEEE: see *Institute of Electrical and Electronics Engineers.*

IESG: see *Internet Engineering Steering Group.*

IETF: see *Internet Engineering Task Force.*

IFIP: see *International Federation for Information Processing.*

IMAP: see *Interactive Mail Access Protocol.*

indirect routing: the process of sending an IP datagram to a gateway for (ultimate) forwarding to the destination.

inheritance: the process whereby the properties of a superior object class are visited upon a subordinate object class.

Institute of Electrical and Electronics Engineers: a professional organization, which, as a part of its services to the community, performs some pre-standardization work for OSI.

Interactive Mail Access Protocol: an application protocol offering mailbox retrieval in the Internet suite of protocols.

interface layer: the layer in the Internet suite of protocols responsible for transmission on a single physical network.

intermediate-system: a network device performing functions from the three lower-layers of the OSI model. Intermediate-systems are commonly thought of as routing data for end-systems.

International Federation for Information Processing: a research organization that performs substantive pre-standardization work for OSI. IFIP is noted for having formalized the original MHS model.

International Organization for Standardization: the organization that produces many of the world's standards. OSI is only one of many areas standardized by ISO/IEC.

International Standards Organization: there is no such thing. See *International Organization for Standardization.*

International Telephone and Telegraph Consultative Committee: a body comprising the national Postal, Telephone, and Telegraph (PTT) administrations.

internet: (Internet usage) a network in the OSI sense; historically termed a *catenet* — a concatenated set of networks. The Internet is the largest internet in existence.

Internet: a large collection of connected networks, throughout the world, running the Internet suite of protocols. Sometimes referred to as the *DARPA Internet, NSF/DARPA Internet,* or the *Federal Research Internet.*

Internet Activities Board: the technical body overseeing the development of the Internet suite of protocols.

Internet Assigned Numbers Authority: the entity responsible for assigning numbers in the Internet suite of protocols.

Internet Community: anyone, anywhere, who uses the Internet suite of protocols.

Internet Control Message Protocol: a simple reporting protocol for IP.

Internet Drafts: a means of documenting the work-in-progress of the IETF.

Internet Engineering Steering Group: the group coordinating the activities of the IETF.

Internet Engineering Task Force: a task force of the Internet Activities Board charged with solving the short-term needs of the Internet.

internet layer: the layer in the Internet suite of protocols responsible for providing transparency over both the topology of the internet and the transmission media used in each physical network.

Internet Protocol: the network protocol offering a connectionless-mode network service in the Internet suite of protocols.

Internet suite of protocols: a collection of computer-communication protocols originally developed under DARPA sponsorship. The Internet suite of protocols is currently the de facto solution for open networking.

interpersonal message: a structured electronic mail message exchanged between two MHS user agents, consisting of a well-defined heading and one or more arbitrary body parts.

IP: see *Internet Protocol.*

IP address: a 32–bit quantity used to represent a point of attachment in an internet.

IP-connected: the subset of the Internet community which can exchange IP-based traffic.

IPM: see *interpersonal message.*

IS: either *intermediate-system* or *International Standard,* depending on context. In the latter case, such a document is named as either "ISO/IEC number", if it represents work under Joint Technical Committee 1; otherwise, it is named as "ISO number".

ISO Development Environment: a research tool developed to study the upper-layers of OSI. It is an unfortunate historical coincidence that the first three letters of ISODE are "ISO". This is not an acronym for the International Organization for Standardization, but rather three letters which, when pronounced in English, produce a pleasing sound.

ISO/IEC: see *International Organization for Standardization.*

ISODE: see *ISO Development Environment.*

LAN: see *local area network.*

local area network: any one of a number of technologies providing high-speed, low-latency transfer and being limited in geographic size.

maximum transmission unit: the largest amount of user-data (e.g., the largest size of an IP datagram) that can be sent in a single frame on a particular medium.

media address: the address of a physical interface.

media device: a low-level device which does not use a protocol at the internet layer as its primary function.

Message Handling System: a store-and-forward third-party facility for deliverying arbitrarily structured electronic mail messages.

Message Store: an entity acting as an intermediary between a MHS user agent and its local message transfer agent.

Message Transfer Agent: an application entity that offers the message transfer service.

Message Transfer System: a collection of connected message transfer agents (MTAs).

metamail: An openly-available implementation of MIME.

MH: An openly-available implementation of a user-agent for UNIX.

MHS: see *Message Handling System.*

MIME: see *Multi-purpose Internet Mail Extensions.*

MS: see *Message Store.*

MTA: see *Message Transfer Agent.*

MTS: see *Message Transfer System.*

MTU: see *maximum transmission unit.*

multi-homed: a host or gateway with more than one network attachment.

Multi-purpose Internet Mail Extensions: The format for multi-media contents in the Internet community.

name: an identity associated with an entity of some kind. In the context of an IP network, a name is a textual identifier.

name server: an entity which maps a name to its associated attributes.

naming authority: an administrative entity having the authority to assign names within a given domain.

National Bureau of Standards: see *National Institute of Standards and Technology.*

National Institute of Standards and Technology: the branch of the US Department of Commerce charged with keeping track of standardization. Previously known as the *National Bureau of Standards.*

NBS: see *National Institute of Standards and Technology.*

network: a collection of subnetworks connected by intermediate-systems and populated by end-systems; also, (Internet usage) a single subnetwork or a related set of subnetworks in the OSI sense.

network byte order: the Internet-standard ordering of the bytes corresponding to numeric values.

network layer: that portion of an OSI system responsible for data transfer across the network, independent of both the media comprising the underlying subnetworks and the topology of those subnetworks.

Network News Transfer Protocol: the application protocol offering news article transfer service in the Internet suite of protocols.

network-identifier: that portion of an IP address corresponding to a network in an Internet.

NIST: see *National Institute of Standards and Technology.*

NMS: see *network management station.*

NNTP: see *Network News Transfer Protocol.*

NPSDU: *normal data presentation service data unit*

NS: *network service*

NSAP: *network service access point*

NSDU: *network service data unit*

NSF: *National Science Foundation*

NSF/DARPA Internet: see *Internet.*

NSSDU: *normal data session service data unit*

Open Systems Interconnection: an international effort to facilitate communications among computers of different manufacture and technology.

OSI: see *Open Systems Interconnection.*

partially-qualified domain name: an abbreviation of a domain name omitting ancestors common to both communicating parties.

passive open: the sequence of events occurring when an application entity informs TCP that it is willing to accept connections.

PCI: either *presentation context identifier* or *protocol control information,* depending on context.

PDAM: a *Proposed Draft Amendment* to an International Standard. If ratified, the Proposed Draft Amendment advances to Draft Amendment (DAM) status.

PDU: see *protocol data unit.*

PE: see *presentation element.*

physical layer: that portion of an OSI system responsible for the electromechanical interface to the communications media.

POP: see *Post Office Protocol.*

port number: identifies an application entity to a transport service in the Internet suite of protocols.

Post Office Protocol: an application protocol offering mailbox retrieval in the Internet suite of protocols.

PPDU: *presentation protocol data unit*

PRDMD: see *Private Directory Management Domain.*

presentation context: a binding between an abstract syntax and a transfer syntax.

presentation context identifier: an integer identifying a particular presentation context active on a presentation connection.

presentation layer: that portion of an OSI system responsible for adding structure to the units of data that are exchanged.

Private Directory Management Domain: a Directory management domain *not* run by a PTT authority. See *DMD* and *ADDMD.*

Private Management Domain: a MHS management domain run by a private organization. Each PRMD must contain MHS routing information to its parent ADMD. In addition, by bilateral agreement, a PRMD may have MHS routing information to other ADMDs and PRMDs.

PRMD: see *Private Management Domain.*

protocol control information: (conceptually) the initial part of a protocol data unit used by a protocol machine to communicate information to its peer.

protocol machine: a finite state machine (FSM) that implements a particular protocol. When a particular input (e.g., user request or network activity) occurs in a particular state, the FSM potentially generates a particular output (e.g., user indication or network activity) and possibly moves to another state.

PSAP: *presentation service access point*

PSDU: *presentation service data unit*

pseudo-header: a 96–bit quantity used by a transport protocol in the Internet suite to guard against misbehaving implementations of IP.

PTT: a *postal, telephone, and telegraph* authority.

QOS: see *quality of service.*

quality of service: the desired or actual characteristics of a service; typically, but not always, those of the network service.

QUIPU: a pioneering software package developed to study the OSI Directory and provide extensive pilot capabilities.

quoted-printable: A MIME encoding language which is largely readable by humans, but provides some protection against character mapping by message transfer agents. See also *base64.*

RDN: see *Relative Distinguished Name.*

reassembly: the process of recombining fragments, at the final destination, into the original IP datagram.

Relative Distinguished Name: the final component of an entry's Distinguished Name, consisting of one or more attribute/value pairs.

Reliable Transfer Service Element: the application service element responsible for transfer of bulk-mode objects.

remote operation: an action invoked by one application entity but performed by another.

Remote Operations Service Element: the application service element responsible for managing request/reply interactions.

remote procedure call: a synchronous remote operation.

replication: the process of keeping a copy of data in order to improve performance, either through shadowing or caching.

Request for Comments: the document series describing the Internet suite of protocols and related experiments.

resource record: a unit of information associated with a domain name.

retransmission: the process of repeatedly sending a unit of data while waiting for an acknowledgement.

RFC: see *Request for Comments.*

RFC Editor: the entity responsible for publishing RFCs in the Internet suite of protocols.

RFC-822: The format for electronic mail messages in the Internet community.

richtext: A simple text formatting language.

RO: see *remote operation.*

RO-notation: a set of extensions to ASN.1, defined using ASN.1's macro facility, that convey the semantics of remote operations.

ROSE: see *Remote Operations Service Element.*

router: a level-3 (network layer) relay.

RPC: see *remote procedure call.*

RTSE: see *Reliable Transfer Service Element.*

SAP: see *service access point.*

SDU: see *service data unit.*

segment: the unit of exchange in TCP.

selector: a portion of an address identifying a particular entity at an address (e.g., a session selector identifies a user of the session service residing at a particular session address).

service access point: an artifact modeling how a service is made available to a user.

service data unit: user-data passed through a service access point.

service primitive: an artifact modeling how a service is requested or accepted by a user.

session layer: that portion of an OSI system responsible for adding control mechanisms to the data exchange.

shadowing: a form of replication in which a well-defined unit of information is copied to another name server, allowing that name server to authoritatively process transactions regarding that information.

Simple Mail Transfer Protocol: the application protocol offering message transfer and submission service in the Internet suite of protocols.

Simple Network Management Protocol: the application protocol offering network management service in the Internet suite of protocols.

SMTP: see *Simple Mail Transfer Protocol.*

SNAcP: see *subnetwork access protocol.*

SNDCP: see *subnetwork dependent convergence protocol.*

SNICP: see *subnetwork independent convergence protocol.*

SNMP: see *Simple Network Management Protocol.*

SNPA: *subnetwork point of attachment*

socket: a pairing of an IP address and a port number.

SPDU: *session protocol data unit*

SSAP: *session service access point*

SSDU: *session service data unit*

Stefferud's three body problem: $G_{2,3}(G_{1,2}(m)) \neq G_{1,3}(m)$

subnet: (most unfortunate Internet usage) a physical network within an IP network.

subnet mask: a 32–bit quantity indicating which bits in an IP address that identify the physical network.

subnet-number: that portion of an IP host-identifier which identifies a particular physical network within an IP network.

subnetting: the process of using IP subnetting procedures.

subnetwork: a single network connecting several nodes on a single (virtual) transmission medium.

subnetwork access protocol: a protocol used to access a particular subnetwork technology.

subnetwork dependent convergence protocol: a protocol used to augment the service offered by a particular subnetwork technology to the OSI network service.

subnetwork independent convergence protocol: a protocol used to provide the network service between two end-systems.

SYN: the synchronize bit in a TCP segment.

TCP: see *Transmission Control Protocol.*

TCP/IP: see *Internet suite of protocols.*

TELNET: the application protocol offering virtual terminal service in the Internet suite of protocols.

three-way handshake: a process whereby two protocol entities synchronize during connection establishment.

TLV: *tag, length, and value*

TPDU: *transport protocol data unit*

transfer syntax: a description of an instance of a data type that is expressed as string of bits.

Transmission Control Protocol: the transport protocol offering a connection-oriented transport service in the Internet suite of protocols.

transport layer: that portion of an OSI system responsible for reliability and multiplexing of data transfer across the network (over and above that provided by the network layer) to the level required by the application.

TSAP: *transport service access point*

TSDU: *transport service data unit*

UA: see *User Agent.*

UDP: see *User Datagram Protocol.*

upper-layer protocol number: identifies a transport entity to IP.

URG: the urgent bit in a TCP segment.

urgent data: user-data delivered in sequence but somehow more interesting to the receiving application entity.

User Agent: an application entity that makes the message transfer service available to the user.

User Datagram Protocol: the transport protocol offering a connection-less-mode transport service in the Internet suite of protocols.

user-data: (conceptually) the part of a protocol data unit used to transparently communicate information between the users of the protocol.

Virtual Terminal: the OSI virtual terminal service.

VT: see *Virtual Terminal.*

WAN: see *wide area network.*

WD: a *Working Document.* If ratified, the Working Document advances to Committee Draft (CD) status, if relating to a new work item; or, Proposed Draft Amendment (PDAM) status, if relating to an existing standard. As a part of the advancement, a number is assigned to the resulting CD or PDAM.

well-known port: a transport endpoint which is documented by the IANA.

wide area network: any one of a number of technologies providing geographically distant transfer.

X.121: the addressing format used by X.25–based networks.

X.25: a connection-oriented network facility (some say that's the problem).

X.409: the predecessor to Abstract Syntax Notation One and the Basic Encoding Rules.

XDR: see *External Data Representation.*

Bibliography

[1] Vinton G. Cerf and Edward A. Cain. The DoD Internet Architecture Model. *Computer Networks and ISDN Systems*, 7(10):307–318, October 1983.

[2] Jon B. Postel. Transmission Control Protocol. Request for Comments 793, USC/Information Sciences Institute, September 1981. See also MIL-STD 1778.

[3] Jon B. Postel. Internet Protocol. Request for Comments 791, USC/Information Sciences Institute, September 1981. See also MIL-STD 1777.

[4] Jon B. Postel. Simple Mail Transfer Protocol. Request for Comments 821, USC/Information Sciences Institute, August 1982. See also MIL-STD 1781.

[5] Craig Partridge. Mail Routing and the Domain System. Request for Comments 974, Bolt, Beranek, and Newman, Inc., January 1986.

[6] David H. Crocker. Standard for the Format of ARPA Internet Text Messages. Request for Comments 822, University of Delaware, August 1982.

[7] Marshall T. Rose. Post Office Protocol: Version 3. Request for Comments 1225, Performance Systems International, Inc., May 1991.

[8] Brian Kantor and Phil Lapsley. Network News Transfer Protocol. Request for Comments 977, University of California, San Diego, February 1986.

[9] Paul V. Mockapetris. Domain Names — Concepts and Facilities. Request for Comments 1033, USC/Information Sciences Institute, November 1987.

[10] Paul V. Mockapetris. Domain Names — Implementation and Specification. Request for Comments 1034, USC/Information Sciences Institute, November 1987.

[11] American Standard Code for Information Interchange. American National Standards Institute, 1977. ANSI standard X3.4.

[12] Jon B. Postel. TELNET Protocol Specification. Request for Comments 854, USC/Information Sciences Institute, May 1983. See also MIL-STD 1782.

[13] Jon B. Postel. Introduction to the STD Notes. Request for Comments 1311, USC/Information Sciences Institute, March 1992.

[14] Lyman Chapin. The Internet Standards Process. Request for Comments 1310, BBN Communications Corporation, March 1992.

[15] Jon B. Postel (editor). IAB Official Protocol Standards. Request for Comments 1280, USC/Information Sciences Institute, March 1992.

[16] Joyce K. Reynolds and Jon B. Postel. Assigned Numbers. Request for Comments 1060, USC/Information Sciences Institute, March 1990.

[17] Robert T. Braden. Perspective on the Host Requirements RFCs. Request for Comments 1127, USC/Information Sciences Institute, October 1989.

[18] Robert T. Braden. Requirements for Internet hosts — Application and Support. Request for Comments 1123, USC/Information Sciences Institute, October 1989.

[19] Robert T. Braden. Requirements for Internet hosts — Communication Layers. Request for Comments 1122, USC/Information Sciences Institute, October 1989.

[20] Robert T. Braden and Jon B. Postel. Requirements for Internet gateways. Request for Comments 1009, USC/Information Sciences Institute, June 1987.

[21] Message Handling Systems: System Model-Service Elements, October 1984. International Telegraph and Telephone Consultative Committee.

[22] Information Processing Systems — Text Communication — MOTIS — Message Handling: System and Service Overview. International Organization for Standardization and International Electrotechnical Committee, September 1988. Draft International Standard 10021-1.

[23] Message Handling: System and Service Overview. International Telegraph and Telephone Consultative Committee, 1988. Recommendation X.400.

[24] Norman Z. Shapiro and Robert H. Anderson. Toward an Ethics and Etiquette for Electronic Mail. Technical Report R–3283–NSF/RC, The Rand Corporation, July 1985.

[25] Subject: `Internet Domain Survey Results`.
From: `nisc@nisc.sri.com`
To: `namedroppers@nic.ddn.mil`
Date: `Sat, 2 May 92 2:28:33 PDT`
Message-ID: `<CMM.0.90.2.704798913.nisc@phoebus.nisc.sri.com>`.

[26] Mark K. Lottor. Internet Growth (1981-1991). Request for Comments 1296, SRI International, January 1992.

[27] Paul V. Mockapetris. DNS Encoding of Network Names and Other Types. Request for Comments 1101, USC/Information Sciences Institute, April 1989.

[28] Craig F. Everhart, Louis A. Mamakos, Robert Ullman, and Paul V. Mockapetris. New DNS RR Definitions. Request for Comments 1183, Transarc, October 1990.

[29] Mary K. Stahl. Domain Administrators Guide. Request for Comments 1032, SRI International, November 1987.

[30] Mark K. Lottor. Domain Administrators Operations Guide. Request for Comments 1033, SRI International, November 1987.

[31] Marshall T. Rose. *The Little Black Book: Mail-bonding with OSI Directory Services*. Prentice Hall Series in Innovative Computing. Prentice-Hall, Englewood Cliffs, New Jersey, 1991. ISBN 0–13–683210–5.

[32] Ralph Droms. Access to Heterogeneous Directory Services. In *Proceedings of the IEEE InfoCOM*, June 1990.

[33] Michael F. Schwartz. Resource Discovery and Related Research at the University of Colorado. Technical Report CU-CS-508-91, Department of Computer Science, University of Colorado at Boulder, January 1991.

[34] Michael F. Schwartz and Panagiotis G. Tsirigotis. Techniques for Supporting Wide Area Distributed Applications. Technical Report CU-CS-519-91, Department of Computer Science, University of Colorado at Boulder, February 1991.

[35] Ken Harrenstien, Mary K. Stahl, and Elizabeth J. Feinler. NIC-NAME/WHOIS. Request for Comments 954, SRI International, October 1985.

[36] David P. Zimmerman. The Finger User Information Protocol. Request for Comments 1288, Rutgers University, December 1991.

[37] Michael F. Schwartz and Panagiotis G. Tsirigotis. Experience with a Semantically Cognizant Internet White pages Directory Tool. *Journal of Internetworking: Research and Experience*, 2(1), March 1991.

[38] Marshall T. Rose and John L. Romine. MH.5: How to process 200 messages a day and still get some real work done. In *Proceedings, Summer USENIX Conference and Exhibition*, pages 455–487, June 1985. Portland, Oregon.

[39] Marshall T. Rose, Einar A. Stefferud, and Jerry N. Sweet. MH: A Multifarious User Agent. *Computer Networks and ISDN Systems*, 10(2):65–80, September 1985.

[40] Marshall T. Rose and John L. Romine. *The Rand MH Message Handling System: User's Manual*. Department of Information and Computer Science, University of California, Irvine, November 1985. MH documentation set.

[41] Marshall T. Rose. *The Rand MH Message Handling System: Administrator's Guide*. Department of Information and Computer Science, University of California, Irvine, November 1985. MH documentation set.

[42] Marshall T. Rose and Jerry N. Sweet. *The Rand MH Message Handling System: Tutorial*. Department of Information and Computer Science, University of California, Irvine, May 1985. MH documentation set.

[43] Marshall T. Rose, David J. Farber, and Stephen T. Walker. Design of the TTI Prototype Trusted Mail Agent. *Proceedings, Second International Symposium on Computer Message Systems*, September 1985. Washington, D.C.

[44] Marshall T. Rose, David J. Farber, and Stephen T. Walker. Design and Implementation of a Trusted Mail Agent. In *Proceedings, 8th International Conference on Computer Communication*, September 1986. München, FRG.

[45] Marshall T. Rose and Einar A. Stefferud. Proposed Standard for Message Encapsulation. Request for Comments 934, University of Delaware, January 1985.

[46] Nathaniel S. Borenstein and Ned Freed. Multipurpose Internet Mail Extensions. Request for Comments 1341, Bellcore, June 1992.

[47] Frank J. Wancho. Digest Message Format. Request for Comments 1153, USAISC-White Sands (WSMR), April 1990.

[48] John S. Quarterman. *The Matrix: Computer Networks and Conferencing Systems Worldwide.* Digital Press, Bedford, MA, 1989. ISBN 0–13–565607–9.

[49] Mark Horton and Rick Adams. Standard for Interchange of USENET Messages. Request for Comments 1036, AT&T Bell Laboratories, December 1987.

[50] Shannon Yeh and David Lee. Message Posting Protocol. Request for Comments 1204, Netix Communications, Inc., February 1991.

[51] Mark Horton. UUCP Mail Interchange Format Standard. Request for Comments 976, AT&T Bell Laboratories, February 1986.

[52] Steve E. Kille. Mapping between Full RFC-822 and RFC-822 with Restricted Encoding. Request for Comments 1137, University College London, December 1989.

[53] Anne Westine and Jon B. Postel. Problems with the Maintenance of Large Mailing Lists. Request for Comments 1211, USC/Information Sciences Institute, March 1991.

[54] David H. Crocker, E.S. Szurkowski, and David J. Farber. An Internetwork Memo Distribution Facility — MMDF. In *Proceedings, Sixth Data Communications Symposium*, pages 18–25, November 1979.

[55] Douglas P. Kingston III. MMDFII: A Technical Review. In *Proceedings, Summer USENIX Conference and Exhibition*, pages 32–41, June 1984. Salt Lake City, Utah.

[56] Ronald L. Rivest. The MD5 Message-Digest Algorithm. Request for Comments 1321, Massachusetts Institute of Technology, April 1992.

[57] Mark R. Crispin. Interactive Mail Access Protocol: Version 2. Request for Comments 1176, University of Washington, August 1990.

[58] James Rice. Interactive Mail Access Protocol: Version 3. Request for Comments 1203, Stanford University, February 1991.

[59] Mark L. Lambert. PCMAIL: A Distributed Mail System for Personal Computers. Request for Comments 1056, Massachusetts Institute of Technology, June 1988.

[60] Franklin F. Kuo, Debra P. Deutsch, Harry C. Forsdick, J.J. Garcia Luna Aceves, Naja Naffah, Andrew Poggio, Jon B. Postel, and James E. White. Multimedia Computer Mail — Technical Issues and Future Standards. In *Proceedings, Eighth Data Communications Symposium*, pages 191–196, October 1983. North Falmount, Massachusettes.

[61] Jonathan Rosenberg, Craig F. Everhard, and Nathaniel S. Borenstein. An Overview of the Andrew Message System. In *Proceedings, Frontiers in Computer Communciations Technology*, pages 99–108, August 1987. Stowe, Vermont.

[62] Jon B. Postel. File Transfer Protocol. Request for Comments 959, USC/Information Sciences Institute, October 1985. See also MIL-STD 1780.

[63] Karen R. Sollins. Trivial File Transfer Protocol: Revision 2. Request for Comments 783, Massachusetts Institute of Technology, June 1981.

[64] John H. Howard, Michael L. Kazar, Sherri G. Menees, David A. Nichols, M. Satyanarayanan, Robert N. Sidebotham, and Michael J. West. Scale and Performance in a Distributed File System. *Transactions on Computer Systems*, 6(1):51–81, February 1988.

[65] *The Simple Times*: The Bi-Monthly Newsletter of SNMP Technology, Comment, and Events. Send a note to the electronic mail address `st-subscriptions@dbc.mtview.ca.us` for subscription information. ISSN 1060-6068.

[66] Keith Moore. Representation of Non-ASCII Text in Internet Message Headers. Request for Comments 1342, University of Tennessee, June 1992.

[67] U.S. Federal Information Processing Standards Publication #46–1: Data Encryption Standard, December 1988.

[68] U.S. Federal Information Processing Standards Publication #81: DES Modes of Operation, December 1980.

[69] Burt S. Kaliski. The MD2 Message-Digest Algorithm. Request for Comments 1319, RSA Laboratories, April 1992.

[70] U.S. Federal Information Processing Standards Publication #113: Computer Data Authentication, May 1985.

[71] American National Standard: X9.17: Financial Institution Key Management (wholesale), 1985.

[72] RSA Encryption Standard (version 1.4). RSA Data Security, Inc., June 1991.

[73] John Linn. Privacy Enhancement for Internet Electronic Mail: Part I - Message Encipherment and Authentication Procedures. Request for Comments 1113, Digital Equipment Corporation, August 1989.

[74] Steve T. Kent and John Linn. Privacy Enhancement for Internet Electronic Mail: Part II - Certificate-based Key Management. Request for Comments 1114, BBN Communications Corporation, August 1989.

[75] John Linn. Privacy Enhancement for Internet Electronic Mail: Part III - Algorithms, Modes, and Identifiers. Request for Comments 1115, Digital Equipment Corporation, August 1989.

[76] Marshall T. Rose. Proposed Standard for Message Header Munging. Request for Comments 886, University of California, Irvine, December 1983.

[77] Stephen E. Kille. Mapping between X.400(1988) and RFC 822. Request for Comments 1327, University College London, May 1992.

[78] Peter B. Danzig, Katia Obraczka, and Anant Kumar. An Analysis of Wide-Area Name Server Traffic. Technical Report 92-504, Computer Science Department, University of Southern California, May 1992.

[79] Nathaniel S. Borenstein. Computational Mail as Network Infrastructure for Computer-Supported Cooperative Work. In *Proceedings, Computer-Supported Cooperative Work*, 1992. (to appear).

[80] Marshall T. Rose. The Future of OSI: A Modest Prediction. In *Proceedings, IFIP International Conference on Upper Layer Protocols, Architectures and Applications*. IFIP WG 6.5, North-Holland Publishing Company, May 1992. Vancouver, Canada.

Index